A MANUAL
of EUROPEAN
BIRD KEEPING

A MANUAL
of EUROPEAN
BIRD KEEPING

FRANK MEADEN

BLANDFORD PRESS
POOLE   DORSET

First published 1979

Copyright © 1979
Blandford Press Ltd,
Link House, West Street,
Poole, Dorset, BH15 1LL

British Library Cataloguing in Publication Data

Meaden, Frank
  A manual of European bird keeping.
  1. Birds – Europe
  I. Title
  636.6   SF461

ISBN 0-7137-0935-7

Set in 11/12pt Monophoto Ehrhardt
Printed in Great Britain by
Fletcher & Son Ltd, Norwich and bound by
Richard Clay (The Chaucer Press) Ltd.
Bungay, Suffolk

CONTENTS

Contents

FOREWORD

For anyone who sets out to write a book covering a great range of related items, the resulting work is likely to be one of two types. The first type appears more frequently. Its author probably has a sound and wide-ranging knowledge of the subject, but insufficient time often imposes a restriction on the material which could be included in the book; so the author must turn to other sources. A work of such a kind, when compiled from up-to-date and accurate sources, is a most useful book, but it is often the case that compiling information of this type highlights some rare species for which there may be only one or two available facts. Much research is then required, going further and further back through the literature until the original may be discovered, as maybe a report of observations made perhaps a century ago! In such circumstances, the great importance of first-hand observations is all too apparent.

This brings me to the second, and much rarer, type of book: the primary source work. Such a book is based on the broad, personal knowledge of the author and few people have the fortune or persistence to gain the necessary breadth of experience that makes such a work possible. Frank Meaden is one of those happy exceptions, and in this book he offers his own hard-won knowledge.

I have come to know him as a man who has the avicultural equivalent of what is called 'green fingers' when it occurs in gardeners; I suppose 'feathered fingers' would be the avicultural term. Certainly, his great ability to care for birds is one that many people find it difficult to emulate. By pursuing a keen interest in the keeping of native birds over many years, and with a constant determination to learn more, he has gradually built up a personal and practical knowledge of a surprising range of species. I think he shares my feelings that knowledge, in a subject that you care about, is something to be shared. The information that he has gained has been freely imparted over the years to those who have come to him for help. I am very pleased that he is now able to offer it to a much wider audience.

By its very nature, a book of this kind is a very personal thing, and to some extent must be an individual and idiosyncratic account coloured by the range of the author's experience. Should one think that it is open to criticism on this account, any such consideration is surely outweighed by the importance of the original information and observations that become available. Thus, even the potential critic is likely to turn to it as a primary source of information!

I know that Frank Meaden has always been concerned about the way in which birds are kept. I know too that he will share my view that this book should not only help people to keep and breed birds with greater success, but also encourage enthusiasts to provide better conditions and greater care for their birds. If it does this, then all the time and effort will have been well justified.

Colin Harrison

PREFACE

Even after two score years and ten of practical bird keeping, I still try to keep an open mind on all aspects of this subject, although I must confess to adhering very firmly to beliefs in certain areas where well tried methods have a high degree of success. Inevitably, when writing on a technical subject in which there is a vast diversity of opinion and practice, one must write from one's own point of view and practical experience. Some may gain the impression from my comments regarding experiments that I have become hide-bound, adhering rigidly to theories and principles. On the contrary, however, it is my open-minded attitude which often causes problems, for in any experiment I carry out I investigate all implications of the collected data and endeavour to understand unexpected phenomena as well as accepting the overall picture.

It has been suggested that I give a short account of my life, and, through no false modesty, but since the reader will be interested in aviculture I shall confine the autobiography to the events which explain my interest in the subject. My introduction to bird keeping goes back as far as memory can recall: my father had a seemingly infinite capacity to store knowledge of all living creatures, and since horses would not fit in our garden and too many dogs did not fit in his income, birds proved the favourite. My earliest recollections are of a nest of song thrushes which I hand raised from a very young age with the assistance of an early rising grandmother; as a matter of interest, one of these birds was still singing strongly when I went into the army as a young man. Apart from these and other specimens where I had been told 'these are yours', my first very own bird, from choice, was acquired when returning from a fishing trip with my father, a keen angler. As we neared home I saw a flash of yellow and green in front of a car: it failed to emerge from the other side and in the road I found the still form of a cock greenfinch; picking up the 'corpse' I held it carefully until home indoors, when suddenly a slight movement indicated that only stunning had occurred. This greenfinch never flew strongly again but lived for many years in a cage with a canary hen and they annually produced their hybrids for five or six years; his death was not until I was on the point of leaving school.

I continued bird keeping—stimulated by a father's interest—and watching wild birds in Windsor Park and the surrounding Berkshire, Buckinghamshire and Surrey countryside as a child, and then later in life I studied with the intention of becoming a veterinarian. I took over the research side of a firm producing pet foods a few years after demobilisation from the army, and, with aviaries gradually extending in a suburban back garden and then in other gardens after moving house, the interest never waned.

A true love of the four seasons and all living things was instilled in me from childhood and I developed a constantly searching and enquiring mind. My aims seemed clear enough: whatever country I was visiting or resident in, birds became the subject of study. Eventually I settled for keeping birds of the western Palaearctic regions and trying to discover the factors giving success in keeping and breeding these birds—particularly with regard to replacement diets, and endeavouring to produce strains of bird which would thrive and breed under aviary conditions. Over all those years—from the age of five—I have kept numerous varieties, many of them abroad; gradually, with established residence in England, the choice was dictated—I would keep native birds, or at least those of western Europe.

Part Two of this book is a list of those European birds which have formed part of some experiment in either breeding or feeding; I have coded it with a reference relating to success or failure in breeding (see page 65 for details). With dietetical experiments, of course, one has to accept that breeding cannot be successful on every occasion: a lack or an excess of some foods contribute quite easily in such matters and this is why a well-balanced food intake each day is essential. Although variety is important, a change in the additives, rather than the tried and tested basic food, is best, otherwise losses may result with a consequent need for frequent restocking.

Many of the rare species mentioned in these pages, such as hoopoes, bee-eaters, wrynecks, Dartford warblers, barred warblers, pine grosbeaks, long-tailed rosefinches, have been presented by friends abroad, zoological organisations and universities for the furtherance of my studies. I write this book with the sincere and optimistic intention of contributing to the knowledge of bird keeping, and to enable those who wish to keep and breed our native birds to achieve greater success. I believe this to be important for a number of reasons: because of the pleasure that can be derived from doing so; the beauty of such creatures; for the greater and more intimate knowledge of these birds which can be gained from close association with them it is vital that despite increasing urbanisation people should be able to know and therefore care about birdlife: opportunities to observe and live with birds, which in an urban environment would not be possible because of the effects of poisonous sprays, etc., can thus be achieved. The knowledge of bird keeping may assist those whose work involves, or who wish to save, injured birds or deserted nestlings. Finally, of course, we depend on the bird keeper and breeder to save endangered species.

Frank Meaden

PART ONE

*General information and advice
on choosing birds, housing, feeding
(including insect culture),
hand-rearing, 'meating off',
pairing and nesting.*

INTRODUCTION

Although, in the past, birds of European species were relatively easy to obtain, the reduction of bird populations as a result of increasing urbanisation and careless use of insecticides has given rise in the United Kingdom to a need for strict legislation controlling the catching of live birds. Bird keepers, nowadays, therefore often suffer some frustration in trying to acquire certain protected species. However, ample facilities do exist whereby those who genuinely wish to breed birds may apply for licences permitting them to take from the wild limited numbers for the purpose of aviculture. With the possibility of an even greater scarcity of native birds, conservation, rather than the pleasure gained from watching them, is the finest motive to begin bird keeping.

In the United Kingdom all birds with the exception of a few species—at present for example corvids and starlings—are legally protected in one way or another. My own work with birds has, in the main, been greatly assisted by the appropriate authorities' granting me licences to take wildlings for research work; likewise a number of foreign governments have allowed me permits to have specimens taken in their countries for the same purpose. I am grateful to all who have helped me in this manner as I owe so much of my existing knowledge to their kind co-operation.

Since protected native birds may not be sold indiscriminately, and in order to make allowances for those who breed birds and do hope to dispose of them by sale, the Bird Protection Act permits the sale of birds which have been bred in aviaries, provided that as nestlings they have had closed rings put on them. A closed ring is a metal ring which can be passed over the foot of the young bird, and will move freely on the shank of the adult specimen but cannot be removed over the foot once the bird is fully grown. There is, of course, nothing to prevent one from keeping unringed birds if one wishes to have them for pleasure, study or research in one's own aviaries, or merely to give away any surplus bred from them.

Whilst the ringing of young birds is essential in the U.K. for the person wishing to sell stock, I have not ringed one of my own birds for many years; I have certainly done so for other people, as I do not like to see a novice attempt this job without some prior experienced guidance. Indeed I have never encouraged a new-comer to bird keeping to commence ringing for a number of seasons as it is common for the parent, when cleaning the nest, to take exception to the rings as foreign matter and throw the offending bands out, together with the much sought-after young.

The birds in our family aviaries are never ringed because in large enclosures which are densely planted, a number of accidents can occur: rings can so easily become caught up on a twig of a nest site, a loose piece of wire or even growing shrubs, whereas birds that are housed in cages or indoor flights seldom meet with such accidents. It can be heart-breaking when one has finally succeeded in breeding a few of a much longed for species to find losses through ringing. It is also a sound general principle to keep interference with breeding stock to a minimum until one knows them intimately.

Keeping any form of livestock is a responsibility; and the husbandry involved cannot be shirked or avoided at any time: when the decision is made to keep and breed birds, the onus is upon the keeper to house the stock under sound hygienic conditions and to feed them a reliable diet. Aviaries must be constructed with the welfare of the inmates in mind, and it is a moral responsibility of any bird breeder to keep the stock in the safety of comfortable enclosures: the life-span under such conditions can be increased to three times that of wild individuals and some aviary bred varieties have now appeared with brighter plumage and increased size. Whereas natural wild species live in constant fear of predators; undergo many hardships and perils during migration; endure hard winters foraging for enough food to survive, and may even face possible death from toxic chemicals whilst resident here or transient when migrating, aviary stock need not, if their keeper's cage is up to the required standard, encounter any such risks and should in time, with increased domesticity, provide ready breeding strains.

Having decided to keep and breed certain birds, one must next consider which species, whether for example seedeaters or insectivorous or some of each, and then the actual variety or collection; here it would be wise to consider one piece of advice in particular, if in real earnest about breeding birds: success is far more likely if you keep only one pair in an aviary. Certainly some of the common, more easily bred, varieties will no doubt breed successfully in a large collection, but so many young never live to leave the nest under this arrangement. It is difficult to justify such waste. Those who pin their hopes on rearing under such conditions must be prepared to face the inherent risks of many losses.

With regard to simplicity of the care involved, most insectivorous birds are easy to keep in good health just so long as they are fed correctly and not over-crowded. Some will require a shed-type shelter attached to their aviary to which they may retire in cold weather; others need gentle warmth and, probably more important, extra light during the winter months. Due to the vast amount of small live insects required by newly hatched nestlings, however, insectivorous birds are not 'easy' to breed. It is useless offering maggots to those just out of the egg: the skin is too tough. They require something soft like the small green caterpillar from the oak or the cabbage. Even the mealworm can, at this time, be given only in a small size (larger if white at the skin-shedding stage). Incorrect feeding does by no means certify failure in all cases—some birds will break up insects more than others—but it is of great importance that one should know of the numerous suitable insects which can easily be bred in vast quantities. There is the wax-moth, of which there are three sizes. One chooses from the Greater, the Lesser and the American depending upon the birds being bred. There are locusts and crickets, and many other species of small insect apart from these can be cultured. Caterpillars, too, can be cultured or supplied commercially. It will help to grow vegetation which encourages greenfly in an enclosure: hops are very good since the underside of the leaves becomes densely infested with these insects which are relished by seedeater and insectivorous species alike when rearing is in progress. Even a help of horse manure in an aviary will attract much wild insect life if kept reasonably moist. Bee or wasp grubs are sometimes obtainable and are highly nutritious items to offer. Wood ant 'eggs', easily collected in certain areas, are one of the finest foods it is possible to obtain.

Success to one person can mean the rearing of one or two stunted young birds: to others, only where a full brood of the young are flying and not discernible from the parents is success felt to be achieved; patience and perseverance are essential factors and of the utmost importance. It is always wise to compare notes with other breeders and to study wildling habits. A holiday spent observing a particular species in the wild habitat and compiling data for reference when later attempting to breed that bird, can be an immense help and perhaps influence the outcome of such efforts. Very often I have seen the comparative beginner to bird keeping be successful in a first breeding where older hands have failed, most likely due to a keenness to learn, and a willingness to take advice and to try, for example, new methods of feeding. So many of us, even farmers who have kept livestock for many years, have fixed, unflexible ideas.

When the term 'migrant' appears in this book it refers to those birds migrant to North-West Europe. Depending upon the latitudinal area where the bird keeper resides and the local weather conditions the housing of birds will vary in both winter and summer. Winter roosting temperatures should not be below 50° F (10° C); feeding time should be extended with artificial lighting. The more delicate varieties wintering in tropical areas when wild, need temperatures no higher than 60° F (15° C) as long as their feeding periods are lengthened. Excess heat from direct sun rays during the warmer months can be avoided by complete shading of the roof with shuttering or climbing vines or by positioning an aviary beneath a suitable tree. This is, however, rarely necessary where normal temperatures do not exceed 90° F (32° C) in the shade, but, humidity is vital at high temperatures.

There are some birds which one may leave outdoors all the winter, provided that they have a dry shed-type shelter to remain in if they so wish. Some nights they will roost outside, but if their food is habitually placed in the frost-free area of the shelter, they will use it more often. There must be some form of illumination, natural or otherwise, to ensure that they can enter, as birds such as we are considering do not normally enter dark or semi-dark shelters. Mention here should be made that of the species which may be housed in this manner those allowed the use of outdoor flights during winter are invariably the foremost in spring song and also breeding condition. This difference can at times be quite remarkable to witness: if one keeps a number of the same species some of which are housed in one manner and others which must stay indoors all the time due to limited suitable housing facilities, one can observe the value of the outdoor life in the general condition, the spring moult and the bloom on the plumage. Although the vast majority of migratory birds tend to be treated as semi-tropical during the winter months, the cold seems in fact to have little effect where they are allowed a little extra feeding time by artificial lighting; they will enter a shelter to feed in the light and so very often remain inside near their food supply. The daily exercise out of doors, the rain and even winter sun seem all to play a vital part in their health. Whilst this method of housing is suitable and even desirable in temperate regions for the hardier birds, it should not be attempted in cold regions without considerable experience in bird husbandry.

All native birds when healthy, at home in their daily surroundings, and with adequate food available of the type needed to rear young, will at some time in spring or early summer reach that phase of their life-cycle where it is normal for them to reproduce. The study of birds during this season alone is well worth every penny of their keep for the whole year. Each season will bring with it something of interest, for keeping and breeding or studying birds can be one of the most fascinating and absorbing of pastimes.

In spring one must plan the pairings: there is always a period here of doubt, then pleasure on finding that a pair accept one another and courtship takes place. There is rarely much time spent waiting for results: fit birds, particularly hardbills, will nest quite soon after pairing. All birds at this time should be receiving a richer diet. The extra light of longer days will soon have its effect and males will be heard singing and claiming their territory. A watchful eye on the female of any pair is wise at this time: despite all the precautions imaginable one can occasionally find a hen having trouble with her first eggs owing to chilly nights. If it occurs more often then it can be a sign of the bird's being too fat, either by faulty feeding or lack of exercise; early nesters are normally the ones to suffer from this problem. Dry warmth will normally assist the passing of the egg.

Later, when incubation is almost completed and the time for hatching fast approaching, be especially observant for egg shells to appear on the aviary floor, feeding shelf, or sometimes the furthest point from the nest site: be hopeful that it is the young hatching and not the eggs being thrown from the nest. Very tactful observation is necessary now and it can be most rewarding when allowing one to see the female feeding young. The time and care spent during the vital stage of the next few days in providing suitable rearing foods and the confirmation that there is a ready acceptance of such foods tend to involve one very deeply.

Summer gradually turns to autumn and this is the time to take advantage of nature's generosity and collect from the wild harvest of berries, fruits and seeding heads, for the moult of birds, although a completely normal and uncomplicated function if fed correctly, must never be allowed to deteriorate into the malady it can become with bad husbandry.

The breeding of native seedeaters, providing one remembers that they have not been domesticated to the same degree as, for example, the canary, is a fairly simple matter if kept under near natural conditions in outdoor aviaries with suitable foods and adequate nesting sites and materials. Although there is often a temptation to have mixed collections it is not the best method of propagating any strain of bird. There have been many times when I have bred quite successfully from goldfinches, siskins and redpolls on the colony system, with only one variety to an aviary, sometimes up to six males and double that number of females being housed in an enclosure of adequate and often generous proportions. Pairs of bullfinch, hawfinch, chaffinch, brambling and most buntings will invariably produce large quantities of better quality young when in an enclosure of their own. Quite apart from having to share much needed livefood for rearing— and it disappears in a short while with a number to eat from it— one cannot keep a really good record of parentage under the colony breeding system. It can be useful for some particular group studies and can be achieved with the first three finches mentioned.

Pairs of the other finches listed and the buntings are better bred in their own aviaries, and most important of all, never with their own kind. It must be realised that in the wild where any bird is even only mildly territorially minded it can chase from its selected area another bird which it may feel is interloping. Under aviary conditions this is frequently impossible. Death or any sort of injury in an aviary through fighting for territorial rights is unpleasant and unnecessary and is completely the responsibility of the bird keeper. A little extra thought when planning the pairing can make obvious the risks of housing certain birds together. If in doubt take advice from an experienced bird keeper and always err on the side of caution.

A bowl of insects in the morning may last a pair with young the best part of a day: the same amount in a mixed collection could disappear in an hour or so and for the remainder of the time until the next feed what are the young to be fed upon? Under such conditions it is grossly unfair to class the parent birds as bad feeders and blame failure upon them. Assess the birds' needs correctly, provide the necessary, leave them alone and it is very surprising just how often the pair are successful.

Throughout the year make a note of each item of behavioural interest, even commonplace occurrences can all be entered upon a simple index card. Do not record merely the number of eggs or young, but also the date paired; when the site was selected or accepted; nest materials used; even the behaviour of both parents throughout the breeding season. In this way a whole family history can be built up often proving very useful in successive years. Where one is genuinely prepared to build up experience, such records will show each bird's characteristics, their likes and dislikes, every success and, when failures occur, not just the failures but frequently an overall picture illustrating the causes of such failures.

An aviary need not be just an obstruction to the view, a frame covered in rather hard-looking wire; with planning many enhance a garden and blend extremely well with their surroundings. The reader will belong to the already converted but a pleasant-looking structure can give everyone a far better impression of bird keeping in general, than a stark ugly one. The facility for free flight, without too much in the way of perches, encourages the birds to more exercise and the perches if erected by the owner should be around the outer perimeter and where shelter is provided. With ample natural growth there is less need to offer such perching arrangements except beneath the roofed portion where very little will grow. Almost any wood will suffice, beech being very good as it can be cleaned so easily: dowelling or any bought timber should be discarded in preference for natural twigs and branches.

HOUSING

For sheer aesthetic pleasure, large aviaries of grand proportions, well stocked with interesting subjects, do have much in their favour. This was the custom many years ago among those more affluent people who appreciated the company of birds. Such an enclosure can be very attractive as a show-piece: many in the old days were large conservatories holding a variety of trees, shrubs and plants from distant countries together with collections of birds. Only but rarely, however, were birds stocked with thoughts of preserving the species: conservation was not seen as the important subject it is today. If one has unlimited space at one's disposal, one can still have large enclosures—birds will certainly benefit from ample wing exercise and to some it is essential for advancing breeding condition—however, the mixing together of many species or too many birds in a confined space is to be frowned upon, for when kept in large numbers the majority of species seldom breed as freely or numerously as they would in the wild or if given an ample-sized aviary to themselves. Today conservation must take precedence over aesthetic considerations.

We must then, if serious in our attempts to breed birds other than the common finches, provide the pairs with individual breeding quarters; some of the finches can be left to reproduce in large numbers providing that they are in collections where considerable thought has been given to their fellow inmates, the provision of large neutral feeding areas and adequate nesting sites.

Certainly one will find that the vast majority of insectivorous varieties will require their own enclosure when contemplating reproduction under controlled conditions: it is not merely territorial instinct which dictates this, but more the adequacy of the right type of food at just the right time, when any young are actually being reared (the critical period is then the first six days):

a mixed collection means shared rations; one unit per pair means controlled feeding. It is that simple.

Large walk-through aviaries are very popular where collections are open to the public and I like them, too, for privately owned collections as the birds do tend gradually to gain a greater confidence. They may be used when colony breeding or if one has decided to maintain a collection of varying species. Such aviaries can be extremely attractive when well planted, but, with regard to aviary vegetation, remember that whereas with insectivorous birds almost any type of flowering plant, shrub or tree may be utilised to either visual or insect culturing advantage, seedeaters housed in a like manner would cause excessive damage to growing vegetation. In their aviaries it is far better to grow those items which either provide food in themselves (see Feeding section) in their berry or fruit growth, or which attract insect life which most birds require when breeding is in progress. A number of feeding points should be provided in an aviary of this type.

The walk-through aviary can be shaped to suit one's choice, the landscaping of the property, or the ground available for this purpose: the basic essentials are to choose materials for their durability and to give ample thought to the actual planning beforehand. Remember that discussion with other bird keepers and visits to a number of collections at the planning stage will allow one to usefully benefit from other people's experience.

New or used scaffold tube, timber, solid steel rod of one centimetre diameter or over, perforated angle and small-bore pipe can all serve very usefully in the construction of aviaries. Bricks, new or secondhand, ornamental stone and building blocks should be considered once the general plan has been decided upon. If you are using any steelwork, even if it was once galvanised, a certain amount of wire brushing will be necessary to remove rust, and it must then be painted with an anti-rust solution. Where a smaller enclosure is contemplated, a visit to a local scrap metal yard will frequently solve one's constructional problems as many of them can supply the basic frame materials at low cost.

Sometimes one can effectively combine the use of timber and metal. Timber railway sleepers offered for sale can be sawn lengthwise by a local mill to provide strong well-preserved uprights that will last many years; positioning one of these uprights at each multiple of their length with slightly thinner sections linking them and secured to the upper ends does form a strong frame for a walk through, merely requiring the wire covering, and timber boarding at the outer perimeter at ground level for wire fastening at the base. The main resulting impression is of a very open-type aviary, suitable for all-year use where resident species are concerned and sufficient evergreen roosting facilities exist for their shelter. Always beware of too large an unsupported area, particularly on the roofing section, where wire may tend to sag. Make use of straining wires for support where risk of heavy winter snowfalls are likely and limit unsupported wire roofing to one square metre. The end result can be a complete garden under wire and when tastefully planted the wire itself is very unobtrusive. Certainly this type of aviary can provide opportunity for studying one's subjects under pleasant conditions.

As previously advised there can also be disadvantages. After a good breeding season, one may wish to catch up certain of the inmates: many a frustrated hour have I spent crawling under shrubbery only to see wanted specimens re-emerge in a far corner. It can assist if inner corners are constructed in such a manner that they include a wire enclosure into which birds may be driven: a canvas or net as used over soft fruit can then be dropped over the exit and catching be made simpler. Even a feeding area which incorporates four wire doors normally held close to the roof and which may be lowered to take wanted specimens can prove helpful on such occasions.

This type of aviary is not suitable for more delicate migrant species which have to be caught annually. The experienced bird keeper would not use an extremely large walk-through type of enclosure for migratory birds. There are many reasons including the facts that it is essential to catch up birds at times and that it is difficult, unless a shelter is provided—somewhere into which the birds freely enter for food and so can be held during the colder months, to keep a close check on stock which could be of higher risk rate.

This kind of aviary is altogether more appropriate for colony breeding of seedeaters if some study is being made of them as a group, or for a few insectivorous birds that may be kept and bred in close harmony: waxwings will breed more effectively in such a manner; redwings too give little cause for concern when in a family number; hoopoes and even bee-eaters will be happy in colonies.

Few would use such a large enclosure for only one pair of birds unless a serious attempt was being made for a first breeding of some importance for research. One can house a few wisely selected mixed pairs of resident insectivorous species in such large aviaries: a number of neutral feeding areas must be provided along with much growing vegetation, such as shrubs and small trees, pampas grass, raspberry canes, currant bushes, heathers, brooms, hops and very thick undergrowth in corners and outer perimeters. Nest boxes of a wide variety of types in abundance must be made available and perhaps a floral assortment of shrubs decorating the central area will assist in providing territories. All this adds up to a highly interesting pastime for the bird keeper but it must be said that the breeding results in such aviaries are frequently rather disappointing. Even remembering the wide range of cover to encourage insect breeding, and siting heaps of horse manure or compost here and there, with the consequent occupational insect hunting for the birds, there is often a higher rate of mortality from fighting in these large aviaries. It is completely natural for some birds to select a territory and be prepared to fight to the death to hold it, and one must remain ever alert for any over-aggressive individuals: do not delay the removal of a bird in such circumstances.

Where one decides to keep mixed pairs in this manner, it is of some considerable importance to recall the methods of nesting in the wild and to avoid housing together pairs that may compete for sites. Try a tree hole nester, a ground site pair, those which may select a site in low vegetation. When attempting to breed small insectivorous birds there are so many factors playing against success that one must give great consideration to their well being lest we contribute to their failure.

If the birds are merely for public exhibitional purposes in this type of aviary, anything other than the more common varieties is only justifiable if adequate catching points are incorporated in the construction.

Due to the vast area a walk-through-type aviary can involve, it is vital during early planning and construction that one gives sufficient thought to security, and to the exclusion of vermin. The use of rubble and concrete foundations all around the outer limits, ideally a path entirely surrounding the enclosure with the inclusion of a few courses of bricks on which to erect the outer frame stands, can help to keep out rats, weasels and even fully grown mice. The entry of very young mice is another problem;

they frequently enter when small and grow to adulthood inside, thus unable to escape even if wishing to do so; they breed and one has the family to contend with. The regular use of traps, harmless to birds, is helpful, and a wise precaution at all times.

With numerous shapes and types of aviary to choose from, it may be hard to decide which, but do not rush the planning stage. Keep maintenance to a minimum: the renewal of wire, timber, wood preservative treatment, all must be considered: they are time-consuming tasks that one invariably finds need doing at the same moment as the aviary is required for breeding birds. Endeavour to construct so that all panels are interchangeable: in this way one can be removed quickly and a replacement set in position in a matter of minutes, the worn portion needing attention being concentrated upon later, away from the aviary site, at leisure. Plan according to good ideas seen elsewhere: consider simple methods of feeding in the dry for winter months; built-in observation points; regular supplies of fresh water—all are well worth investigating and can mean much to the person who has other duties to attend to in addition to maintaining avian stock.

A type of aviary rather common in the keeping of parakeets—long flights more or less open to the weather joining at one end a warm shelter in which they feed—can very easily be adapted to the needs of native species, preferably in single pairs or perhaps a limited number of birds. The extra thought and the planning in the early stages of building can mean far more time to enjoy or study the inmates of the enclosures once installed and when leisure hours are at a premium.

Considerable success has been achieved using rows of aviaries built in series. When doing so, it is advisable to house totally different species adjacent to one another. In six such aviaries, we could house the following without any undue risk of bickering: in consecutive enclosures place bullfinches, accentors, greenfinches, tits, goldfinches, and finally wagtails. In this manner a number of birds can be studied and bred in quite a limited space.

Among other types of aviary there are those of wire on a simple wooden frame, made to move from a soiled patch of grass to a new site, perhaps solely for use during the breeding season. More sturdy structures have draught-proof quarters of shed-like shelter, and some are even attached to a birdroom with indoor flights for the inmates' use. I personally favour the row of aviaries as illustrated (Fig. 1) which simplifies feeding and watering during hard weather. The 'party-wall'-type division between each adjoining aviary cuts wire costs and with one pair to each it offers complete control. Where wishing to do so, one could build it with linking doors so that in autumn after the breeding season, the row of aviaries became one, giving greater freedom to stock and allowing maximum flight room.

The initial costs need not be great for aviary erection. Even the simple wooden frame covered in wire, joining four posts top and bottom with boards from post to post, with a door at one corner and a little roofing at each corner to provide the barest of shelters can be quite attractive when, for example, covered by climbing roses, and it will house a few pairs of breeding birds. This type of enclosure built into the corner of the garden, takes up very little room and can provide hours of pleasure and educational interest.

My own choice of aviary is shown in Fig. 1. It provides shelter in a feeding and roosting corridor which affords storage space and good observation points. The shelter itself is situated over either a cupboard or open range which comprises storage space. It would have roof lighting over the passageway rather than the shelter and each indoor shelter can have a glazed portion sited above the entrance hole. Beneath the shelter should be a heavy gauge wire false base sited above a sloping solid base, edged at the corridor with plastic guttering. This assists in catching waste food, droppings and excess water, generally helping to maintain cleanliness: brushing and washing of the wire base remains the main chore. From the feeding corridor I prefer to see a further window or wired section between the birds' shelter and the passageway. Wire is preferable since it allows warm air to circulate in the building as a whole.

The outdoor aviaries are seen to have a low brick surround and brick pillars at each corner: this would naturally require some form of foundation, but, as some sunken concrete is needed anyway as a vermin deterrent, it need not be additionally very expensive, especially if tackled by oneself or a group of interested friends and helpers. The wooden frame set within the pillars for fixing the wire into place can be removable so that simple re-wiring operations may be made at a much later date, or they could be fixed in position with bolts set into the brickwork. With such a design the strong old secondhand timbers look very well and once climbing roses or similar decorative vegetation become

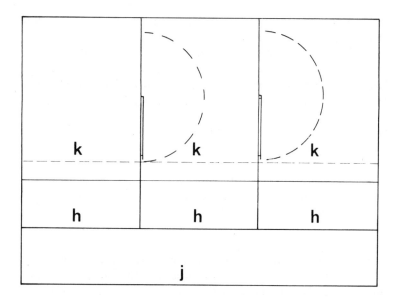

Fig. 1 Side view of a suggested 'in rows' aviary layout: (*a*) roofed feeding corridor; (*b*) shelter with feeding hatch; (*c*) outdoor aviary or flight; (*d*) storage space or unit; (*e*) brick base and piers; (*f*) optional observation windows; (*g*) overlapping roof.
Plan of the same aviary: (*h*) three shelters; (*j*) roofed feeding corridor; (*k*) three outdoor flights with indication of doors for use in autumn and winter, when aviaries are opened up into one large enclosure. Note that entry into the outdoor flights could be through the rear of the storage space.

fully established it will blend in with most gardens. Electricity should be laid on by a professional tradesman or advice sought on this. Although rather limited lighting and possibly heating may originally be in mind, make sure the wiring is adequate to cover further heating if insect culturing or the use of an electric drill or other tools is foreseen. If for finches only, the front of the shelter could be open or have removable sections. If open fronted, however, there should be a generous overhang of roof to stop rain blowing in to the detriment of the structure and inmates.

Where large aviaries are constructed in temperate climates such as that prevailing in England, one must remember that the weight of snow in winter can be considerable. Upright posts and cross members should be planned with this in mind and with thirteen millimetre wire mesh, an effort should be made to ensure that this remains taut at all times. Wire flapping in the breeze, or sagging wire on an otherwise attractive enclosure can ruin the effect.

Try to have roof lighting in the bird rooms: this will provide the maximum amount of natural light. The only drawback is excessive heat in summer months but in almost all cases birds will be in the outdoor part of the establishment at this time. I like to use a birdroom for wintering most insectivorous stock but allow them the daily use of the adjoining outdoor aviaries leading from this. The most delicate I house indoors all the winter.

Adequate thought should be given to installing the ventilation for any birdroom: an even temperature should be aimed for, but with most species a minimum of discomfort will be experienced as long as the feeding hours are extended. Indoor flights in a birdroom are preferable to cages although it may limit one to a lesser number of birds. However, more species will live amicably together in a close proximity during the winter than at any other time although this must never be used as an excuse to crowd birds in any compartment.

When constructing any aviary or birdroom, the incorporation of a safety compartment is always a good investment. It is a method of security whereby one enters through one door, closing it afterwards, before entering the enclosure proper, and closing the second door. At times birds can become so tame as to be a nuisance and no doubt when a bird does fly off it will be the most valued specimen—it is always so. The use of a safety compartment eliminates such worries and it is well worth the small loss of space it entails. Quite often escapees can easily be coaxed back to an enclosure whilst some have been known to live in the area for years, daily returning for food.

We will later look at another way of studying and breeding birds termed liberty breeding, a truly fascinating procedure and extremely educational when time can be afforded to study the behaviour of the liberated and returning breeding stock. Frequently when over-stocked with the more common of finches we have liberated a number then found that we still had to feed them in the garden because of their dependence and stubborn refusal to leave the premises, but of course such trust from birds can give great satisfaction and interest to the bird keeper. I have known birds actually draw blood attempting to get through the wire endeavouring to return to an aviary in which they were reared. One group of young accentors caused much concern through this, even though they were fully self-supporting and it ended only with transporting them into the country for release.

FEEDING

With such a varied collection as the native avifauna of Europe to select from it will be obvious that many different diets may be required. There will be even more to choose from!

The use of any natural or man-made food cannot be proven ideal when used over only a short period: even through the four seasons of the year it will not necessarily show its deficiencies or for that matter where certain items are being supplied too generously. If one has a proven method of feeding and the birds moult in good colour with no long-drawn-out spells of rough feather; winter well with regular short bursts of song; where a spring moult is normal, pass through it with excellent results and reach breeding condition in early spring; if successful breeding is achieved and they have completed a full cycle on such food, then do not be in a hurry to change. By all means make trial additions of other foods, whether insects from home culturing or purchased, or the man-prepared foods which are available in abundance today. We cannot all be experimenting dietitians and spend a life time pursuing the many varied diets, otherwise so much in other spheres would be neglected. Take advice from more experienced bird keepers who have bred a variety of species consistently over the years.

Feeding for breeding can be vastly different from feeding for exhibition purposes. Weight can be put on any good body bone structure, though not skull or brow, and this may be required for competitive showing of stock. It is not, however, conducive to longevity, propagation or general well being; laziness or the inability to exercise the body brings advanced obesity and a shorter lifespan and a consequent drop in the production of healthy young to carry on the strain.

Aim for a diet which provides a regulated food intake: certain birds will endeavour to take their fill of favourite foods to their own detriment: do not allow it if at all possible. If giving a seed mixture, ensure it is well balanced, with not too many fattening seeds; thin it out with clean screenings. Screenings are the wild seeds extracted at source by the farmer at harvest time, when threshing the grain for domestic use—unfortunately they are not very readily available nowadays. Remember that so many seeds available today are completely foreign to our stock; we offer only a substitute diet in all cases. If a softfood or insectivorous mixture, make absolutely certain that it is mixed thoroughly with the additional and plentiful use of greenfoods: vegetable protein is as vital to their health as to that of any other creature. Animal protein as we tend to provide it comes mainly from one source, but consider supplementing this. Imagine an owl feeding off one rat or an equal weight in mice; the rat provides one each of liver, heart and stomach, the latter usually holding a quantity of undigested vegetation of farinaceous items, whereas a number of mice would offer a wider variety and greater number of nutritious organs. Ox heart and liver can be used but a few locusts, wax-moth larvae, mealworms and aphids will provide more variety. Aim always for a wide variety of foods. Trace elements can be missing so easily from a diet and the resulting deficiency not be noticed for quite a long time. Give thought to what the actual insects have eaten: there is always an amount of undigested food in them which is transferred to the feeding bird.

Variety is just as essential for seedeaters, but with the use of vegetation which has been proven nutritious for human consumption, it is easier to be sure they are being fed correctly; free food, which nature provides and which was used to a far greater extent by our forefathers, is obtainable by all. For the town dweller it may well mean a trip into the country in autumn for collecting and storing seeding heads, but he too can grow much in the way of natural food in a small town garden, tubs, boxes or conservatory. Those in outer suburbia or in the heart of the country have everything at their finger-tips. A library book on wild plants may assist if necessary: the ever-common dandelion, chickweed, sowthistle, comfrey, water-cress, ripened dock seed will be useful. Some may be stored in seed or berry form. Greens such as dandelion and comfrey can be dried for use in softfood during winter months.

To supplement the wild plant life, man-prepared mixtures are convenient. Foods eaten by birds vary greatly from one part of the world to another: even from district to district there can be vast vegetational differences. Nevertheless in the wild most birds can obtain the minimum requirements for a well-balanced diet. Our aim is to provide a similarly nutritious alternative if the birds' health is not to suffer through a build-up or lack of certain elements and this can sometimes happen so gradually as to be undetectable until too late. Our general well being, health and ability to live as we wish results from the selection of a balanced diet. We are able to achieve this quite easily, both for ourselves and, where big business is concerned, for our stock, whether cows, pigs, horses or dogs. There has been ample research to ensure that their catering needs are met. But who has ever worked out the bare necessities of the Dartford warbler or any other small bird?

Fortunately over the years, more so since the subject of conservation has been taken seriously, bird foods have improved: today, with the addition of fresh fruit, vegetable matter and fish or meat protein, a number of good basic diets can be safely relied upon to not only keep adult birds healthy but also to rear nestlings to maturity without signs of rickets or fear of other complaints caused generally by malnutrition. Food must, of course, provide all that is required for full growth, but it must also supply nourishment for the ample maintenance and repair of the body. Each body carries out the wonderful process of turning the food intake into materials and energy essential to its growth, its survival and ability to reproduce. Without going into too much detail, for many chapters could be written on this subject alone, as essential as water and oxygen are carbohydrates, fats, proteins, minerals and vitamins. In some cases excess is passed through the body, in others too rich an intake can prove harmful. A gradual deficiency can kill as too can excess over a period. It will be seen that the advantage of a varied diet is that where one item is failing another can sometimes rectify the balance.

I was asked once to provide details for the Royal Navy of a bird food which could quickly be prepared from readily kept items whilst at sea and which could be fed to migrant species of birds which frequently land on vessels in an exhausted condition. This can be achieved quite simply and I include it here for use in an emergency: do remember that it should not be used over any great length of time. It is useful where a damaged bird is handed in for attention and is unexpectedly accepted without prior warning, when adequate food has not been obtained. Almost any farinaceous matter, such as finely ground grain or flour, wholemeal, maize meal, wheatmeal, etc. can form a basis. To this should be added a little soya flour; finely minced dry meat or fish, generous amounts of grated cheese, a little dried milk or liquid if available. Olive oil, soya oil, corn oil, sunflower oil can all be used to dampen the dry mixture; finely minced fruit such as household currants, sultanas, apricots, prunes may be added. I have even used sardines (in oil) in emergencies and so many ordinary stored items of human foods can be put to such good use if a little thought is first given to the normal intake of the casualty, that there is really never a need for bread sop to be forced down an injured bird's throat. All such foods should end up crumbly moist and sweet smelling: honey, moist sugar or glucose apart from their nutritional value often help to make such an emergency food more palatable.

For regular feeding one cannot do better than to obtain a food from a good, well recognised source and provide the fresh items, which cannot be stored easily, oneself; remember that young birds require more calcium in the food than an adult; an adult bird will invariably obtain much from food and insect life taken in an aviary. Bird keepers with keen angling friends will be able to provide fish or the cleaned out portion: this can be steamed and mixed into insectivorous foods providing a valuable addition and much variety to a diet. The use of fresh fish fry such as small minnows as a bird food is very good: these placed in a shallow container will often be fed by adult birds to their young. Almost everything of redstart size upwards will take advantage of their provision.

The inexperienced bird keeper often makes the mistake of hatching out a multitude of maggots into flies. Unless a fly is fed on honey or glucose water from the time of hatching it has little in the way of nutritional content and should therefore not be fed in any number to birds; the odd few taken do no harm, but with a steady diet of them a bird will soon show signs of malnutrition. I have been horrified to hear of how so and so's birdroom is full of flies and his birds eat voraciously from them. Inevitably, a few days later one hears of the birds' having a membrane closing over the eye and severe eye irritation setting in; if caught in time I have recommended the use of Abidec (Parke Davis) a vitamin supplement, one drop direct to the beak of a softbill every few hours, combined with the force-feeding of mealworms or wax-moth larvae. However, prevention is always better than cure.

Even among a group as small as the Corvidae the required diets can vary greatly from one bird to another. One can easily understand how such a large family as the warblers, grouped together in these pages for convenience, need to have a widely varied food intake, some needing a far more vegetable-based diet, others extra fruit, whilst those such as the small leaf warblers keep in better health when receiving extra milk in their diet, the latter helping to replace the minute insect life taken in the wild. Milk can, indeed, be used to dampen almost any softfood to the benefit of the subject but in the case of willow warblers and chiffchaffs a high protein invalid food supplement can be mixed with milk and given in small quantities in addition to the basic softfood ration.

One advantage of feeding softfood is that where it is deemed necessary to include any colouring agent just prior to and during any moult, it is a simple matter to do so. There are many colouring agents to choose from, mostly harmless vegetable-based ones which are used in human foods.

Many softbills will take soaked household fruits such as currants, sultanas, raisins; where it is available, the fruit of the elder can be dried for winter use in this manner and one can freeze many wild fruits and berries collected during the autumn wild harvest: these simply need to be removed from a freezer, as would domestic food, well before use. Apricots, figs, dates, prunes, dried apples and pear, may be minced finely and included in the softfood regularly: they are almost all highly nutritious foods which will be appreciated since taken quite naturally in the wild by many species.

The inclusion of comfrey, the brassicas, spinach, dandelion (root, leaf, flower and stalk) chickweed, young nettles or even the top couple of centimetres or so of the more adult plant, all chopped finely or minced before use can be added to the food of any insectivorous species: some will benefit from a more liberal use than others. All bird breeders who keep hardbills should include in their quarters growing comfrey, cabbage, spinach, dandelion, etc. Keep a supply steady during the whole growing season. The remainder of the time, during the winter months, winter cabbages or Brussels sprouts may be left for them to eat from. Old cabbage stalks have always been planted in my enclosures as they invariably flower and seed and the pods are avidly taken by almost all finches during the time they are rearing young.

Hops may provide only a limited harvest of seeds and over only a short period of the year, but another useful function which must not be forgotten is their attractiveness to 'greenfly' (aphids). Whether hardbill or softbill, the aviary inmates will eat these small insects with much pleasure. Blackfly seem not so popular, although some individual birds, regardless of species, seem to enjoy them. Dessert apples should always be available to seed-eaters and insectivorous, minced in the food mixture for the latter, and whole or quartered for the seedeaters.

The use of insects such as mealworms should not be essential during the winter months as the correct insectivorous mixture ought to be adequate. The livefood should be looked upon more as a bonus. Although it is pleasant to see wintered stock acquire a tameness and confidence through the daily proffered insect life, be it mealworm, wax-moth larvae or locust, even such mites as goldcrests can be kept in excellent health for a number of years during which time they receive no mealworms at all in their diet: in the old days such a thing was unheard of; mealworms were considered essential to keep birds singing.

We have, under licence, taken goldcrests from the nest at the time of hatching, keeping them in a wooden box lined with two and a half centimetre thick polystyrene, the nestlings being held together in soft paper tissues. The young goldcrests have been reared on wax-moth larvae and softfood, the latter being specially adapted for their needs. There were many additions to this diet and it was varied as they progressed and started to peck at the food for themselves. They were, finally, gradually 'meated off' and fed on the softfood alone and were maintained on this staple diet all their lives (almost five years) merely taking small insects during the summer months when released into outdoor quarters. This illustration of feeding is used to show that a softfood may be up-graded sufficiently for such a purpose. It is not recommended for general use—these birds were taken for research purposes—but their normal estimated life-span in the wild would be a mere eighteen months. During the time they were experimented with, they received many additions to their basic diet, the most common being English Cheddar cheese, finely grated; fish roe was used quite extensively as were a number of high protein invalid foods supplied for the purpose by their various manufacturers.

During the winter months when birds are frequently housed indoors behind glass, one can make good use of rosehip syrup and a number of other such supplements, intended for human consumption. They are easily adapted for bird use and can be given either in a drinking font, mixed in water, or in the daily food intake; do avoid putting such rather sticky items in water containers in which birds can attempt to bathe, for the plumage becomes soiled and unpleasant for the bird. Many names such as Virol, Marmite or the baby foods of strained beef extract, spinach, and such like will be known to the reader: these have all been used at various times with excellent effects and use of items proven in nutritional value makes feeding a much safer task. The manufacturer will often provide an analysis of his product and go so far as advising where necessary upon a recommended percentage of the food intake.

Insect Culturing and Collection

On discovering that an insectivorous pair of birds have young, many people tend to offer immediate large quantities of mealworms and such like. If this food is too readily available when the young have just hatched, their appetite, small at this initial stage, is very soon sated and it is then, when they fail to gape, that it would seem the parents have an impulse to eject them from the nest. An offspring which lies still and does not gape, seemingly dead, is removed.

In the wild, birds must hunt food to live and rear young and of course the close proximity of food dish and contents in an aviary obviates this necessity; this is one of my reasons for recommending that almost all livefood is cut into pieces and mixed with the daily softfood mixture. There are further methods possible whereby a certain amount of hunting can be introduced: some small insects, very simply cultured without any elaborate laboratory conditions, can be tipped into a tray holding about one or two centimetres of wholemeal wheat. This depth will hide some, but it will take a short while only for a bird to become aware of their presence. While the parent has the time-consuming task of hunting, a newly hatched nestling has time to digest the previous feed and be ready to gape for the next. I have used both these methods and others yet to be described and a personal preference is still to mix the cut up livefood with the insectivorous mixture: it matters little how wild my aviaries become, or how much natural insect life is produced in the vegetation of them, the constant search for pieces of mealworm or moth larvae in the softfood at every feed ensures there is no diminishing intake and gradual aversion or rejection development, with fresh 'meating off' operations becoming necessary each autumn, with the decrease of wild insect life.

Those able to spend a few minutes each month on insect culturing will have a wide variety of food to augment daily basic intakes. Few of these insects are a complete food in themselves but all can be extremely valuable when used in conjunction with other foods. The main essential is a birdroom cupboard or small room—even a disused wardrobe can be converted—which should be maintained at a steady 75° F (25° C). The foods needed for insect culturing are all easily available and the subjects themselves need very little attention: from choice I check my own supplies almost daily but only because I am interested in the process. The life-cycles vary from one species to the next, but average between thirty and fifty days. The female of some species can lay thousands of eggs, so giving a good yield for a small initial financial outlay. Very little attention to the process is needed. Keeping such an insectary at the recommended temperature in the birdroom itself ensures that the room remains warm but not hot, seldom if ever exceeding 50° F (10° C) and thus certainly not too warm for any avian inmates; I have very often utilised this excess warmth, escaping through vents into the room, for the general benefit of the birds and my own comfort during the colder months.

Professional entomologists and pest research establishments with fully equipped laboratories at their disposal, experimenting upon the control of insect pests, breed their specimens in large glass containers. These stand in trays of oil so that any escapees do not travel very far. We, however, are dealing with harmless creatures so there is no need to take elaborate precautions: in most cases where birds are kept, such an escape would become a happily anticipated event.

Plastic confectionery jars in use today are ideal for our purpose, although moths, when breeding, need a container from which they may drink, otherwise their short lives will become even further limited and little will be achieved in the way of insect production. There are three well-known methods of providing drinking facilities for the moths and I have used them all quite effectively. A glass test-tube can be placed inside the main container with the moths; this tube should be about fifteen centimetres long and needs a loose-fitting cork which allows a strip of blotting-paper to be placed in the tube full of water so that the end protrudes above the cork: the capillary action of the water rising will enable the moths to drink from the end of the strip. The tube of water could hold a shaped piece of sponge rubber instead, once again protruding from the top but filling the tube entrance to prevent the moths' drowning. The third method is to make a horizontal slit two and a half centimetres wide by a quarter centimetre just below the jar shoulder, and fix a water container to the side of the jar with strong adhesive tape: place a strip of blotting-paper through the slit with the lower part outside and hanging in the water reservoir. I would remind the reader that it is only moths which need to drink and any hole such as the slit just mentioned should be covered with adhesive tape when only larvae are using the bottle. They can be a nuisance if they escape: it happened once and they entered a nearby thermostat, pupating inside and welding the points together with their silky-like cocoon so that the heater was permanently set on.

The plastic lids of these confectionery jars are a screw-on type and can have a section cut from them and a piece of fine metal gauze fixed in position with adhesive tape. Very thin flexible wire gauze can be held in position with strong elastic bands. This air vent must be of metal as cloth will be eaten through in a very short while. In some cases I have cut a circle from the lids and, with the handle removed, secured a woven wire tea strainer over the hole. Unless one provides rolls of corrugated paper or similar material to assist pupating, the larvae will mass at the top and stop the flow of air.

Having prepared a number of jars in this manner (to commence I would suggest between three and six for a normal small collection) the next thing is to obtain the nucleus culture. Do prepare the breeding jars first; I have seen a number of such cultures die off where the reception and food supply had not been amply considered.

The food should next be prepared and it will vary according to which insect is being raised and what it will finally be used for. My own choice for a good all-purpose food is the American wax-moth: it takes a good quality food which is subsequently passed on to the birds and it can be harvested at any stage between its minimum and maximum growth: it can be anything from a small caterpillar-like grub to a creature double the diameter of a mealworm and a good two or three centimetres long with a skin as soft as the green caterpillar from oak or cabbage. It needs merely the gentlest pressure to burst and is certainly superior to the tough skin of a maggot or the shell-like covering of the mealworm. Its culture, along with that of several other useful creatures, is described below. Each culturing jar will need approximately a half kilogram of food.

Ephistia cautella

A common European meal moth, fast reproducing and requiring a minimum of care, it is readily taken by any small insect-eating bird. It is sometimes found breeding in a box used for housing mealworms, or maybe in a seed bunker. It is small with variegated wings and the larvae are white with a brown head; the overall length is in the region of one centimetre when fully grown. An ideal culturing agent is five parts (by weight) whole wheatmeal, to one of glycerine, and a generous sprinkling of a yeast for bird or animal preparation. Each female when breeding should lay anything up to two hundred eggs over a seven-day period. Their life-cycle is on average forty-five days at the recommended temperature and conditions. To assist at the pupating stage, coils of corrugated paper rolled from strips of two centimetres width should be a great help. If two or three of these are put in each jar not many will be lost at this stage.

Anagasta kühnella

This is the Mediterranean flour moth and very similar in appearance to the above moth. The larvae when fully grown are the size of the caterpillar found hanging by a thread from the oak in late spring. In colour they are pale pinkish-white, soft skinned and always welcome when offered to hardbills as well as insectivorous varieties. The feeding is simplicity itself since only whole wheatmeal is given, with a sprinkling of yeast. They should reproduce in more or less the same quantities as the aforementioned variety. Again the provision of the corrugated paper rolls will greatly help when the pupating stage is entered. The life-cycle is approximately fifty to fifty-five days.

Achroia grisella

This, the lesser wax-moth, is native to England. The larva reaches a maximum of one and a quarter centimetres in length. The little extra work involved in the food preparation for these is well worth the effort. Even in the fully grown stage just prior to pupation, the larva is readily taken by goldcrests whenever they have the opportunity. In hand-raising experiments, the larvae have also produced excellent results. The nourishing foods which make up the culturing medium for this moth are as follows: six parts by bulk of whole wheatmeal, six parts rolled oats, one part glycerine and one part honey. When mixed to a crumbly consistency, add a sprinkling of yeast and mix well into the food. The food medium should end up moist but not of a gluey nature and even when it has been given rather on the moist side, the larvae have been produced in good quantities.

Galleria melonella
The greater wax-moth can be treated in an identical manner to the last variety. This one will reach one and a half centimetres in length and be proportionally fuller in girth. Again we produce very soft-skinned larvae and this is vitally important where newly hatched young birds are concerned, whether they are to be reared naturally by the parents or by the keeper. An ideal nucleus culture would be about two hundred moths or larvae, but if using the former remember to provide drinking facilities.

Achroia melonella
The American wax-moth can be fed on the same food as the two closely related varieties previously mentioned, but there are other food mixtures which can be used, none accelerating production or increasing the size but possibly improving the general condition of the insect and consequently the breeding strain. In the wild these wax-moths will invade a badly infected beehive where the swarm has been considerably weakened and will eat all the honeycomb: this can only be achieved where bees have contracted some disease and are too weak to defend their hive from predators. They really constitute nature's way of cleaning up after an infected swarm has died off. The skin is very thin and the larvae can reach over two and a half centimetres in length and far larger than a mealworm in diameter. Even so any bird seems well able to take them, the smallest of birds beating them against perch or on the floor: certainly only a few sharp pecks render the larvae hors de combat! Other mediums such as wheatmeal, rolled oats, brood comb, yeast and honey, or Farex, yeast honey and glycerine have been used satisfactorily.

Carpophilus dimidiatus

The com-sap beetle is only about one sixth of a centimetre in length but it produces a larva just about three times this length. Despite this rather small size, birds seem to enjoy them. Where one offers an experimental handful of their food medium, holding dozens of the larvae, birds do certainly make a feast of them. I collect them in the normal way by placing a carrot in their container over-night: it is a simple matter the following morning to lift the carrot, best cut in half length-wise, and find hundreds of these larvae feeding on the vegetable. I used to shake them into a shallow dish, to which I would add two or three drops of cod liver oil, not only to prevent any escape but to render the insect harmless, since they are capable of eating their way out of a cardboard box. The manner in which I saw redstarts swallow them whole and alive make me wonder whether it might be harmful and now I use only minute quantities of the oil, as very small doses will do no harm. The food for rearing this insect need be no more than rolled oats but I did always add a good spoonful of molasses and a little yeast. Because of their diminutive size their content seems unlikely to be of great nutritional value yet it does provide variety if included in an otherwise rather austere diet.

Tribolium casteneum

This rather distant relative of the mealworm, which can be friend or foe, depending upon its use and method of being fed to one's birds, is the rust-red beetle, which, unlike the mealworm, can be fed in any numbers. This is another insect which I have always treated first with a minute quantity of oil; the oil can be corn oil, olive, sunflower oil or cod liver oil. As a member of the family Tenebrionadae it is most likely the commonest pest of stored goods, being found in cereals and their products, oilseeds, even bones and in particular many oriental dry foods. It is a lighter colour than the previous beetle and measures something like a quarter of a centimetre in length. It produces a larva over double this when fully grown and at this stage it resembles the mealworm and could quite easily be mistaken for it. As a relative of this insect it has the same distinctive flavour and seems quite a favourite with birds. Wholemeal wheat and rolled oats with a small amount of molasses and yeast will produce large quantities of this insect. As with most small insects which go through a pupating stage, rolls of corrugated paper in the culturing jars seem to greatly assist them through this part of their growth.

Tenebrio molitor

The mealworm is valuable as long as it is not used to excess so that the bird's digestion is abused. Given in excess it can cause gout where the kidneys fail to eliminate certain waste and uric acid crystallises in certain areas, particularly the outer extremities. Used wisely, however, it is one of our most useful foods for birds. I treat them with a few drops of oil before cutting them into small pieces and mixing with the insectivorous birds' basic food supply. The mealworm may be given alive to the hardbill, although I find that pinching the head, thus rendering it stationary is best, so that it will not escape from the food tray or bury itself beneath the seed and so be missed by the bird it is intended for.

Excess moisture is the main danger to guard against when culturing this insect. If one uses a container made of glass, tin or plastic, which does not breathe as does a wooden box, the urine of this insect will build up and cause a deterioration of the food supply, possibly with fatal results for the culture. Minute insects resembling a white dust will form over the surface of the container and breed on the decaying food and in such an environment the mealworms will soon die.

A dry, well-aired container; a small amount of carrot so that there is always a little available in a fresh state, never being allowed to accumulate or to begin rotting; a small quantity of rolled oats and wholemeal, with a little molasses and a good sprinkling of yeast mixed well to a dry crumbly mass are all that is required. Remember that the beetle is able to fly so construct the box, if of wood, with a lid of very fine mesh wire gauze in a tightly fitting wooden frame, or, if using a confectionery jar as previously described for moths, lay it on its side so that a maximum surface is obtained. Into such a jar or box lay a double sheet of canvas sacking and on top of this place a heaped tablespoonful of the prepared food and a slice of carrot.

Now to start a culture place about fifty to one hundred beetles in the jar and add a label outside showing the date. Six weeks from that date the beetles' productive life of egg laying is more or less ended. The beetles can be collected, killed and frozen, passing them through a mincer at a later date and adding to the food of redstart-sized species and above, but never that of the small

35

warblers or goldcrests. The eggs will be left on the canvas and on the base of the jar and the basal side if placed as suggested. Place a half kilogram of the prepared food in the jar and stand on end or side in a warm site. The newly hatched mealworms will soon show themselves and as soon as they grow to just over a centimetre place a slice of carrot or apple in with them. Do not overdo this for fear of excess moisture which will arrive with the first signs of rotting.

If there are about a dozen jars in use then there should be no need to purchase this insect, unless a very big stock of softbill birds is being maintained. Start one new jar every month and a steady supply should be available throughout the year.

A word of warning should be given on the old-fashioned method of breeding mealworms by placing them in a tea-chest amid two or three old sacks and large quantities of food. The mealworm is cannibalistic and many at the pupa stage, when most vulnerable, will be partly eaten. If one has such a box containing mealworms at their various stages of growth, the population will reach a certain point, then move no further; of each beetle's eggs laid there will be hundreds which never reach maturity. The method recommended above ensures that no beetles are left to prey upon the smaller and earlier stages. All will grow more or less together therefore eliminating even further the possibility of any cannibalism.

The simplest method of removing beetles is to remove the carrot for two or three days, then place a large slice in the jar late one evening: the following morning almost every one of them will be on the carrot and the removal of this should also take the bulk of the beetles with it. The remainder will have to be removed by hand at that time to be sure of a good harvest.

Fly Maggot

So many varieties of fly exist that if one makes a hole about the size of a pencil in a fresh egg and then stands the egg in a dry warm spot with the hole uppermost, within a very short while a horde of maggots will fill the egg, the result of a fly having laid her eggs in the opening provided. Although not suggested as a method of culturing, this illustrates how simple it is to produce these insects.

It is most important to know what food the maggot has eaten. This larva is not very nutritious when kept for any length of time as it then has to live on its own fat and the food content therefore lessens. It is vital with many maggots commercially bred for angling that they be cleaned thoroughly by being placed in bran for about five days after having been removed from the source of their food supply. A maggot raised on fish should be a little more nutritious than one grown on meat. A supply can easily be produced during warmer months by using fresh fish each time. Do not allow the food to build up with left-overs from a previous hatching and rearing. A bucket holding bran or sand, or a larger container such as a barrel may be used. Over this hang a bag made of curtain netting into which has been placed the fish. Place a lid over the whole bag and container below, so that no rain may fall on it. Flies will invariably visit such an attraction and within a few days there will be hundreds of small maggots. As these grow to the stage where they no longer wish to feed but only to pupate, they will leave the fish and fall in the container below. Normally it is only when the old used fish is moved that they will give off an offending odour: the bag and the remains of the fish can all be buried in the garden and a new start made with fresh fish. The gamekeepers of years gone by hung the birds of prey, shot in defence of their pheasants, on the nearest wire fence and the consequent maggots falling from these were welcomed by the birds. One seldom heard of a case of botulism in those days for with a fresh carcase for each breeding it was most unlikely to ever occur.

When feeding birds with maggots, there are a few additives which one can use to improve the nutritional content and the general value of this creature: to a cup of maggots add ten drops of cod liver oil, then sprinkle with calcium lactate, Vionate, Casilan or Complan. The oil must be used sparingly—too much can do more harm than good—though the small quantity mentioned will add a slight film to the maggots' surface and ensure that the other fine powders adhere to them. The calcium is to make certain sufficient reaches the nestlings; the last three mentioned items are all excellent in their own fields. Used in this manner, the almost worthless stored maggot becomes rich in nutritional value, the fine powder being passed to the nestlings.

Bee and Wasp Pupae
These are exceptionally good food value although culturing is not

possible and an apiarist should be consulted. There are usually a certain number of bee grubs wasted in any apiary establishment and they are well worth the little effort in collecting them, either for immediate use or for freezing. They may be given whole to large birds, cut into pieces for smaller species or minced for the very delicate billed specimens. Likewise the grubs of wasps are a useful addition to a bird's diet and an enquiry at the local council pest control office may be helpful. Ask if there is any chance of getting the wasp nests removed by the department. Even after extermination of the swarm, the larvae should be untouched by the chemicals used since each is sealed in its own little cell. Check, however, with the pest control official that the chemical is not a liquid which has contaminated the sealed grubs. Using a pair of tweezers one can open up the full cells and gently remove each grub. These can be fed immediately or frozen for future use.

Locusts
Large plastic aquaria, quite reasonably priced, are easily available and one of these or a wooden-framed plastic container, or even an unwanted aquarium of glass can be used for the bulk of the locusts. A lid should be made of perforated zinc in two separate pieces one of which will hold the electric bulbs which provide the necessary heat and the other, smaller if possible, will act as the door for feeding, watering and removing the females which have been fertilised. Two bulbs are recommended in case one should fail during use causing loss of breeding stock. Carbon filament bulbs give more heat and adequate light for this purpose and it is advised that a qualified electrician should install such equipment as this kind of bulb in particular needs a good heat-resistant holder and cable near the fitting.

A main breeding compartment and separate hatching jars are suggested; the adult locusts are kept in the former where they should receive fresh grass and a small shallow dish of bran daily. A sponge protruding from a small glass bowl of water will supply all drinking needs. Have a confectionery jar ready for the fertilised females, when they are ready to remove from the main culture and place moist sand in it to a depth of about ten centimetres. A small piece of sponge in a dish such as a cage drinker with water, and sufficient grass for each day should be supplied making sure that stale grass does not build up and cover the sand base. The female will insert her abdomen into the sand as far as she can reach, then lay her eggs. She will gradually extract her body until the last eggs are just below the surface of the sand and will then seal the egg 'tube'; before putting her back with the adults give her an opportunity to lay other eggs. Such a container as the confectionery jar can take up to five fertilised females, but only if placed therein on the same day or over a period of two days: the eggs in one jar will then all hatch at the same time. Allow just over the two weeks' expected period for hatching. The most suitable breeding temperature is about 80° F (26°–27° C), so if housed in an insectary which is controlled at this the bulbs fitted to the adults' container need be for lighting purposes only, allowing them roughly sixteen hours per day. The moistened sand for the eggs to hatch in is made damp only on the one occasion prior to the fertilised female being placed in the jar. The sand should be made just sufficiently damp so that when gripped tightly in the hand it retains that shape when released but will crumble under the least pressure. Newly hatched young locusts may be fed directly to birds but I prefer to see that they eat grass beforehand, and then I do not feed them to the stock until at least twenty-four hours old: almost all birds can cope with this insect when at this stage, except perhaps treecreepers and goldcrests. For these smaller birds, young locusts can be minced and added to their mixture.

One should be careful when considering unconventional forms of food. There was a time many years ago when I wondered if one could breed the beetle from which cochineal is prepared, a small insect reared on cactus in Mexico. I had visions that this might enable certain birds to retain colour which is frequently lost when in confinement. Later in life, when visiting Mexico, I admired the many flowering cacti I saw but left the insects to their own devices after I had investigated the cacti's skin texture. Spiders can be collected but not bred in vast quantities. Crickets can be bred in a dustbin containing pages of newspaper rolled into balls, and fed on rolled oats and wheatmeal at about 80° F (27° C).

Ant 'eggs', particularly those of the wood ant, are a nutritious item too good to be missed if local to one's home. I have moved whole nests into aviaries, the best time being the month of May, and watched them soon rebuild with the material I packed with them in large plastic bags: they started breeding shortly afterwards. They can be fed by filling a jam-jar with wholewheat meal on to which should then be poured hot water containing melted crystallised honey and a little yeast. Allow this to set once more and cool before placing near to their nest. They will soon make determined inroads into the food. Lay the jar on one side to prevent rain destroying the food supply. A long cane can be used to reach the top centre of the nest when the 'eggs' are available. If the top layer is removed at this time and the 'eggs' spread, birds will soon arrive on the scene for their share of this food. On the other hand this excellent addition to the basic diet can be collected at the wild site. Lay a sheet of canvas in a sunny spot on the ground at least six metres from the nest and fold over the edges to form a flap of about ten centimetres all round. Place a few small sticks or dead leaves under the edges of this flap and then gently remove the top of the nest where the largest 'eggs' are stored. Shovel a heap into the centre of the canvas sheet and the ants collected with the 'eggs' will speedily remove them to the shade of the flap all around the outer edges. It is a simple matter to brush them gently into a container from here.

A butterfly catcher's net swept over the uppermost grass-heads and flowers of a field, the contents being removed to a plastic sack or large bag will in a very short while provide a host of insect life. Bees will soon escape if the net is held upwards for a moment or so, open, so that they may carry on their work undisturbed. A plastic collection jar or bag should be taken on any trip to the country lanes or fields. Even a stroll in the garden can be rewarding for the birds as a glance under rockery stones, and in borders often produces a fair amount of woodlice. Leaves harbouring aphids, and heathers shaken over a plastic sheet or in a bag can usually give forth dozens of small spiders and other creatures suitable for any nestlings in the rearing stage.

Small fish fry can sometimes be collected by the bucketful and can be stored in the freezer or fed minced in softfood to birds of redstart size upwards. Provide a few each day alive in a shallow dish so that parent birds may help themselves as they wish. They will then be seen to hammer the fish well before offering it to their young.

Where permitted one can use moth traps at night and gather a multitude of insects as well as moths. However, do keep a watchful eye on the species of moth taken: today we are so short of many that a little care in the conservation of these is the duty of everyone.

Whiteworms can be cultured quite easily but I find few birds prefer them to the insects mentioned above. Those who do wish to breed them should firstly prepare a breeding container: plastic seed trays are ideal for this purpose. Obtain some peat, sufficient for each tray intended for use; sterilise this in the oven, then fill the trays and keep them moist taking care that no other insects can enter. Have a sheet of glass for each tray, just large enough to cover it and overlap the edges. Now to obtain a nucleus culture mix half a cupful of wholewheat flour into a paste with water; find a damp, sunless spot in the garden, make a slight depression in the ground and pour the contents of the cup into this; finally place a piece of slate over this. Add daily amounts of the paste, keeping only sufficient available for each day. Many worms will eat this but after a few days small hair-like whiteworms will appear. Keep feeding these until they increase to form a small knot of creatures three or four centimetres across; at this stage gather them and place them in a small tin containing wet moss. Leave them like this for two days then very gently with a spatula remove them to the prepared tray. These trays must be kept in total darkness. They should be fed daily with only sufficient (a tea-spoonful at first) for each day so that the paste does not go sour or rancid; gradually the mass of worms will multiply and once estab-lished will breed quite freely and in large quantities. If the worms tend to 'ball up' when collected for the birds, harvest them at evening the day before, place them in damp moss in the dark and they will be widely dispersed by the morning when required: the moss can be shared between the birds and they will take them as required.

Fruit flies are simple to breed, requiring only one or two squashed bananas in a jam-jar. Keep about six of these active and they can quickly be placed one after the other in aviary or indoor flight. Another method of producing this fly is to use a bottle of Guinness or milk stout. Fix a drip feed in lieu of the stopper, secure upside down and site just below a dish containing a sponge which fills the container completely. The flies will produce eggs and the minute maggot will pupate in the drier crevices of the sponge, producing an insect with reasonably good food content.

HAND RAISING YOUNG BIRDS

This is a method of rearing young birds to the stage where they can ably feed for themselves without assistance other than the daily provision of food, water and other necessities. For most people this can be a problem as working hours, sleep, hours of light and leisure time rarely coincide with the needs of a young, completely dependent bird.

Warmth is as vital as food and we must be sure that during the night when temperatures drop to their minimum, the young bird is kept warm. The use of a nest is far from sufficient and many young birds die solely through their keeper's ignorance of this fact. A box, either of wood or cardboard, will be required; line this to a thickness of about two and a half centimetres with polystyrene which can be cut from ceiling tiles, or obtained from do-it-yourself stores or builders' merchants in sheet form of various thicknesses. The box including the base should be lined fully. One piece is needed for a lid and this should have a hole in it about the size of a pencil. The young bird will need to lie in soft tissues which must be replaced frequently so that wet and cold do not chill the nestling. The excrement sacs, too, should be removed after each feed.

As would be expected, the diets of wild insectivorous and seedeating species vary, not in fact to any great extent during their first few days as both then take animal protein in the form of insects, and a certain amount of vegetable matter, but gradually the seedeating varieties increase their consumption of farinaceous foods and vegetable matter, whereas the insectivorous birds continue on their all-insect diet with the only vegetable content being that of the undigested food of the many insects fed to them.

The ideal time to start rearing a young bird, if from choice, is five or six days old. Only too often the time is not chosen: it is thrust upon us when an accident in the wild causes some kindly soul to bring a bare gaping creature to the door with some such comment as 'we found this, can you do anything to help'. Perhaps in our own aviary we may find a youngster on the floor, apparently dead. Where this happens it can be a case of a hen flying straight from the nest and dragging an offspring with her. Very often breathing on the youngster held in cupped hands in the warm for a few minutes revives the bird sufficiently for it to commence gaping again. Whatever the cause, whether handed to us or taken specifically under licence for one purpose or another, the task of rearing it is before us.

For the seedeaters I have used insectivorous mixtures made into a paste with milk, to which I have added a pinch of grated cuttlefish or calcium lactate, some cut up mealworms, chopped dandelion, comfrey or a little brassica. Never mix a great deal at a time: use two teaspoons of basic food, with a dozen mealworms and about half the equivalent of vegetable matter as softfood. Add milk to bring the mixture to a cream if the bird is very young, or crumbly-wet if five days or over. This can be fed to the bird either by spatula, shaped at the end, or by a syringe: I have used one originally intended for icing cakes, and adapted the nozzle by enlarging the small round hole. The spatula, although taking a little more time, is probably the best for the inexperienced as the food should be placed as far down the throat as possible whilst the bird is gaping: a syringe can tend to choke the subject in the hands of the inexperienced. If it is used, however, always point the nozzle well down the throat on the bird's right-hand side, towards the crop; after a short while one can fill the crops of a dozen youngsters in almost that many seconds.

Try using Farlene (Glaxo), a baby food which has been extensively used for young birds with good results. Add to it the above recommended extra ingredients and the bird should thrive if fed frequently enough. It is always far better to feed little and often, but always in the endeavour to keep the crop packed full at all times from early morning until one retires for the night. Then the box containing the young bird, or birds, should be placed near some form of heating: an airing cupboard will suffice if the door is left ajar for fresh air to reach the box air vent.

When the young hardbill reaches the stage where he greedily makes a grab for the food being offered, provide a shallow dish holding some of the rearing food and sprinkle a little maw seed on top of it; add a further shallow container holding some soaked seed which should include red rape, teazle and also a small amount of hemp if the finch is other than bullfinch, chaffinch or brambling. If the hand-reared specimen is one of these three members of the finch family substitute a few cut up mealworms on top of the soaked seed for the hemp.

When the subject has been eating this food regularly, in addition to the food fom the spatula or syringe, for about a week, one should then offer the normal seed mixture one offers their stock, but always in a soaked state. Keep the bird on this and the rearing food until it has fully moulted. As soon as the bird is observed to be eating properly from its dishes, offer leaves of dandelion, comfrey or any of the brassicas, not too much at a time but enough to last the day without souring; with the completion of the moult the bird can be run into an outdoor aviary after first having been introduced, for a day, by the cage hanging just inside the enclosure door.

The hand raising of insectivorous species is no more difficult. Start off with a small amount of good quality high protein softfood, or Farlene, as a base. To this quantity of, say, two teaspoonsful add a dozen cut up mealworms, a pinch of grated cuttlefish powder, or calcium lactate, and about a third of the amount of the basic softfood, of finely chopped greenfood such as dandelion, comfrey or spinach. Then add milk and before stirring add one drop of Abidec. Mix the whole to a cream and always feed softbills with a spatula.

At the age of six days one can start giving, well mixed in the softfood, some finely grated Cheddar cheese. If a grater is not making it fine enough pushing small pieces through a metal tea strainer with the thumb will render it suitable for mixing in the food; start at about twenty-five per cent of the basic mixture and increase gradually to form a third of the whole food within a week of starting.

As the bird progresses so too can the diet gradually change. In addition to the mealworms mixed into the food, offer from tweezers a few wax-moth larvae between meals of softfood; these should have had their skins burst or heads squeezed with the tweezers before the birds eat them. The time will come when the young bird will peck at the food as it is offered on the spatula and from this moment it should be caged; it will soon begin to take food from a shallow dish. I like to give a container rather larger than a saucer and sprinkle it with the food in a little more crumbly texture and add some grated cheese and a few meal-worms cut into pieces. Then, in a small area in the centre, I place about ten or twelve maggots and cover them with a clear upturned glass: I keep an old broken wine glass for this purpose with the broken stem ground down. The bird's attention will be constantly drawn to the movements, and as it pecks at the insects inside the glass the bill will slip and come into contact with the food; this encouragement to feed is also used in 'meating off'. The moth larvae can be increased to ten or more a day and the mealworms should be correspondingly lessened to five per day. The required calcium will now be provided by the softfood or the Farlene although this latter basic, if it has been used, should have been discontinued in favour of the softfood intended for general use at the time of the bird's being caged; at that time it will still be taking the rearing food from the spatula as well as commencing to peck at food.

As soon as the moult is complete in these birds, endeavour to give them a few weeks outdoors in a smallish aviary where one can keep an eye on their general health and behaviour. The winter quarters will vary from species to species but the majority can be allowed outdoors on good weather days, and some all the time just so long as they can re-enter the warmer atmosphere of an indoor shelter. Bathing facilities should be available to them from the time they begin to eat for themselves. As their self-supporting age is reached they can be given Abidec in their drinking water twice a week until the end of the moult. Even whilst hand raising is in progress there is much more which can be added to their diet, but for simplicity I have kept to an easy to prepare mixture for rearing and general feeding. Consulting the entry for the particular species in Part Two will give a more comprehensive list of suitable foods.

'MEATING OFF'

When any bird is taken, under licence, from the wild, some knowledge is necessary to prevent dietary shock which can be fatal.

One can usually house seedeaters individually, or with a tame inoffensive bird in a box-type cage. To the drinking water add a few drops of a vitamin food supplement. The seed mixture should be as varied as possible and soaked to the point of sprouting. A week or so on this diet, together with wild foods and the bird can be given a mixture of dry and soaked seed on a fifty/fifty basis. The only time adult hardbills should be collected from the wild is in the early autumn or winter time. A few mealworms and maggots in a shallow dish will often be taken but it depends upon the species; wild foods of the bird's choice should never cease to be available at least for the first month under controlled conditions.

The insectivorous bird requires a little patience in the way of a constant alertness to the situation. Watch what is happening, not by standing in front of the new specimen but by quick glances at the food dish each time one is in the vicinity of the cage.

For those who are prepared to make a special effort, I would advise the construction of a 'meating off' cage, which ensures the safety of the subject and helps immensely in weaning freshly taken insectivorous specimens on to a man-prepared diet. Having used a cage such as that described below for many years I can vouch that it adequately fulfils its purpose. Firstly make a cage base in the form of a box about eight centimetres deep. Its area should be roughly that of a canary double breeding cage. This base should be constructed with two drawer trays so that the finished cage is easy to clean. Purchase some softwood approximately one and a half centimetres square in section and from this construct a frame (Fig. 2) to fit the upper rim of the cage base sides; when glued

46

and panel pinned together, this frame should be secured to the base with about six small flat brass hook and eye catches, two either side and one at each end. This frame should incorporate two doors, one for feeding and watering, the other for removal of the bird without handling or undue chasing or shock. When structurally complete, cover the entire frame and doors with a very finely woven nylon material, almost as closely woven as linen. Secure this by gluing the frame one side at a time, placing the material in position and pinning taut on the frame until completely dry.

Fig. 2 'Meating off' cage construction details: (*a*) frame; (*b*) base and perches.

This 'meating off' cage can be used for even the most difficult species. Adult goldcrests can sometimes prove troublesome, but in a suitable cage even fruit flies cannot escape. Young locusts, blow flies and moth larvae remain nearby tempting any inmate until eaten. Give drinking water containing Abidec. A shallow container a little larger than a saucer should be covered with a thin layer of a high protein softfood, comprising about fifty per cent steamed and minced ox heart and liver and plenty of grated cheese. A little extra cheese should be sprinkled on top and upon this should be cut several mealworms. Leave the centre of the dish bare and in the space place half a dozen mealworms and about a dozen very lively maggots and cover them quickly with an upturned clear glass as described above so that the birds will peck at the glass and as their bills move downwards they will come into contact with the foods.

There is no excuse for losing a bird taken from the wild: even a box-type cage with a piece of butter muslin or even hessian or linen hung over the front will give the bird that required security it needs in the first day or two. Ensure that the material allows adequate light to reach the bird. After a few days this cloth can gradually be raised.

The time taken to 'meat off' a bird varies with the individual as well as the species: I have seen wagtails and nuthatches eating within moments of being placed in a cage with food. I do not like to see any body weight loss at all, and if feeding is carried out correctly, any bird should be eating reasonably well within two hours. Correct feeding involves renewal of the cut up mealworms and a supply of more cheese four or five times daily. A bird should be treated like this for at least two weeks and by that time ought to be eating everything that is offered. Always see that the softfood and cheese are being eaten in quantities denoting a healthy appetite before lessening the number of mealworms and always check the birds' advised diet before catering for them; some may need fruit, others sunflower seed, berries or a particular variety of livefood.

Finally mention may be made that nuthatches should not be put in a cloth 'meating off' cage: they will ruin it within an hour. Use a box cage with lengths of bark secured to the inner sides or propped up with the base very near the food dish.

PAIRING, NESTING AND NEST SITES

General information on this subject may prove useful in addition to the specific comments on each species in Part Two. Some pairs of birds can be placed together and no sign of bickering will ever be noticed, but I would hasten to add that a further pair of the same genus can be freed in another aviary and murder be committed within minutes. The very first thing to realise is that one cannot attribute to birds the human process of thought: because some action is logical to us, we tend to imagine a bird will think likewise. It may well be so in some cases, but we must respect that if a pair we had thought ideally suited does not wish to contemplate family raising duties at a particular time it is better to treat them to a gradual courtship than risk one bird mauling another.

Many birds benefit from being housed in an aviary adjoining that of their prospective mate. At first they may completely ignore the bird on the other side of the wire, or even attempt to attack or threaten it at every opportunity. However, over a period, with advanced breeding condition, there should be a noticeable change in both birds. With longer days, more sun and a richer diet, the opponent for each crumb of food, the antagonist for a favourite perch, the challenger to the territory, slowly becomes more attractive and nature will take its course in time; what we must do is watch for the perfect moment to open a dividing door.

First study the wildlings: does the male choose the site of nesting operations? Is it he who first arrives from migration and stakes out a territory? What is the 'key' that unlocks a mating reaction and acceptance? There is always one and when you know your birds you will be able to breed them in aviaries. The problem in breeding is not pairing but providing the right substitute food for newly hatched nestlings for at least the first five days.

49

Fig. 3 A finch nest site which will act as a deterrent to any mice reaching a nest or disturbing a nesting hen in any way. This sketch illustrates the way in which the site can simply be made with the use of bamboo cane, nest basket, wire and conifer branches in its construction. A short length of plastic pipe pushed into the soil will hold cane in position and prevent it from rotting.

The moment to pair could be when a male enters a nest site and displays to the female, and she attempts to follow him despite the wire division between them. If she remains uninterested at the far end of her aviary, wait a little longer; nature does: in the wild the male would probably chase her from the territory if she showed this lack of response, then await another female's arrival, attracting and calling her with his song. In an aviary he cannot chase her away and we must here bend natural law a little as we can rarely provide another female in just the right condition. A few more mealworms daily, the concentrated vitamin we should plan for any bird lacking in condition, the male's song, all will play their part in this little drama.

One example does not prove a general rule, but robins can be wretches for fighting between themselves at times other than during the breeding season when a pair will seem the most devoted of couples. We hand raised three, liberating the odd one when certain we had selected a pair: they were housed as mentioned above in adjoining enclosures and in this instance we placed a nest box in the hen's aviary. Originally they had fought at every opportunity and indeed I had at one time to separate them forcibly by hand when they were clutched together and ignoring my presence. Gradually with the male's constant song the female used to follow his movements although still in her own aviary: the arrival of a wild pair to my garden hastened things a little as the males spent much time fighting through the outer wire; perhaps this action, so natural in the wild, prompted a reaction also from the hen and she was eventually seen entering the hollow log nest site in her aviary and the male was doing his best to reach her at these times: it was then that a door was opened in the dividing partition and from that moment it was all plain sailing. We eventually had four clutches of eggs and far more young robins around the place than I ever intended. I would mention here that each lot of young had to be removed due to the male's attacks upon them once they reached a self-supporting state. These same young were finally released to the wild when observed taking enough wild insect life to be self-supporting. We liberated them on alternate days: in all probability some were chased from the area by local birds but one of the original pair still resides nearby and visits the garden on occasion.

The common redstart can be an example of difficult pairing, and yet I have known someone who bred them in a very large

Fig. 4   Various log and box sites.

Fig. 5   A timber site using a sheet of roofing felt and lengths of bean-sticks for the roof.

flight cage, certainly something I would not recommend. On the other hand I have never had any difficulty in the pairing of black redstarts, seldom witnessing even the slightest bickering. Nightingales, wheatears, barred warblers have all earned themselves a bad name in this respect and yet I have known pairs of each so very peaceful, gentle and devoted in appearance.

The important point is timing: with characters as diverse as humans', birds cannot be predictable in their actions: they must reach their peak of condition to be paired without risk. No matter how long one keeps and breeds birds, there is not one man alive who 'knows it all'; one just cannot give precise instructions and say, 'do things this way and success will be yours'. We have all come across the odd person who believes they have all the answers, but if it were all so easy we might as well keep white mice: the challenge to learn from one's studies is in itself a great attraction, but, were the truth admitted, the longer one keeps and studies birds the more one is made aware of one's limitations.

All birds require daily bathing facilities: the importance cannot be over-stressed. It is essential for general fitness and for firmness, colouring and well-being of the plumage, but it also contributes to breeding condition and one must never ignore anything which assists in reaching this required peak of condition.

When pairing birds for the breeding season it must be realised that the adults have to be one hundred per cent fit to obtain young of an equal or better standard, or even to obtain full eggs. For this reason, the food supply prior to the beginning of the season should be of high nutritional value. The hens in particular should have sufficient flying space available to obviate any undue fatness, subsequent egg binding and even failure to lay. The insectivorous species should have extras in the way of live insects though not too many mealworms and these should be cut in half or at least killed at all times. The seedeaters too must now receive a few mealworms: at first cut these up on top of their seed supply and as soon as they are seen eating them—they can have a daily supply—just pinch the heads of the insects before giving them; in the case of hardbills this is not a safety precaution but merely to prevent them escaping before being eaten. If the seedeaters have been receiving sweet apple, plenty of dandelion, chickweed, or even spinach, comfrey and brassicas of all kinds where wild plants are not available, they should now be coming into full song and

Fig. 6 Nest box made from willow branches or similar sticks, for finches and large softbills.

Fig. 7 An 'off the ground' site made from two flower pots rolled in roofing felt (also a piece between the pots), then covered in beansticks, wired in position, and the ends half closed with short pieces of stick, assembled as shown.

chasing their hens. Offer plenty of mineral grit and cuttlefish; another useful item not often used is rock salt, as offered to cattle to lick. It is amazing to see how much time is spent by birds steadily nibbling at a block of salt.

Before the eggs are due to be laid you should make certain that they will be fertile, with healthy chicks hatching, by supplying all the essential nutrients well in advance. This should be not merely the month before, but prior to the moult and right through the colder months. Many bird keepers complain of clear eggs, developing chicks dead in shell and similar 'ill-luck', but these things can be eliminated: do not discard adult birds for these reasons but rather analyse your feeding prior to the nesting season. For any chick to develop from an embryo, all the vital requirements for its growth must be present in the egg to provide it with the strength needed for ultimate hatching and the first twenty-four hours of the nestling stage.

Sometimes a freshly imported bird or pair will nest and hatch young, only to lose their nestlings after appearing to search everywhere for something that is missing. I have seen this with a few birds from Russia and can only conclude that when first imported they are unused to our vegetation and tend to search for that which they are used to. This problem has in my own experience sorted itself out the following year and I have always been glad that I did not dispose of the birds for lack of ability in rearing: the errors were mine not the birds'. When rearing is in progress, it is often customary for the parents to slacken off feeding around midday, not stopping fully but resting between journeys whilst young too tend to nap: they resume again in earnest at 3 p.m. or so and it is important to make sure that there are sufficient of the right foods for them to feed the young prior to the long night ahead, and some, too, for an early morning feed next day, whilst their keeper is still asleep.

The pairing of hardbills is often a simpler matter than that of certain insectivorous birds. Normally a pair of hardbills, either alone, in a trio or even under a colony system will accept each other without undue risk of fatalities occurring. It is normal for the earlier provision of extra rich food supplies, mealworms, dandelions and the growing plant life in their enclosure and even sprouting seed to take effect on their condition in conjunction with the extra sunlight and longer days. There are, of course, occasions when a pair do seem to dislike each other, but it is rare

Fig. 8   Hanging nest box made from bean-sticks and two squares of wood covered first in felt.

Fig. 9   Using three flower pots or more (block bottom holes), site on a mound of gravel for drainage purposes, plant grasses, etc., then carefully place rocks in position to hide all but small entrance holes. Will prove ideal for wheatears, pied wagtails, etc.

indeed for harm to result unless they are large birds such as the hawfinch, or there are more than one pair of the same species together. Do not place the same trust in softbills.

In the wild state excellent examples of a species may quite possibly choose poor quality partners, but in aviaries when pairing, the best two can be paired, ensuring, as near as is possible, good quality young. If this can be carried out year after year one can build up a quite impressive quality of stock. At times during my liberty breeding experiments, when using such specimens, the young have benefited even more by this compulsory pairing system of ideally matched parents together with the subsequent natural diet collected by them from field and orchard: these two advantages improved a strain noticeably. Let me here add that liberty breeding is still really in its infancy for the re-taking of the parent birds, as wild specimens, is limited to those with official licences. I do not recommend beginners attempting it unless, even with a licence to do so, funds are unlimited to replace possible truants or genuine losses through predators and, sadly, the latter can be frequent.

There are no hard and fast rules for nesting that one must follow. When birds have nested interference should be avoided; one should ensure that no nest is sited where it may become tinder dry, but apart from these points it is difficult to aid them as birds can be as perverse where nest sites and nesting are concerned as any animal or human on their worst day.

Avoidance of too much disturbance to nesting birds is as wise in an aviary as in the wild; certainly there are pairs which constitute the inevitable exception which proves the rule, particularly where birds have become finger-tame over a period in an enclosure, always accepting the proferred mealworm or other favourite item of food. On the whole, observation from a distance is more satisfactory to bird and man: an ever alert eye is frequently necessary to be certain that young are being fed correctly and regularly but this is easily achieved without undue and obvious attention.

Nests should not be allowed to dry out too much for moisture in a nest, the warmth of the parent's brooding body and the slight clinging dampness which occurs all play their part in successful hatching; so often one sees a hen bath and return to the nest a few minutes later. I well recall an old friend of my father's, a real countryman, and a breeder of exhibition Yorkshire and Norwich

Fig. 10   Artificial hedge of varying heights to suit many species, made from bark-covered timbers and finally filled with heathers, conifers, evergreens, etc.

Fig. 11   Even a bare bush or bundle of branches can be covered by beans, sweet peas, etc.

canaries in his day. He used shallow dishes of water in his breeding cages into which were placed the old type terracotta flowerpots, one to each cage, with an earthenware nest-pot in the top: his explanation always seemed reasonable enough at the time: the damp assisted the hatching. The more one thinks on it, the more feasible it seems. From that time onwards I have always attempted to provide nest sites, although not fully open to the elements, not completely sheltered either, and I have no complaints to make about developing chicks failing to hatch.

A mouse climbing near a sitting hen at night can easily frighten her from her nest with a resulting loss through chilled eggs. We have looked at the problems of keeping mice out of aviaries in the aviary building section, but we can still do various things to combat this menace inside the enclosure. Rodent poisoning can be effectively practised so long as one makes certain that birds cannot reach the poisoned grain, and that mice cannot carry it from its site to a place where birds may partake of it. Traps that take mice alive can be a good investment but the very small ones can escape even from these. With a little thought one can provide many nesting sites that are almost certainly mouse-proof. Make use of plastic rainwater pipe, ensuring that one end is firmly held in the ground. Block the open end to prevent any inquisitive insect-hunting bird from disappearing and erect sites on top. Two such posts can be used for the more complicated sites. We all like to give such birds as wheatears a natural site and those who are always free of vermin are very fortunate in being able to do so. However, many are less happily situated and for those sites such as those in Figs 4, 5, 7 and 8 can be fabricated. The wheatear will readily accept such a site even though not on the ground.

The small plastic cold-water pipe can be used as illustrated in Fig. 3 for finches and even many softbill species: using roughly half a metre of this pipe, push it well into the earth of the aviary floor and into it new sites can be slipped as required; the site is nothing more than a wicker nest-basket, bamboo cane and a few small branches of fir, evergreen, bracken or heather. Select bamboo canes that will just slide into the plastic pipe; split these at one end into four near enough equal sections to a depth of about forty centimetres and secure a nest basket about half-way down with the four split sections near enough equally spaced around the basket; then wire the topmost end of these sections together to form an eight centimetre square. The twigs or branches to

Fig. 12   A further type of constructed hedge.

Fig. 13   Flower pot and brick site among vegetation.

Fig. 14   A bale of peat covered in seeds, grasses, plants, etc. with nesting holes.

provide birds with their required seclusion can then be gently slid through the square at the top, out past the basket and tucked in again beneath the wicker site. Use thin twiggy pieces and the canes will not split further. Thin gardening wire can be used to secure the sections a little way apart below the nesting basket so holding the twigs in position.

Mice will not usually climb the bamboo canes when a site is constructed in this manner. But beware of positioning it too close to the aviary side, whether timber or wire as they will certainly jump the small space so conveniently provided, by climbing to a point above the site and leaping from it to the nest. House mice which frequent many aviaries are very adept climbers and jumpers, far too frequently being one jump ahead of the bird keeper and thus earning many a hen a bad reputation as a breeding bird, or causing blame to fall on a cat when it may even have been after the mouse.

With a little imagination many types of site can be constructed, but if the pair of birds is really fit they will frequently make use of something completely surprising. I well remember a pair of tree pipits which had some beautiful sites provided in a large aviary, planted very tastefully and affording them all the seclusion they could wish for, but they chose to nest in the open on a shelf and reared successfully there. Figs 3 to 15 showing a number of possible sites for a fairly wide variety of aviary inmates, the reader should be able to select or amend some designs to suit his birds' purpose.

Do not offer too much in the way of nesting materials to begin with as it invariably becomes soiled as it is played with. Provide small quantities of various materials such as teased-out fibrous string, coconut matting, horse hair, dog hair, cow hair, dry grasses of very fine thin type as found with moss in dense undergrowth, small tufts of cotton-wool, moss, birch twigs and heather twigs. Wherever anything is over eight centimetres in length, apart from the twigs, make sure to cut this into shorter lengths to obviate the danger of birds entangling their legs; this can so easily destroy a season's hopes, even if not causing the death of the bird.

A quick check in one's record book or card index at this time will tell exactly what any particular bird made use of the last time that it nested. A lot of time and frustration can be saved when fully aware of a bird's choice. Frequently it will be found that pairs, or at least the hen, will wait until after a shower, when basic

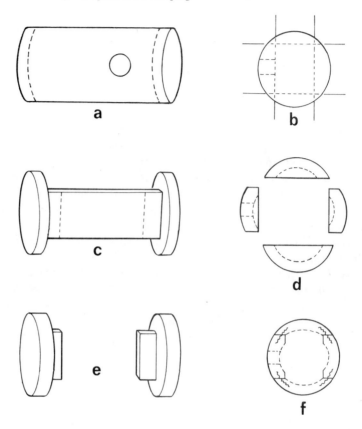

Fig. 15 A simple method to make log nest sites: (*a*) illustrates where to cut the original log with four right-angle (90°) cuts each end; (*b*) gives end view of this; next chisel off four sides of log carefully to leave as in (*c*); (*d*) gives an exploded version of the four sides; saw the log as in (*c*) to finish as shown in (*e*). Join the four sides together again in correct order (*f*) with special timber connectors, obtainable from almost any ironmonger. The two ends can now be replaced and fixed. A square roof can be attached if to be placed in very open site in an aviary. The size of the entrance hole will depend entirely upon the species it is intended for; better too large than small is a good maxim.

nesting materials are damp and pliable, before choosing the materials. They prefer the lining materials to be reasonably dry but where twigs or the coarser grasses, mosses and fibrous materials are used these are appreciated in a moist condition which can more easily be moulded to the required shape. After a quick downpour of rain, or the aviary floor is hosed, I have often seen birds readily use nesting materials which had previously been ignored for days.

Make use of wild vegetable down if accessible, but treat sheep wool from barbed-wire fences with a little caution as I have seen many accidents from its use: either cut it into pieces about two centimetres long or leave well alone.

Birds like the nuthatch will need mud for closing the nest box entrance and also any cracks and crevices they find in their nest box which allow the light to enter: the thrush family use mud, too.

Many varieties have their own favourite materials: the nightingale likes oak leaves, dead and withered from the previous year, to provide wonderful camouflage for its nest low in growing vegetation. This will often be amid nettles or low growing bramble but often I have had them nest in other sites, once using a flowerpot left on its side. Even so their choice of materials is inherited and oak leaves remain the favourite mixed with grasses and a little moss.

For long-tailed tits offer many fine mosses, spiders' webs by the dozen, collected on a thin hooped stick, fine feathers, small pieces of cotton wool, lichen, small pieces of tissue paper about postage stamp size and first rolled in moistened hands. They like dense honeysuckle to nest in, or bramble, a thick hawthorn or similar site in which they can weave the walls of their nest to form the foundation for the warm, snug, fully feather-lined nest.

Often where a ground nesting bird is wary of a ground site, perhaps due to nightly prowling mice, I have found them accept a biscuit tin fixed on its side to a mouse-proof climbing post. A few nail holes around the top edge and green turves inside will sometimes coax the pair into using it. The holes in the roof let in sufficient water from rainfall to keep the grass inside green and provide them with ample seclusion. I have seen whinchats take to this site within an hour of its installation, though a more unlikely whinchat site I can hardly think of. These bogus sites, that can be made absolutely mouse-proof are a great asset, so do not give up hope when the birds reject orthodox nesting arrangements, just the right vegetation, an exact replica of an observed site in the wild, etc. They will often adapt: they even have to do so in the wild with man's urbanisation of the countryside.

Observation of behaviour and record-keeping at this time can be well worthwhile. Indeed without accurate data it all seems rather pointless and there is so much information still needing to be passed on. Do practise this observation very discreetly so that one's presence cannot be objected to by the nest owners. Sitting outside the enclosure with a pair of binoculars trained on the site will tell much: one does not have to see into the nest to gather information. Most information can be gained from seeing who comes and goes and what they are carrying to and fro.

Having illustrated suitable nesting sites for finches, buntings and insectivorous birds, I would merely emphasise the fact that they all have minds of their own, particularly in regard to what meets their immediate requirements when nesting. The presence of nocturnal wandering mice, often unsuspected by the bird keeper, can, for example, cause normal ground nesting varieties to seek higher sites or the furthest possible point from vermin. One cannot always blame such untoward behaviour on prowling mice, however, and one must beware of attributing one's own frame of reference to the birds. A mid-height shelf in an aviary must be much the same to a bird as a bank site in the wild and a half open fronted box will provide similar security to the roots of an upturned tree.

PART TWO

Keeping and breeding details for individual species. The author's successes (and failures) are indicated for each species according to the following key:

† Adult birds hand reared
* Pair nested
** Eggs laid
*** Young hatched
**** Young reared to maturity
‡ Liberty bred species

FINCHES AND BUNTINGS

We may make certain generalisations about the group of finches and buntings before considering under separate headings certain birds which require more specialised advice and slightly different management at certain seasons of the year or stages of their lives. Where pairs are housed individually, one pair to an aviary, life can be very simple. Where mixing is involved, a kind of permutation is sometimes required, certain species being 'high risk' specimens as compared to other more placid types. We must remember to observe all birds as individuals: one can keep a dozen pairs of one variety and find that one male or female is as homicidally inclined to one or more of his kind (or others) as the worst in human criminal history—observation will tell us where our trust is being misplaced: if suspicious act quickly and isolate the offender. Having offered that advice, one can go for many years without having to actually heed it, but the odd rogue can do much damage in a short time if not apprehended.

There are some finches which can be colony bred: goldfinches, siskins, redpolls, crossbills, and, with a slightly lesser degree of success, greenfinches. The only real disadvantage of this method is the inability of the bird keeper to identify true parentage of the young or maintain any accurate records of stock. It depends entirely for what purpose one is keeping the birds: if merely for the aesthetic enjoyment of the aviary inmates' company I suppose it can be justified; if for behavioural studies, it may be essential; were one attempting to improve and maintain a true strain of birds by selective pairing, however, then it is pointless. Bullfinches, chaffinches, bramblings, yellow hammers, hawfinches and most buntings should either be housed one pair to their own aviary or one pair to any mixed collection. In some cases they can be very territorially inclined when breeding, sometimes not even waiting for another inmate to cause offence

67

before attacking it; it is obvious that such behaviour is in no way conducive to breeding harmony, even in a large aviary.

Those birds housed together all winter as a mixed collection stand a far better chance of living in peace during the breeding season in a large enough enclosure than a motley crowd placed together at the last moment with little thought given to their well-being or future safety. At times a little belligerence by bullfinches when actually selecting a nest site and forming their territory will die a natural death with their having identified that area; quite often things will then remain peaceful throughout the season, the other birds treating the stronger ones with a certain amount of respect. This pecking order is normal and as long as no physical harm results can prove most interesting to observe. Similarly aggressive behaviour can be expected from the other birds I have listed as being best paired in their own enclosure: some may indeed breed amicably without worrying others but the individual bird keeper should keep an ever-watchful eye on birds of this type.

The nesting sites can be varied but on the whole need only be nest baskets or suitable growing or installed vegetation to provide natural nesting site choice and facilities. Those requiring different sites are the birds expected to choose ground, rock crevice, or hole positions for nesting, merely a few of the buntings. Many of the birds under this heading will prefer shelf-type sites, or bush sites, but unless absolutely certain that one's aviaries are free of mice these should not be erected as they could become one of the worst encouragements and difficult areas to clear of vermin without also putting a stop to breeding operations as a whole. The majority of finches and buntings will accept a basket site or build their own natural nest in a simple site without such elaborate measures being undertaken. However, in very large enclosures, perhaps the walk-through type where it may be open to a number of people entering, more secluded sites are usual to ensure some degree of security and success.

The diets of this group of birds vary so greatly in the wild that it is almost impossible to give an exhaustive list here. All will survive on the accepted finch mixture as sold commercially but in the wild few of these seeds would be taken by many of them: it is a substitute diet and a fairly well balanced one, but it should be understood that many of the ingredients are not conducive to longevity in the subject. There are so many natural foods that can be obtained or grown to provide variety that one should endeavour to cater for the individual's natural needs a little more closely.

Some birds will over-eat of a certain favourite seed and may become almost addicted to it. Variety of course is necessary, but one should not confuse a varied with a well-balanced diet. Before even a general assessment of the nutritional value of individual seeds, or diets, can be made, it is first vital to learn of the chemical composition of such foods and the effects of the substances they contain. As a large proportion of the human diet should contain animal and fruit and vegetable nutrients, so too should the birds'. But birds are no more wise than humans in accepting the items we know they should have, and the bird keeper's task is to make items such as carrot, celery or their juices palatable to the finch or bunting family. Apple is in fact easily introduced to the finches. The use of mealworms helps greatly and most birds will accept them after experimentation. The cutting-up of this insect on their seed is usually enough to ensure that it is taken avidly at all times: we can then introduce the necessary moisture to mealworms by giving them carrot, apple and celery and, if this becomes a general habit then a certain amount of the required substances will reach the bird in the undigested portion of the mealworms' food. The reference to fruit and vegetable juices is meant as an illustration; they are important, but so are many other foods of proven use; malnutrition in even its mildest form, cannot be cured by seed alone and one should make it one's business to learn which foods provide which nutrients and therefore prevent certain diseases. Mineral deficiency, for example, causes several diseases which can be easily avoided. There are, I believe, in the region of ninety minerals in the twelve basic organic minerals and if our birds get their required supply of each daily they will never suffer this particular deficiency. A basic knowledge of the constituent elements of the commonly available foodstuffs should be acquired by all serious bird keepers.

Brambling (*Fringilla montifringilla*)****
General description
This bird is about thirteen centimetres long and is very closely related to the chaffinch though the general appearance is far darker, the neck and head being marked with black streaks and

from the throat downwards the chest is a rich tawny orange; there is a winter and summer plumage, so that from the breeding season onwards the male's head and back of neck will be almost jet black. They are simple to sex at all times, the hen resembling so much the chaffinch female in her colouring.

Habitat

Although belonging to Northern Europe and Scandinavia where they nest in similar sites to the chaffinch, this bird's breeding range appears to be moving south; they are a frequent winter visitor to the British Isles arriving in their thousands, but native habitat is mainly birchwoods. On migration they tend to flock in open country but often near beeches or hornbeams.

Aviary

As with most species of seedeater, the minimum recommended aviary for breeding should be two metres long by the same height and one metre wide: longer dimensions will assist during mating display flights. A roofed portion should be included to provide shelter from heavy rainfall with a little dense evergreen foliage for roosting: this may be grown in their quarters with no ill-effects since they do not usually damage such foliage.

Food

In the wild the brambling will live almost exclusively on insects during the breeding season when, however, they will also take many seeds from the ground. The young are reared on insects of all kinds and the adult birds frequently take seeds from opening conifer cones and rely during winter months on beech seeds where available and ground seeds during the harder weather. From this one can see that we have a species here which will readily take insect life often all year round; they will even catch insects on the wing. The provision of insects in their diet simplifies catering arrangements and ensures a high protein food intake. The seeds should include screenings or collected wild seeds dried for out of season use, plain canary seed, grass, lettuce, all the brassicas, a little linseed, small amounts of maw and gold of pleasure and dock. They will rarely eat seeds from growing plants in the wild and although their doing so under controlled conditions is a result of failure to provide a totally adequate substitute diet, they do surely benefit from them since they must replace, or partly so, certain natural foods. Some bramblings will readily eat softfood especially if its introduction is assisted by its

70

being sprinkled with maw seed or some other favourite seed of the individual bird. Any young birds will require a large number of insects in order to fledge properly.

Breeding
With a mixed collection the brambling must be watched until the individual's behaviour has been noted: the males, and at times females, can become a source of trouble; not normally of a spiteful nature, they do often become aggressive whilst breeding operations are carried out. More often than not, in the case of successful rearing, certainly with full clutches, my birds have had an enclosure of their own. Provide the pair with natural nesting sites by growing an elder in the aviary; when quite bushy in appearance, run a string or wire fully around it at the largest part and tighten it, pulling in the branches to form a tightly knit area; some hens will more readily commence building a nest if a basket containing a moss lining is inserted at this point. When building without the aid of a basket they will require a number of thin birch twigs or similar; I have seen heather twigs taken, also beech and fine dead twigs of honeysuckle. Give roots, moss, dog or cow hair, horse hair, too, if cut short; feathers may also be used but it depends upon individual choice as some line nests fully with hair; it could well be more normal in their original colder climate to use more feathers for warmth.

The provision of plenty of insect life, mealworms and any other obtainable items of such high protein value will bring the birds into breeding condition and one will soon hear that raucous call of the male urging his mate to nest.

Bullfinch (*Pyrrhula pyrrhula pileata*)†*****‡
General Description
The British bullfinch is unmistakable for any other bird in the wild by his jet black cap and bib; slate blue-grey back; white rump; black wings and tail, and the rich carmine chest and underparts, the latter being present only in the male: the female has a brownish pink chest with browner back, and the young resemble her in colouring. The length is about sixteen centimetres. One can sex young bullfinches just prior to their fully entering the moult when the males first identify themselves by a slate grey streak behind each shoulder, well in advance of the first breast streaks, of red.

Habitat

Originally more forest dwelling than today, now common throughout almost the whole of Britain in woodland, thickets and orchards, the latter much to the professional fruit growers' dismay due to their terrible depredations on fruit buds. They often frequent gardens in the suburbs and here, too, they will strip fruit buds from many trees; despite this we invariably see many rotting apples on orchard ground in the autumn.

Aviary

Again we can use the standard minimum recommended aviary size. These birds are very easy to cater for, but they can be very aggressive and territorially minded. Having once asserted their full authority over the other inmates, however, they often get on with their own domestic duties and ignore other birds. Due to the food requirements of a nest full of young bullfinches, however—a host of insects in the initial stages of growth—I prefer to give them an enclosure to themselves. The aviary should provide adequate shelter for the winter to shield them from inclement weather: they are hardy birds but live far longer and remain in good health at all times if a dry draught-proof shelter is available to them. Because of their tiresome habit of de-budding so many shrubs and plants, they are limited to very particular growing vegetation: elder will survive but it does not provide what is normally accepted as a good nest site for the bullfinch, so they should have a wicker nest basket placed in a dense part of its growth. They will greatly benefit from many kinds of edible vegetables such as comfrey, cabbage and spinach; hops will also grow despite the constant pruning, providing insect life, and seeds later in the autumn.

Food

Sunflower is a firm favourite and a good flesh building seed and it does not cause birds to run to fat inwardly as does hemp: for this reason I never give these birds the latter seed. When soaked well, groats will be eaten and the germ is highly valuable. Once again endeavour to make use of screenings and many wild field seeds: that wonderful conditioner, dandelion, should be given as soon as the seeding heads become closed after blooming and on the point of opening to disperse the seeds; at this time there is no better food for advancing condition. Give a mixture of seeds containing sunflower, groats, small amounts of rape and other brassicas, a very little linseed and niger and as many wild collected seeds or screenings as can be obtained. Highly appreciated are the twigs from hawthorn, fruit trees and bushes, just when the buds become swollen and ready to burst open. In fact, so long as the leaves are young and tender, such cuttings as blackcurrant and raspberry will be taken throughout the year. Even my roses, which go unsprayed, provide an odd feed now and again: they take the green-fly and any shoots they can find. I find that a pigeon conditioning seed when well soaked and on the point of sprouting, has many seeds that prove acceptable to bullfinches, for their own use and for feeding young once the nestlings have advanced from the insect diet to part insect and grain stage at around eight to ten days. My own bullfinches have, over the years, become fond of soaked household currants: these are given when no other berries or wild fruits can be collected from hedges. I leave them in water over-night, then strain them and include in their seed. During the autumn one can collect many wild fruits such as hawthorn, rowan, and numerous others and the bullfinch receiving such attention will moult out far superior to any other; these fruits are often given in small quantities to their young when rearing. Animal and vegetable proteins are the aim in the bullfinch diet and more important than grain as a basic food. Soaked teazle when they are rearing and in that change-over period from insects to seed will prove the most useful seed in addition to the soaked sunflower.

Breeding
Bullfinches require little in the way of nest sites and the fact that they may make only a mere shadow of a real nest is often our fault: we cause so many of the hindrances which occur when attempting to breed birds; we expect too much adaptation over too short a period. Give the bullfinch adequate thin pliable twigs, plenty of rootlets to choose from, horse, cow and dog hair for lining purposes and they will then build a nest which will hold eggs. Where wicker nest baskets are used, the amount of twigs needed will be correspondingly less, but they do still search for such items and after a heavy shower when such things are at their most pliable watch these birds carry them around looking for a suitable site: such a nest basket need not be covered from view with evergreen branches, heather or conifer; it needs merely one or two sprays in

front of it and some kind of shelter above to stop direct full rain falling upon nest or occupants.

Northern Bullfinch (*Pyrrhula pyrrhula pyrrhula*)†*****‡

General Description

This northern bird, or the 'Siberian' as the older bird keeper still calls it, is different only in size and a few minor habits from the British bullfinch; the colouring is certainly brighter than the British bird and it is larger, too. I have handled so many over the years that I would say there are two distinct body types: one very long, which although slightly slimmer appears far more so, due to the extra length, and the shorter, very rotund bird, longer than the native here but also very much thicker set. Some of these birds seem giants when compared to the smaller race and despite a brighter, more vivid, red on the chest of the male, a far greyer back to both sexes, a whiter wing bar and larger areas of these colours together with the white of the rump, they are identifiable to one and all as bullfinches.

Habitat

Northern Europe and Siberia in forests of coniferous trees, they tend through sparse tree and shrub growth in the very far North to breed closer to each other than the bird we know here; even in aviaries they tend to be a little better tempered or at least more tolerant of their own kind. Even when in the North they nest low and they do require far greater amounts of twigs than the British bullfinch. Some nests I have seen in Finland were immense, almost reminiscent of a dove's nest.

Aviary

The enclosure to breed these birds would be identical to that advised above. Although used to intensely cold conditions it does not have such wet weather to contend with therefore provide a shelter to protect it especially from damp. This northern bird still retains its taste for buds and for this reason only the growth of the previous subject's aviary should be included in this bird's enclosure.

Food

The food choice of all the races of the bullfinch from England across Northern Europe, Scandinavia, Russia and Asia to Japan seems to be common under controlled conditions: buttercup seeds, chickweed, charlock, dandelion, dock, dog's mercury, fat-hen, meadowsweet, pansy, sowthistle—the seeds of all these are eagerly sought; the fruit and seeding pips of bramble, rowan, apple, raspberry; buds from many conifers, hawthorn, elm, oak, blackthorn and many soft fruiting shrubs.

During rearing one can see them gradually filling their food sacs until the throats bulge: these pouches are never used at other times, apparently shrivelling back to normal when not feeding young; I have one or two hens which take softfood for their young in rather large quantities and I have observed at close quarters how they pump from these food sumps into the gaping youngsters' beaks; it at first amazed me that so much was being taken on each visit to the softfood as until then I had only heard tell of these food sacs and was incredulous.

The northern bullfinch does not require anything different from the British bullfinch in the nature of its food supply. When newly imported, mine bred with little encouragement, but the first year they seemed to spend much of their time during rearing searching for some foods which were not available in my aviaries; I checked with others who also had these birds in their care and found we were all experiencing much the same behaviour from these birds. In subsequent years they behaved normally or, I should say, appeared to have adapted to our food supplies: apparently something had seemed missing when breeding here the first year which, in many instances, caused high losses among nestlings.

As for all my birds I tend to soak the seed mixtures: this does not in any way increase their nutritional content but it does tend to make them more easily digested by both young and adult, and, more important, means one can include other seeds not normally given to finches. Some pigeon conditioning mixtures contain seeds slightly larger than those normally taken, but in the soaked and sprouting or near bursting condition they are taken by almost all finches and help to vary the diet. In rearing, insects of many kinds, including caterpillars, mealworms and wax-moth larvae, are taken in large quantities; next comes the soaked teazle and sun-flower with the mixture of seeds as before, and whatever wild foods can be gathered at this time, with great care being taken to ensure cleanliness when collecting the latter.

Breeding
No difference is needed in the nesting sites to be provided for the

larger bullfinch from the North: their selection of the nesting materials does include a greater number of fine twigs, from beech, birch and heather; anything very thin and pliable will find its way to the rather bulky platform that these birds will construct. A few more will be woven in to form the boundary wall and they will then accept rootlets and animal hair. Coconut fibre may also be used in nest construction.

Such a large proportion of aviary bred bullfinch hens, particularly of the larger races, are used for hybridising with other finches or canaries that it is essential to breed many more of this beautiful species in the future to offset the hybrid losses, otherwise, with the numbers of hybrid breeders increasing, there will soon be a shortage of the pure strain.

The males can be very possessive of nesting sites and have a reputation for being aggressive towards other finches; for this reason a wary eye should be kept on all aviary inmates of a mixed collection in his company while he is in breeding condition. Of course there are numerous examples of cases where no trouble occurs. I have bred from four and five pairs in a five by thirteen metre aviary without a loss of feather: all were genuine Russian bullfinches and each had taken up a territory since early December of the previous year. I believe the secret of the success on those occasions was the neutral feeding areas, with no nesting sites adjoining them, and the introduction of all the pairs at the same time.

I have over the years acquired a great faith in early pairing of birds and their introduction into selected breeding enclosures. It enables birds to build up a confidence in their keeper and familiarise themselves with usual sights in the neighbourhood: dogs, other birds, general movement of the passers-by. The sound of the male's rather sad and melancholy single call note changes with the season's longer days. The song proper when it commences is almost as though the male bullfinch is chuckling with delight; the low attractive bubbling, although often made by a hen, usually announces his attentions to his mate, as he swings his tail from side to side, ducking and bowing whilst sidling towards her.

The eggs are slightly larger from this bullfinch, with markings much the same but with a tendency towards heavier reddish-brown spots; incubation takes about the same time and yet seems a shade sooner and I believe the growth of chick and feather growth are advanced in this larger variety. To be sure of these theories whilst all the time one is endeavouring to introduce all the body-building foods one can, is a little difficult and far more controlled research, with numerous pairs, is essential to prove or disprove them.

One of the rearing foods first accepted by these birds is sow-thistle which I have seen in Finland, other Scandinavian countries and on the Russian border, so it is quite probable that they are already familiar with it as a food for this particular purpose.

Cirl Bunting (*Emberiza cirlus*)***
General Description
This cannot be confused with any other bunting: the grey top of head, black throat and grey-green band across the chest identify it clearly. Both sexes show an olive green rump. The length is about sixteen centimetres. The female lacks the grey and black about the head and is a paler brown all over.

Habitat
This bird can sometimes be found in similar surroundings to the yellowhammer. However, whereas the latter will invariably sing from a low bush, the cirl bunting will select a tree, often isolated from others and standing out in fairly open country; they frequent hedgerows and farmland where they gather much of their food from the ground.

Aviary
Almost all the buntings have a tendency to chase the females a lot during courtship and for this reason a lengthy aviary should be the aim of any bird keeper wishing to breed them; I would like to think of an enclosure with a minimum length of four metres and two metres wide. Provide thick, low-growing bushes, not in the corners but standing well out from both the ends and sides of the enclosure, but also give one or two high nesting sites as these do on occasions seem to appeal to cirl buntings in aviaries. Where the low sites are concerned, allow long grasses to intermingle, growing in and around the bushes which should be about a metre high.

Food
Most of the buntings, despite their love of livefood, are coarse feeders when it comes to grain feeding: plain canary seed, corn,

grasses of all types, pinhead groats, the brassicas, millet, screenings and a good quality insectivorous mixture will all help to keep them in good condition. Most of their natural feeding is done from the ground but in the aviary always endeavour to keep the food on a mouse-proof post site.

Breeding

I have had these birds nest and lay eggs but on that occasion something removed them from the nest one night. Shortly after that I passed them on to another bird keeper; one nest was made in a low bush and eggs laid, the second attempt was in a high site but no eggs were ever found. The nest was made of grass, moss, roots, and lined with animal hair, the first one being at a height of seventy centimetres or so, built quite naturally without help.

In the wild these birds rear entirely on insect life and if success is to occur in an aviary they should have their own enclosure with adequate supplies of any insects that can be obtained. My adults were extremely fond of young locusts, wax-moth larvae, mealworms and maggots and all but the last would be suitable for the rearing of young.

Corn Bunting (*Emberiza calandra*)**
General Description

This is the largest of our buntings and a good male can reach over seventeen centimetres in length. The hen is always a little smaller and this applies to all the buntings which I have kept or studied in the field. They are not only long birds but very thickset with a tendency towards plumpness. To describe them as completely brown may sound rather uninteresting but it is not meant to, for with their dark streaking they are most attractive creatures; my corn buntings were brought back from abroad and were never what one could call tame, but I have had hand-raised specimens which were so sure of themselves that they walked over my feet in the aviary.

Habitat

As the name would imply, the corn bunting inhabits arable ground, the stout bill being ideal for the corn that it takes. The penetrating song can be heard from afar across a number of fields, a rather wheezing and jangling one but welcome to the country lover. The flight will be noticed to resemble the sparrow's.

Aviary

Remembering that the courtship flight involves much high speed chasing, these birds should have an enclosure no smaller than for the previous variety of bunting with the bushes again about one metre tall and with plenty of long grass. There should also be fairly large clear areas with one or two gravel patches pressed flat to the ground surface.

Food

As well as corn, offer plain canary seed and grass seed of any variety. Some brassicas will be taken as too will a host of low growing seeds from weeds edging the hedgerows of fields; some vegetable matter will be eaten but insects remain the apparent favourite. A surprising number of hawthorn berries are taken when in the over-ripe stage. Where possible offer screenings.

Breeding

Having hand raised many of these birds I can vouch for the necessity of much livefood and calcium lactate powder sprinkled on it, but I have never reared them to maturity in an aviary as I have not kept many over the years. The pair which nested for me and laid eggs was perhaps not in full breeding condition as the eggs were infertile. The nesting sites require bushes of medium height with plenty of long grass around and growing into these bushes. For any success the birds should be left entirely alone once observed to be nesting. The nest itself is typical of the bunting family, very untidy looking, consisting merely of grasses, moss and animal hair lined. Mine was built in April, a little early, and a perhaps the reason for infertility in my own pair.

Reed Bunting (*Emberiza schoeniclus*)****

General Description

When in breeding condition the male is very striking with completely black head; lower chest and belly white; the back a rich brown and heavily striated; in winter the head is browner. Both sexes have a clearly defined moustachial streak, but the female is far more brown and streaky in appearance, as too are the young; these birds are just about fifteen centimetres in length.

Habitat

Although most of these birds are to be found in disused gravel pit areas, well reeded freshwater streams and marshy areas, I have encountered many in quite open country devoid of anything larger than a narrow stream. In winter months they will move into farmyards and often to suburban gardens in the company of sparrows.

Aviary

The two metres by one metre enclosure will suffice for these birds' requirements. Provide a shelter of sorts on a small section of the roof, the rear and a few centimetres down each side, just at the furthest part of the aviary from their human visitors: this will prove ample for them to retire to in inclement weather or if at all shy.

A small pond in the aviary, or sunken large old-fashioned sink, with heaped up soil on two sides, the latter being planted with sedge, water iris and long grasses, will give a very natural setting for these birds, but, appearance aside, when fully matured, the sedge and grass should give one or two ideal nesting sites.

Food

Feeding as with most buntings is very little trouble, and, with adequate supplies of livefood, they invariably come into breeding condition in plenty of time; the basic supply will consist of plain canary seed, brassicas, millet, pin-head groats, many wild seeds and screenings along with a rich insectivorous food. The usual additives can be well mixed with the softfood and they should also have a daily quota of livefood: this can be varied a great deal throughout winter and late summer but during the breeding season they must have wax-moth larvae and mealworms unless a host of wild insects can be obtained; the maggot does not prove sufficiently small and soft skinned for these birds when newly hatched from the egg.

Breeding

These have bred for me on a number of occasions, the young proving quite tame once they have left the nest and acquired some trust in the individual who gives them their daily food, but they never seem to build up a strong rapport with the keeper as do some birds, unless actually hand raised. If wishing to install the nesting sites, give large clumps of heather and bracken of varying heights, from ground up to two metres or so. Push the clenched fist well down into the dense foliage in a few places to give a cup like effect here and there and so form possible nest bases. During the best part of the year these buntings will often forsake most of the seed provided and concentrate upon insects and softfood, but this does tend to vary a great deal from one bird to another. The nesting materials to offer are grasses, moss, swept up dead leaves from the garden, and for lining almost any animal hair, for example dog, cow or horse, in short lengths.

Lapland Bunting (*Calcarius lapponicus*)**, Ortolan Bunting (*Emberiza hortulana*)** and Rustic Bunting (*Emberiza rustica*)

These buntings may only occasionally become available to the bird keeper and although I have kept all of them over the years I would hesitate here to encourage the keeping of them unless for genuine research, or taken under licence for some very good purpose. I would merely add that all can be treated in an identical manner to the Reed Bunting, in all respects.

Snow Bunting (*Plectrophenax nivalis*)**

General Description

In breeding plumage the male is a very striking sight, predominantly showing up very black and white, but during the winter the colour becomes a varying mixture of browns and white, often seeming to depend upon the age of the subject; indeed, when watching a flock, some females and males look very alike until studied closely. The female is slightly slimmer and shorter than the male, being roughly sixteen centimetres compared to his eighteen. She can be sexed easily during the breeding season as she is always a speckled brown but has white underparts and breast; during the winter she, too, acquires more brown in the plumage.

Habitat

Although belonging to barren tundra areas and mountains amid the snow and heather, travelling more inland from the coast in the colder months, it is now nesting in Scotland and it is hoped it will carry on increasing in this reasonably new addition to its breeding range. Not quite as bulky as the corn bunting but very little shorter, this species will be found gregarious with other buntings but mixes with few other birds. It can be seen feeding on the ground taking almost any seed it can find during winter months but reverting almost entirely to insects during the warmer months when they become available.

Aviary
Since so much of the snow bunting's time is spent on the ground it always seems such a pity when one finds them given too small an aviary area to show them off to their best advantage and an opportunity to live as near naturally as possible. They should have a minimum of four metres in length with a width of at least two metres. Their normal nesting site will be in rock crevices well shielded from prying eyes or predators: in an aviary one can quite easily prefabricate very near natural sites with decorative stone from garden centres or even with bricks and cement. They will appreciate the inclusion of heather in their enclosure, but do leave patches of floor clear for their natural foraging habits. The height of their aviary should never be less than about two metres for although spending much time on the aviary floor they will also be seen to fly strongly. Some nest boxes of the half open front type can be given at varying heights. Place a few sprigs or small branches of heather around them as I have known very confiding hens to use such box sites.

Food
Despite their taste for a typical bunting seed diet as advised for the other varieties of buntings, these birds do take softfoods during the months when they are taking more insect life than anything else. Their seed mixture should include kibbled groats, plain canary seed, grasses of all kinds, small millets and screenings. Numerous seeding heads of weeds can be gathered from fields and offered to them and very often with the latter they will wait for the seeds to fall to the aviary ground before collecting them. All forms of insect life are appreciated, even the very small kind of striped snail one finds in nettle beds. I have actually watched them crack these open as if a seed, as does the corn bunting. During the period when young are being reared, however, they will not want anything but insects for the nestlings as this is the only way to rear them successfully. My birds used to take young locusts, mealworms, wax-moth larvae, and any other creature offered.

Breeding
The nest building process of this bird requires that far more

material than is finally used be given: so much seems to get wasted and the end product never looks a work of art, being extremely untidy. But if things progress this far, tidiness matters not a bit. Materials should include dry grasses, moss, dead leaves of all kinds, weed stalks, animal hair, in the case of horse or cow hair cut to seven-centimetre lengths, soft feathers and such like. One of my birds once used a lot of dry chickweed for the base and outer walls. There is a fairly well-established belief among people belonging to snow bunting habitat that these birds mate for their lifetime: I have no proof of this but a well-bonded pair very seldom move far from each other even when with a number of pairs. I used at one time to have six pairs in a far above average-sized enclosure: the inmates fed alongside each other all the time, weaving in and out in many patterns but always sorted them-selves out by retiring together at some time or other in their predicted pairs.

Chaffinch (*Fringilla coelebs*)†****‡

General Description

Reputed to be Britain's most common bird at one time, far fewer, sadly, may be seen these days. The sight of one in his breeding plumage is certainly an admirable picture, a pleasant experience: a brilliant slate blue crown; chestnut back fading to a beautiful shade of rich green on the rump; the dark reddish-pink chest; very dark wings with their white patches shown off to perfection allow this bird to compare well with many tropical species. Both sexes are about fifteen centimetres long but the hen is far browner in all areas. Despite this she is a very attractive subject when viewed in really good plumage and overall condition: the winter plumage of the male is less exciting but nonetheless attractive with reddish-buff head and nape, the back merely a pale chestnut hue.

Habitat

The chaffinch of Northern Europe extends into Siberia. It is a bird of the deciduous woods and the northern spruce woods, but present in garden and park even in built-up areas. Well-grown woodland still has the more dense populations.

Aviary

The standard minimum enclosure will suffice but where space is not at a premium, give a longer flight. The shelter need be little more than a half a metre of roofing with a little cover at the rear and sides for added comfort. The longer flight will be found an asset when the breeding of these birds is attempted. The male is quite a boisterous wooer, such that I think at times I would use a more terse description if I were a hen chaffinch! He can when in top breeding condition continually chase, singing all the time, until his mate agrees that sitting on eggs is far less arduous a pastime.

Food

Feed as recommended for the brambling, its nearest relative. Many seeds are taken on open ground, fallen beech mast being a favourite in all regions where it exists. The more common weeds, persicaria, chickweed and their like, form the bulk of its diet. After the threshing in farmland when the waste was at one time thrown in heaps, the number of chaffinches eating in the area was almost unbelievable, hence their name. During the breeding season, the diet of the adults, although containing many seeds, is basically insectivorous: insects will be taken from the ground, trees and even on the wing, and moths, caterpillars, grubs and small beetles of all kinds are taken for the young. In aviaries we must, if hoping to rear full nests of young, see that they receive similar diets. The seed contents of the mixture which must always be given daily as a basic requirement should contain many of the brassicas, grasses, lettuce, plain canary seed, some linseed and a few grains of hemp. Fallen seeds from wild collected weeds will be taken at all times but this is one of the finches that rarely take seeds from a growing weed and seldom from such plants as the groundsel and dandelion. In an aviary they will do so but only very spasmodically.

Breeding

Having given the pair of birds an aviary to themselves, or if in a collection kept an alert watch for bullying of smaller finches by the male, we can do little apart from providing a high protein insect intake, watching nature take its course and see these birds come into condition. The male will chase the hen quite violently at times, yet when accepted by her he will be one of the most devoted of mates, offering her mealworm after mealworm whilst she broods her clutch. The nesting site usually ends up self-selected, with complete disdain for nest baskets. It matters not if it is a hand-reared bird who has never seen another chaffinch apart from its mate, the nest is a work of art, just as one would expect a wild bird's to be: this sort of inherited knowledge can be absorbing to study in many ways, in all birds. Materials for nesting should include mosses, spiders' webs, as wide a variety of animal hair as possible, a few feathers, small pieces of tissue paper, fine grasses, thin rootlets and lichen; the nest building is an art in itself and well worth using the binoculars to observe. The mating behaviour, the varied courtship postures, the response movements and calls make a fascinating study when time permits. Occasionally a hen will take quite a long while to make up her mind about nesting and the making up of a few more sites will often give her the required impulse, but with this species so much is the result of the courtship: the male's actions quite visibly act as a key to the female's acceptance and nesting.

With the arrival of young, the need for insects must be fulfilled or they will shrink and be lost: the first five days are the most vital as with so many young birds dependent upon animal protein for their existence, so provide all possible in the small insect world.

Chaffinch (*Fringilla coelebs*) The Northern Variety****†
General Description
It is only the appearance of this bird which differs from the foregoing. The habitat varies naturally since living on the edge of the wooded steppes just below the tundra areas, vegetation, nest materials and food must to some extent change with the terrain. However, in appearance the northern bird is larger, in length I would estimate as much as one centimetre. Compare this variation in a bird ranging from fourteen to sixteen centimetres to the same percentage of height increase in a human and the size variation becomes appreciable. The larger bird has correspondingly increased areas of colour; certainly the white wing patches can be very noticeable, the deep plum-red of the breast, the area of green on the rump, the rich back colour. Set one of each side by side and one can very quickly spot the greater colour regions of the body. With the vast movement of chaffinches annually, breeding ranges of immense proportions and their general movements, there is obviously no distinct dividing line but when comparing a bird taken in Russia with one resident in the British Isles the differences are immediately recognisable, and even many Northern European varieties exhibit disparity in size.

Blue Chaffinch (*Fringilla teydea*)

General Description

This is another chaffinch with distinct variation and there are specimens from North Africa and Spain which differ again, but I have never handled the latter. This all blue chaffinch, or to be more exact slate-blue male and dull greyish hen, is quite unmistakable: it completely lacks the pink, brown and chestnut markings of those seen in Northern Europe. Housing, feeding and breeding will be identical, each becoming an almost insectivorous creature with the arrival of the breeding season. Nest materials are very similar, varying slightly from one adapted habitat to another, while sites, too, are only marginally different: where chaffinches have olive groves instead of the hawthorn or other tree, they will use them from habit.

Common Crossbill (*Loxia curvirostra*) and Scottish Crossbill (*L. c. scotica*)****

General Description

These birds are here classed as the one race since it is only through continued and long association with the pine that the Scottish Crossbill has developed its larger bill and this is the only recognisable difference. When describing the adult male as red, the immature male as orange-red and females as olive-brown, one can easily be accused of oversimplification. Really young males are like a young greenfinch, slightly stouter but very speckled; at the first moult he does acquire some orange but at this first stage can be confused with a well-coloured adult female which has a bright face, chest and rump. This, however, is as bright as the female ever normally moults. The adult male is a dark red on head, chest and rump, with the wings and tail dark brown. The young males often show a mixture of shades from yellow through orange to orange-red which to a certain extent depends upon their age and the availability of fir cones during their nestling stage and first moult. The female adult is green but showing a greyish clouding, has a yellowish-green face and rump, is greyish on the belly and very streaked if a first-year bird; these never acquire any true red, merely a shade of yellow-orange at the best, the denser red shades being found only in the males of all crossbill races. They are sixteen and a half centimetres in length.

Habitat

The common crossbill is a lover of the conifer woods and forests and the range of this bird extends over much of Europe, Asia, North America and Canada. The cones of spruce and pine provide the basic food requirements, although buds of conifers are also taken when cone crops fail. Towards the end of the 18th century when coniferous trees were planted extensively and then with present-day reafforestation providing a new habitat, it is not surprising that some years after irruptions from the Continent and Scandinavia vast numbers of crossbills built up in the United Kingdom. They are now quite a common breeding bird: fir cones pulled to pieces beneath pine or spruce usually prove their whereabouts. The cones are not damaged in the same manner as the squirrels' chewing of them; the crossbill neatly extracts the seed with his beak, crossed at the end in a scissor fashion and well adapted for its purpose.

Aviary

Obesity is an enemy of the crossbill in confinement, and one must, if wishing to breed from these birds, provide ample quarters for flight exercise: a minimum would be two metres by one metre and two metres high; if a longer enclosure can be managed so much the better. When in the wild much energy is lost in food collection and to provide a dish of fattening food, available merely for the taking, does not assist in keeping this bird in the best condition for breeding. To start with it is better to place food at one end of the enclosure and the drinking and bathing water as far as possible in the other direction; at least this will ensure the maximum of flight being taken. The crossbill is a large strong finch but can put on weight very quickly with a subsequent loss of general health and virility in breeding. Apart from roosting perches of conifer branches fairly high in the enclosure, their perching need be only one horizontal fir branch at either end of the long aviary. There is no need of shelter except for a slight covered portion of the roof. The crossbill family does not care for too much rain or damp, despite their hardiness against cold weather.

Always ensure cleanliness of perching arrangements; study the roosting area for soiled perches and remove them at once, replacing them with new clean branches fresh from the wild if possible. My reason for this last piece of advice is that the crossbill invari-

87

ably roosts in the same site each night and fouls nearby perches. A microbe which breeds in these accumulated droppings will eventually find its way beneath the leg scales and cause scaly-leg; I have always treated this with five per cent salicylic acid and ninety-five per cent Vaseline, rubbing well into the infected leg once a week for two weeks: this is normally all that is required to rid the bird of the white crusty build-up but if clean new perches are not provided it will soon return. Always keep this mixture away from the bird's eyes and wash your hands after applying it.

The aviary will take on a far more pleasing appearance to the observer and certainly be appreciated by the inmates if it is planted out with conifers: stunted pines are best if the top is removed at about one and a half metres and then kept trimmed during the winter months to prevent its damaging the wire-netting roof; a certain amount of chewing is unavoidable, but if fairly dense at each end with such growth, and cones are collected and offered regularly, only a few branches will die off.

Food
It is a great pity that pine seeds are not commercially sold for bird keepers. This means that one must either collect the ripe, not empty, cones from the wild or mix a variety of seeds suitable for our purpose which is mainly to keep the crossbill in good condition without a build-up of fat catching up on him through his habit of perching between meals. Even a few cones a week will occupy a bird for many hours: the usual seeding foods such as sowthistle, seeding cabbage or any other brassica, seeding grasses, chickweed, dandelion, seeding rhubarb, dock seed when ripe, ripe hops, berries of hawthorn and rowan trees will all be accepted and prove their value in natural feeding, but we must still have a basic seed mixture which should include fifth part sunflower, two-fifths pigeon conditioning seed, fifth part groats and fifth part either wild seed or screenings. If the last two items are difficult to obtain, use one-tenth part finch conditioning seed and make up the balance with half each plain millet and niger.

Breeding
Conifer shelves or groups of conifer branches bunched together to form individual sites are usually acceptable to these birds when in true breeding condition. The nest requires some twigs of birch,

heather, beech or similar fine twiggy pieces up to fifteen centimetres in length; these will be built into a platform on which the nest is constructed. Offer moss, dry grasses, strips of bark-fibre; animal hair from cow, horse or dog brushings will prove ideal; a few feathers are sometimes taken for lining and I have found nearly all aviary nests lined only with hair. Nest baskets whilst not exactly ignored are seldom if ever used for their intended purpose; most of those I ever offered were torn to pieces and strewn around the aviary floor; I believe two only were ever used by birds for actual nesting operations.

Although not able to guarantee the behaviour of these birds in a mixed collection at all times, I have had pairs nest under such conditions without any damage to other inmates. The occasional opened beak threat and the pecking-order seemed firmly established; other birds avoided the nest site. Mine have all appeared quite docile specimens. Even so, for successful breeding an aviary to each pair should be the general aim.

The eggs are bluish-green with brown and brownish-purple spots, and the most I have found in their nests has been four. The young remain in the nest longer than most finches and I have managed to rear them also under foster parents. On that occasion the foster parents were greenfinches which had been hand raised by my daughter when she herself was very young; as a child, hand rearing fascinated her and each year I let her rear a nest of greenfinches, those usually removed (normals) when I was concentrating upon a mutation of greenfinch plumage. These birds invariably received a daily quota of mealworms and grew to like them so much that the daily ration continued into adulthood. A pair of these birds hatched and reared three young crossbills without the aid of any pine seeds or other normal crossbill rearing foods, using daily supplies of mealworms and the usual wild foods and soaked seeds one associates with greenfinch rearing.

Over the years I suppose I have kept about forty to sixty various crossbills, releasing the majority after studying them. They are by far one of our most interesting finches; I have examined hundreds in the field, mostly when I was younger and wished to see if the crossing of the beak tips bore any significance to sex or the type of cone fed upon, etc. The beak tips can cross either way regardless of these factors and there seems no uniformity in this respect.

Parrot Crossbill (*Loxia pytyopsittacus*)†

General Description

Larger than either the common or two-barred crossbills at seven-teen centimetres this bird has a beak of a far heavier type, hooked more like a parrot's and wider in appearance from above, front and below; when observing the skull in a skeleton, the difference is quite remarkable, and the rest of the skeletal frame is slightly larger and disproves the theory of greater body weight merely by flesh. The colour seen from a distance appears more or less the same as that of the common bird of this family, but, when in an aviary one can easily discern a more greyish head in the female and the whitish tips to a male's greater coverts; the call is deeper, more of a 'chop chop' in comparison to the 'chip chip' of the common race. Probably due only to this beak of greater dimen-sions, this bird does look very parrot-like about the head, and all crossbills tend to peer at one in rather a parrot fashion, sideways or as though looking over their glasses. This bird is even more pronounced in this respect and often seems to be pulling faces at its observer.

Habitat

The parrot crossbill is a bird of Scandinavia, Russia and Finland, breeding in these countries and to a far lesser degree in Poland and Eastern Germany and apparently a very rare visitor to Britain. Since they are so similar to the common when observed in the field, there could easily be more visiting unexpectedly. The pine crop of cones is the basic diet, with a supplement of buds, insects and during the late autumn and winter the berries of sorbus and other fruiting trees.

Aviary

It is always difficult to make hard and fast rules with regard to any livestock: breeding is frequently attempted under the most unsatisfactory conditions, sometimes even proving successful, but I would never consider giving a pair of these birds an aviary smaller than three metres long by two and a half metres high, with a width of anything less than between two and three metres. They tend towards laziness if food is always available and they easily develop a rather bad habit of perching for long rest periods between feeds. Provide perches at each end of an enclosure, if possible with food one end and water at the other. By all means plant their aviary as near naturally as one can; stunted pines are ideal for this purpose. Endeavour to give perches from conifers, and as often as possible offer fresh pine branches with many large tightly closed full cones. The work entailed getting the natural seeds will not only ensure an active life but also provide the natural food essential to this bird. Due to their wild diet of high resinous content they are avid drinkers, and even when snow and ice abounds they will still take their daily bath, so do ensure an available source of clean water.

Food

Since the natural diet is almost an all-year round one of fir cone seeds, especially from the pine, the provision of this food is always greatly appreciated. Sunflower is not harmful to them and so can be given in reasonably large quantities. The tendency of all crossbills to eat their fill then sluggishly rest until again hungry must always be remembered, and it is not advisable to overdo the supply of this seed. Place a seed mixture consisting of sunflower, groats, a little niger, a good quality pigeon conditioning seed, in water to soak for twenty four hours; strain before feeding and offer in a deepish bowl: the crossbill often forms a liking for a particular seed and will scatter everything else to the four winds. Some food will remain if a deep seed container is used and the work involved will prove beneficial.

Almost all autumn berries will be taken; the buds of fruit tree prunings or hawthorn hedge cuttings are always welcome as, too, are many seeding grasses, sowthistle, dandelion, chickweed, sweet apple and the pips from apple-cores; from fresh supplies of pine branches they will take every bud with their natural yearning for the taste of pine. Cut up mealworms on their seed supply; then, when they are observed taking them readily, merely pinch the heads of the mealworms; as soon as these are eaten, offer the live mealworm, and once on to this conditioning food, they will remain fit and healthy for many years; when rearing, and the crossbill will certainly breed when really fit, they will need many mealworms for their nestlings. It is mainly these, buds and the soaked sunflower that will then form the basic diet of the young.

Some crossbills will take to softfoods and if these are mixed with milk as the liquid base then it is another way of introducing animal protein in plenty to their diet: I have seen birds which eat avidly of bread and milk, others that take Farex baby food, some that take to an insectivorous mixture if first covered with cut up mealworms on the surface of it before proffering it.

Breeding

As would be expected, these birds nest on pine branches and knowing this one should put one's mind to fabricating either shelves of pine branches or clusters of them firmly secured in a position near the aviary roof. Remember to provide ample conifer above the site to shield it from excess sun or rain; as a bird of the North it finds excess heat unpleasant, so give plenty of shelter.

Breeding condition is reached very early in the year: in fact, this is a bird which nests almost anywhere between December and June.

The parrot crossbill's nest is a much heavier structure than the other crossbills'. It is mainly taken up with twigs which form a platform and lower wall, not merely for strength but to form a barrier against cold. Other materials include grass, moss, bark-fibre, lichen, animal hair and feathers. The whole is a clumsy looking nest but it is highly suitable for the wild habitat. The eggs are bluish-green, heavily spotted with brown and purple. Resulting young will remain in the nest for about twenty-one days.

Two-Barred or White-Winged Crossbill (*Loxia leucoptera*)**

General Description

A very striking effect is achieved by this bird's plumage which is very different from the other crossbills'. It is a little smaller than the common race at fifteen centimetres and darker and brighter of red, but of course it is the double white bar on each wing that makes it so attractive. The bill is smaller and neater looking, but is nevertheless most useful, for the normal food is the seed of the small larch cone. Much daintier in appearance and less clumsy when feeding even in the natural state, I have always been amazed at this bird's hardiness as the range takes it further north than the common crossbill; I have only managed to keep four of these birds and of these only one hen nested and laid eggs. Professor H. B. Tordoff (U.S.A.) bred hybrids between this and the common which proved fertile.

Habitat

In the Old World this bird belongs to Northern Asian Russia and breeds there among the Siberian larch forests, and although it feeds extensively on larch seeds from the smaller more delicate cone of that tree, this crossbill also takes many insects and berries which contain pips or seeds, the rowan being a favourite. As would be expected, nests are made in the larch and are not quite such bulky constructions as the other crossbills' although basically the same materials are used: fine twigs; grasses; moss; lichen and hair.

Aviary

If fortunate enough ever to acquire a pair of these birds, give them a long aviary of at least four metres. I have noticed that this race of crossbill flies far more, and in much lighter fashion, than the others. Two metres high and the same in width would be ideal as a minimum to work to. In all other aspects their enclosure could be a typical crossbill aviary, planted with pine or larch with food at one end and water at the other; a small roofed portion should be provided to shield them from heavy rain and too damp roosting facilities. This bird never chewed the aviary timber in any way, whereas occasionally one of the other races made the steady destruction of the timberwork a lifelong project.

Food

I gave my two-barred crossbills a little more niger than the other crossbills but in all other respects the seed diet was identical, invariably soaked during the months when there were no frosts, and supplied sometimes sprouting in this softened state. All other foods such as dandelion and sowthistle, were taken immediately they were offered. I think they take more fruit quite naturally, not just when the cone harvest fails and I know that mine were particularly fond of apple pips: they still ate much of the apple flesh but when a core was offered they immediately set to upon this to reach the seeds within.

Breeding

If the nesting pattern of my bird each year was anything to generalise upon, I feel that many two-barred crossbills must be lost in the wild to predators. The nest was made on the outer branches on each occasion, in full view of anyone walking along the adjoining path; these birds have little or no fear of humans.

To aid their nesting operations I erected quite elaborate conifer shelves, built in about three tiers, which they almost completely ignored. As if to spite my efforts they built on the very outer edge of one branch. They require fine twigs, mosses, grasses and hair: my birds never seemed interested in feathers for nesting.

At the time of keeping these birds I also had a great surplus of wax-moth larvae and I found that these were often taken in preference to mealworms despite the latter having been gradually introduced by being cut up upon the daily seed mixture.

On the first occasion the male of my pair was not really fit as I had only just acquired him from a continental dealer and the eggs were subsequently clear. In the following years the hen nested and laid but without a male being present and much later when I learned of hybrids having been obtained from pairing these with the common crossbill I wished I had also attempted this. Even if not for the sake of achieving hybrids it would have been very interesting to see how many generations it took to breed back to almost pure two-barred crossbill.

Citril Finch (*Serinus citrinella*)***
General Description
This rather greyish-green bird is rarely seen as an aviary subject, probably because it resides in the high altitude regions of Central Europe. The first impression is that the green is very yellowish but this upon closer inspection is found to be misleading as there is much slate grey in the plumage of both male and female. The underparts are not striated as with the siskin or serin and this exhibits the yellow to advantage. The adult male and female differ mainly by the amount of grey: this in the male is predominantly around the nape, neck sides and even top of head whereas the female has a greyish, slightly more streaked body with much more grey in the chest area in addition to nape and head. The wings and tail are black, or almost so, and there are two dullish green wing bars visible on close inspection. The length is just below thirteen centimetres, and it is of slim build. The juvenile is brownish with shades of green only on the under body: it does not have the wing bars and is often mistaken for other birds.

Habitat
Fairly high mountainous areas among the conifers would be a typical sighting place for this bird where it feeds directly from the

cones. Some of these birds remain in the Swiss alpine regions all the year but many migrate south to France. Grasses seem the most taken seed, but dandelion and many others provide variety and I am not convinced that a number of insects are not used in the rearing of their young although they do offer nestlings many seeds. I have never undertaken crop inspections in the wild. I have found a number of nests high in the trees, resembling those of the goldfinch or siskin in that area.

Aviary
Due to this bird's almost fixed choice of high nesting site, one should consider making a special effort to afford extra height in the aviary; where breeding is the main aim, offer a high flight up to three metres. This is frequently not possible but a gabled roof would provide this amenity: the two-metre length by one-metre width should prove ideal. Bearing in mind the bird's natural habitat and choice of conifer, endeavour to provide spruce cones and fresh branches. Only when this bird feels really at home in its surroundings will it nest; the ground area of natural earth should be well planted with seeding grasses, comfrey and dandelion.

Food
The seed mixture for this bird would ideally be screenings containing plenty of grasses. Not too much niger should be given or they tend to become as addicted to this as many other finches do; the large seeds can be forgotten unless the soaking of seed is undertaken although I have seen citril finches on occasion even work on the large sunflower seed and remove the seed quite easily. Bunches of seeding grasses hung in various sites can prove entertaining as well as beneficial to the birds: they will hang from the stalks in many positions taking from the ripe harvest of seeds, and only when the supply is exhausted revert to man-mixed varieties. Where screenings are available mix in some plain canary, a little niger, small quantities of rape, linseed, gold of pleasure, maw and pinhead oatmeal. Millet will also be taken and I have had birds which took to this seed very quickly, the consumption amounting to almost a third of their daily intake of seed. Some specimens take to a softfood readily once maw has been sprinkled on top and acquire a taste for this food. In aviaries, they do certainly take many insects and I have carried out crop inspections among young and adult birds to find that all took green-fly whenever available.

Breeding

The provision of plenty of conifer branches and rich feeding together with an aviary well shielded from the direct strong sun rays seem to receive this species' approval for breeding. I have seen hens gasping and raising themselves off the nests in an effort to keep cool; they are a high altitude species and I have always kept them as near to their natural habitat as possible. With the birds I have kept, only a few hens have actually nested: in all cases to my own regret they were in mixed collections where too many other birds could interfere with their domestic duties. On at least four occasions I had eggs hatch, but due to other aviary inmates' behaviour, never reared these birds to maturity. They are well worth the attempt since there is much to be gained from studying them, and there appears to be no good reason why, if they can be persuaded to nest and incubate eggs, young should not be reared in captivity as often as from the serin or siskin.

Snow Finch (*Montifringilla nivalis*)

General Description

This Alpine species from mountainous Central European areas is larger than the snow bunting. It is indeed very surprising when one holds them in the hand to find just how large and bulky the bone structure is; yet the bird is rarely plump, just solid. They are very striking specimens and very tame, with little fear of humans. The male in summer shows a rich chocolate brown back, grey head, black throat bib, and whitish belly and underparts. The wings appear very white in flight. On the ground it will be seen that the primaries are black and there are black central feathers to the tail with white each side; this vast amount of white is very conspicuous in flight giving the bird a rather large butterfly effect. The female is much more dull having a browner head and less white in wings and tail. The bills of both sexes are yellow, in the winter turning black as the spring breeding condition builds up; juveniles are rather dull in appearance, but on the whole this bird is a remarkably attractive species. Feeding in the winter months is often in the close vicinity of humans, their presence meaning a source of food for the birds. They frequently feed in quite large flocks, more often than not in the snow where they make an attractive sight. The length is eighteen centimetres.

Habitat

In its Alpine habitat this bird's tameness is its most striking characteristic: it seems to avoid trees and remain on open ground wherever possible. The favoured foods are seeds and insect life as they become available but the winter months with their scarcity of food bring this bird nearer and nearer to man and the scraps of food and crumbs he provides; many tourists in Alpine resorts find this bird's tameness a fascinating item of conversation as he feeds almost at their feet. They seem happiest in the summer, high among the rock crags, but they still remain not too distant from habitation of humans, frequently roosting in a hole in building walls or under the wide jutting eaves.

Aviary

Despite this bird's tameness, one should provide ample aviary space, three metres long by two metres wide and high so that the enclosure gives ample room for both exercise and breeding operations, together with adequate flying area so that one may appreciate its plumage to the full. The enclosure is difficult to build in a like manner to the bird's wild habitat unless it has a back wall; but if this is available it is then a simple matter to build a second rock wall against the first, leaving nesting holes in suitable places for their choice during the breeding season. Quite apart from serving as ideal and natural nesting sites, this rock wall will give them a perfect setting, and a few juniper bushes and heathers planted in the enclosure will provide an almost natural habitat.

Food

Whilst insects are almost the sole food during the warmer months, there is no doubt that seed and softfoods will be readily eaten during the winter. I have always offered the choice of both to this bird and although I have kept only a limited number I have had ample opportunity to study the wildlings. Once again I would suggest screenings as the base of a seed mixture, to which I would add plain canary seed, a little rape, small millets, pinhead oatmeal. I would give seeding grasses as well as the normal wild foods such as chickweed. A few maggots can be given daily and the odd mealworm from hand or placed nearby will encourage the attractive friendliness of this species; during the summer months one can easily increase the intake of livefood and many will be taken of those insects which venture to enter the enclosure.

Breeding
Where breeding is attempted or looks likely, offer plenty of fine dry grasses as the lining of their nest is composed of animal hair and feathers; it is rather a clumsy nest but when one sees the actual size of the adult bird, it can easily be visualised just how much space four or five youngsters will need when fully grown and about to fledge. I have known this bird to use a nest box— the half open-fronted type—but for those wishing to achieve success as near to nature as they are able, rock crevices and holes are the sites to strive for.

During rearing these birds will require much livefood. I have seen most forms taken; the simplest to culture in large numbers are locusts, mealworms, wax-moths; on the few occasions when my birds received wood ant 'eggs' they seemed particularly attracted to them and knowing how these creatures often abound in mountainous regions where fir trees are plentiful, I have little doubt that they take them when available in the wild. The eggs are whitish and from wildling observations there are frequently two broods. Both sexes appear to take turns at incubation and rearing the young is also shared.

Goldfinch (*Carduelis carduelis*)†****‡
General Description
The European goldfinch must be one of the most well-known birds for colour: its many hued progeny when paired with the canary or other finches, all retain a resemblance to the very popular red-faced bird. It is true that there exists wide variation in size and even in brightness of colour throughout Europe but until one wanders to the far side of the Urals no great plumage pattern changes occur. They measure almost twelve centimetres in the British Isles and whilst they decrease in size in more southerly countries they increase in stature to the 'Siberian' or 'Archangel' as those enormous specimens with a hoary-like frosting on their black-topped heads used to be called. The goldfinch has chestnut back and flanks with slightly paler breast markings (called tannings by the aviculturist); the under-belly and cheeks are white and the black crown tapers till the points almost meet the throat; there is a brilliant red facial 'blaze' or mask; tail and wings are of jet black, the latter having broad daffodil yellow bars and the feathers of the wings and the underside of outer tail

feathers are tipped white. Some females are as brilliant as a mediocre male but usually they are a shade duller.

To see a flock of these birds descend upon a patch of thistle or dandelion seeding heads is a wonderful experience for the bird lover. With notes tinkling like bells, the wings flit to exhibit the deep yellow bars to best advantage, in contrast to the red of the mask: it is indeed a bird worthy of all the colloquial and local flattering names bestowed upon it.

The long pointed bill is an ideal tool for obtaining the seeds of the thistle: male and female both will cling to the ripened head and work at the tightly packed seeds though the male with a slightly longer and stronger base to his bill is a little more proficient at this task than his mate.

Habitat
This bird can be found on woodland edge, field, agricultural land and wild moorland and often, too, in many tree-lined avenues and gardens in suburbia. The orchard often frequented for nesting purposes has in many areas been forsaken and preference shown for the odd tree in a garden or even a chestnut growing along a busy road; the dandelion and thistle still remain its choice of foods and it inhabits almost any region where these abound. Since the goldfinch breeds over very nearly the whole of Europe, the habitat does vary with the country in which it lives, breeds, or migrates to during the winter months.

Aviary
There are various methods of housing goldfinches. People who want to form a true strain will methodically pair their birds for excellence of colour and shape; others who may wish to study them in a group may colony breed them, a number of pairs to a large aviary; this is certainly a bird which can be housed more than one pair to an enclosure, providing of course that the dimensions are generous enough to permit it. For one pair the enclosure would be the standard minimum, the length not below two metres, the height the same, and the width not less than one metre: for two pairs add a further half metre to the width; if considering more than six pairs as a breeding colony then one should aim for quite extensive quarters. Endeavour to keep a large neutral feeding area when housing a number of birds in one aviary: there will be far less bickering and the long-term results will be appreciated.

Plant a goldfinch aviary with a number of roots of comfrey and dandelion. These birds can be destructive with regard to shrubs and flowering trees, so hard-wearing items such as elder, hops, or willow may provide perching and cover together with a generous supply of livefood in the way of aphids during the months when most welcome. The goldfinch does not enjoy damp quarters or draughty areas so provide warm dry roosts and plenty of roof shelter, but allow the maximum of roof light to enter their aviary. They require no winter heating but try to protect them from rainfall and draughts: hard frosts when their crops are full do no harm at all. Plastic roofing around the outer edges of the roof and perhaps for an equal amount down the sides from the roof would ensure dry roosts, safety from cats and owls and shelter from direct winds.

Food
This is one of the few birds that does not appear to get too fat on a rich diet though the food supply must not be exceptionally rich or the liver and kidneys can suffer. I still like to keep to screenings when possible with the inclusion of a wide variety of seeds as used in many standard mixtures. One can even add a little hemp. The soaking of seed allows a much wider variety to be offered: some seeds such as those in pigeon conditioning mixtures are often too large and hard for many finches without prior soaking, straining and sprouting. For these birds I would add equal parts of the following to a good clean screenings mixture: teazle, millet, rape and niger, then half part of each hemp, maw, linseed and pigeon conditioning seed; lettuce seed and dandelion is also suitable. Many goldfinches will take softfood once introduced to it by a generous sprinkling of maw seed on top of it and many are quite content with a baby food base to which one can add many further attractions such as gold of pleasure seed and maw. The birds which do take freely of such foods are usually the best rearing ones when breeding is in progress. Occasionally, when a goldfinch begins to lose weight and nothing seems to combat the problem, an introduction of mealworms into the diet, cut up on the seed, will remedy the weight loss and bring the bird back to good health in a very short while; I have even experimented with the use of milk at this time, in lieu of water, and found this also a great help, assisting in the replacement of body flesh, particularly over the breast bone.

Breeding

One of our easier finches to breed in single pairs, trios or on a colony system, these birds will breed successfully if housed and fed well, with adequate additional food for rearing and extra space when a number of pairs are involved: the food supply should be situated in a neutral feeding area. The elder, willow and hops will provide good cover for nesting sites; baskets with a few small branches of conifer secured around them or even clusters of birch twigs surrounded by conifer can be fastened within the growing elders or willows, preferably at near maximum height in the breeding aviary. Natural nests will certainly be constructed where good sites exist but neither of the above-mentioned growing vegetation provides ideal sites for this purpose. With these birds' destructive habits of eating buds of some growing trees and shrubs, it is seldom that the plant matures sufficiently thick in growth for natural nesting without clusters of evergreen being added. Nesting materials are fine dry grass, moss, rootlets, plant down, animal hair, small feathers and even little tufts of cotton wool, the latter being given only in a well teased-out condition, in small fragments. The eggs normally number between four and seven; they are pale blue, finely streaked and spotted with dark purple or red.

With the arrival of nestlings, aphids, chrysalids and mealworms should be provided in plenty. The adults are quite willing to feed these items to their young if well used to them in advance and not suddenly given them for the first time when young hatch; such foods will give the young a very good start in life. Give sowthistle and chickweed but when comfrey and any brassica, even the rape plants growing from wasted seed, are growing in the enclosure, the crops of the young will frequently be seen almost black in appearance, with the contents of these showing through the skin.

The normal soaked seed mixture should now have generous additional proportions of soaked teazle, hemp, safflower and small sunflower seeds remembering that where colony breeding is being practised there will be extra demand and use by others than the breeding pairs. If the goldfinches are housed with other varieties of finches it is advisable to forget the hemp and not include it for fear of obesity, with subsequent egg binding, or respiratory ailments where these are likely: the only exception is where linnets are the only other finches housed with the goldfinches. Keep on feeding the soaked seed mixture, ensuring that continuous supplies of both greenfood and insect life are available right through the moult of the young birds.

Over the years I have many times experimented with rearing goldfinches and I can state emphatically that my best reared goldfinches, native or of the large race were reared entirely on soaked sunflower, teazle, mealworms and comfrey with hardly anything else, except a little human baby food mixed with milk and placed on the food dish.

The collection of wild food when one has birds rearing is a good thing providing the source of supply does not suddenly dry up when least expected. Should this happen, the sudden need for change at this crucial stage is sometimes fatal. It is far better to use basic foods as suggested above and merely augment these items with any of the wild foods that can be gathered. Often there are cases of a supply of chickweed failing just when needed most; the habit of feeding daily from this food as the main supply causes parent birds to search for this item when missing. By using the standard basic items in plenty, one can often pass over such periods of wild food failure with no ill effects.

There is a pale-headed species in Eurasia which hybridises in the wild with our western form. This grey-headed form has a slightly smaller red 'blaze' without the depth of red which occurs in the European race; mention is made of this interbreeding, which occurs in Northern Russia, merely to explain examples of this hybrid form appearing occasionally in dealers' hands.

Northern or Siberian Goldfinch (*Carduelis c. major*)‡****
General Description
The only descriptive difference between this and the native European bird is the vast increase in size with the true northern race. The white of the face is certainly a more snow-like white and there is also a visible amount on the nape, and in relaxation they show more on the rump, as one would expect in the Hornemann, hoary or Greenland redpoll. The impression one gets is that they are far more colourful than the smaller bird, but I feel this illusion is caused by the larger expanse of each hue, the red facial mask, the yellow wing bars and dark tan-chestnut back. Certainly when freshly imported the tannings of the breast are lighter, and the surrounding white on chest and lower belly more prominent but after these birds moult out on a suitable seed

mixture the tannings take on a darker shade. It is when one compares the skeletal frames of these two races that one can get a true picture of the overall increase in body bulk. The twelve centimetre length of the native form against the fourteen and a half centimetres of this race is an outstanding difference. Not all northern goldfinches are this size and as is to be expected the variation in size is not sudden but rather increases gradually as one progresses further north.

Habitat
As the conifer forestation and scrub land of the far North increases so this bird's environment differs from the native goldfinch, and even in aviaries it still prefers the types of food it would be used to in the wild. I would say without hesitation that more insect life is consumed by the northern goldfinch, and they have a great tendency towards mealworms or other livefood at all times, not merely when rearing young.

Aviary
Once again we can breed these birds on the colony system; I would venture to say they are even more inclined towards this manner of breeding due to scarcer nesting sites in the North and that what trees there are seem more confined to areas with more scrub land between, tending to force this closer habitation upon them as it does with the waxwing (*Bombycilla garrulus*). The minimum size for one pair would be as previously recommended for the European race, with the appropriate increases for further pairs or nesting hens; two or three males will certainly be able to fill the needs of double their number of females. Comfrey and dandelion can be planted for their consumption, and elders, hops and conifer for seclusion and the provision of extra insect life as well as perching and roosting facilities. This northern bird detests the rain and damp roosting as much as any bird I know, so offer plenty of dry, draughtproof shelter from wind and driving rain. I often hear these birds singing lustily in the hardest of frosty weather but the moment dampness sets in and they feel its unpleasantness, they are off to a dry roost with just the barest minimum of visits to food supplies. This avoidance of rain does not mean any non-appreciation of bathing facilities, however, and these and fresh drinking water daily are essential for this bird's well being as with almost all others.

Food

This bird has a great liking for mealworms and many other forms of livefood. One still needs to offer the same mixture as that recommended for the smaller race, however, and also some kind of softfood which has been carefully introduced, well sprinkled with maw seed; baby food as intended for humans is readily taken and greatly assists when rearing nestlings. The benefit of this latter item is that once taking it regularly, it is a simple matter to include in the mixing further useful items of one's choice for either moult, rearing or general health reasons. The acceptance of natural animal protein in the way of insects is always an asset; it helps immensely when creating variety in a diet, the various foods that insects have themselves just fed upon contributing in no small way, for apart from the insect itself, there will always be some of the undigested food be it vegetable or other smaller insect life. The wild seeds, berries and greenfood as collected for any other finch, plus thistles in season when the heads are about to lose the seeds, should be given at all times but with care being taken to collect from clean areas where no spraying of insecticides has taken place or fouling by dogs occurred.

Breeding

One should provide conifer nest sites, either in bunches of twigs or in baskets surrounded by a few twiggy branches. A smart site can be afforded by the old-fashioned all-wood roller canary song contest cages with the door removed or wired open to prevent accidents. Fit birds will nest readily. Giving soaked mixtures, including sunflower and teazle and plenty of insect life will almost guarantee success, certainly in getting nestlings over their first week after hatching. Since mealworms are almost always obtainable and nourishing use them as basic supply. Aphids will be present in plenty if the aviary has been planted wisely and these too will be fed to small nestlings. Rape plants grown on the aviary floor will be eaten down to ground level when the parent birds are collecting greenfood for their young. This and other brassicas will make the nestlings' crops look almost black. Comfrey and even transplanted dandelion from the garden will all be given and the young will benefit immensely from this addition to their diet; the provision of foods extra to an austere and monotonous seed diet cannot be too highly recommended.

Greenfinch (*Carduelis chloris*)†****

General Description

Without some reference to the various mutations which a veteran breeder experimented with many years ago, the description of these birds would not be complete. There are lutino or non-melanistic yellow birds with pink eyes; cinnamon specimens showing merely the resulting hues of yellow and brown; silver or grey birds which illustrate only the grey pigment and a further silver or grey phase which shows yellow also, this being in the wings and tail. Now in addition to these, we have a specimen apparently illustrating grey and white; this last bird is almost charcoal grey in appearance, exhibiting no yellow and where one would expect to find this colour, it has white feathers. Whereas the former have all supposedly proven a sex-linked factor, the last has yet to be conclusively proven and may well be of a recessive nature. The late A. H. Scott of Fordingbridge, Hampshire, was the pioneer in this field: he bred many birds of various mutations and I exchanged with him lutino siskins, albino blackbirds, cinnamon thrushes for lutino stock many years ago; it was just after hostilities of 1939–45 that he encouraged me to investigate the lutino and cinnamon mutations of the greenfinch; many of my own rare-feathered mutations of the different species came from other countries.

The normal greenfinch is a very well-known bird with a breeding range covering much of the western half of Eurasia, extending in Russia to 60° N and in Scandinavia to 65° N and found south as far as North Africa and from Ireland to Iran. About fifteen centimetres from bill tip to end of tail, it stands boldly, solidly cone shaped. It is a good coloured specimen, predominantly green and yellow but this varies with the area inhabited. The northern race from Scandinavia and Russia, of which I have kept many, all seemed a little larger though there is not the great difference in size that is found in some finches. It is, however, browner, the yellow in flights and tail still clearly shown but the body colour in both male and female being diffused with lightish brown. The best coloured males are a yellowish-green, slightly shaded with olive, the yellow becoming accentuated on breast and rump. They have bright yellow wing bars, carpal joints and on each side of tail. A female greenfinch is usually much duller in her plumage, browner and having less yellow, yet I have known some almost as bright as males.

Habitat
A bird of forest, farm, woodland, road-side, indeed garden, it keeps mainly to the lowlands. They are now common in winter and one sees them feeding from peanut holders in gardens, placed there for the tit family during hard weather. Wherever there are thickets and tall hedges, particularly hawthorn, this bird will be found. With their strong conical bill they will eat almost any seed, or break berry stones such as that in the hawthorn fruit, in their search for food; of a hearty appetite—bordering on the greedy—they will spend hours on farmyard screenings or spilled grain. If seed is placed in a garden during winter months, they will chase others from the site to secure the choicest foods.

Aviary
The most accommodating of our finches, certainly the more domesticated among them, as a child I bred them in a small cage. Later with advice from others more experienced than I, they were housed in aviaries, where a better physical specimen can be produced. An aviary two metres in length and height by half that measurement in width will house a pair comfortably and provide ample space for breeding operations: on many occasions I have placed more than one female with a male; quite often this can bring good results but, depending upon the character of a bird, sometimes it brings nothing but problems.

Always keep to the rule of having a neutral feeding area when keeping more than a pair together. For everyday use plant the floor space with brassicas and comfrey. As greenfinches are rather destructive little will grow in the enclosure apart from elder, hops and juniper, but if the aviary is enlarged other conifer growth can be included.

A minimum of shelter is required for this hardy species, and as long as he has a dry roost with the roosting perches renewed often to avoid excessive fouling and consequent scaly-leg outbreak, he will remain happy for many years.

Food
A coarse feeder, the greenfinch will live well upon screenings, with extras such as a little groats, wheat, rape, linseed, hemp, niger and sunflower; this mixture should be soaked for at least twenty-four hours and strained of water: offer in this sprouting condition once frosts are finished and carry on until after all adult and young birds have completed moulting and frosts are again

imminent. Provide only dry seed during the winter months. Almost all my greenfinches take a variety of livefood, as does the wild specimen and they will avidly devour growing vegetation as previously mentioned. Hop seeds covered in rich yellow pollen assist them when moulting and I am quite confident their colouring improves immensely from its inclusion in their diet. Give seeding grasses, weeds of many kinds, rowan berries, hawthorn fruit, dock seed and chickweed; give also Brussels sprouts which will be appreciated when other greenfood is scarce.

Breeding

This is one of our easiest birds to propagate in captivity and there is little needed in the way of seclusion for nesting sites. A wicker basket, a few twigs of conifer to shield it and make certain that there is some cover from rain and direct strong sunlight, provides the hen with comfort to carry out her incubating duties and rearing. Offer mosses, animal hair, coconut matting or short lengths of teased out coarse string, a few small wisps of cotton wool, dry grasses, perhaps even a few twigs if a natural nest is being prepared for a fabricated site or one in a growing bush or tree. Once a female decides she wishes to nest, it will be only a day or so before the job is completed. The clutch of eggs, as with most finches, will usually number between four and six.

Many birds will accept some form of rearing food which should of course be introduced long before the breeding season commences. They will give their nestlings much greenfood and live insects; greenfood such as cabbage and comfrey can be taken fresh from that growing in the aviary but many wild specimens exist which are acceptable to seedeaters and can be provided in an effort to vary the diet. During the change over from soaked and sprouting seed to hard seed in late autumn and vice versa in the spring, there should be a period of about fourteen days when the birds receive fifty per cent of each: there ought not to be any abrupt transition from one to the other.

Pine Grosbeak (*Pinicola enucleator*)***

General Description

The largest finch of our region, about twenty to twenty one and a half centimetres, is amazingly tame. I have had these birds direct from the wild habitat of the Arctic circle and Siberia and they have alighted upon my head and shoulders readily accepting sunflower seeds, tugging hair from my head and showing no signs of fright even when I moved around. They are heavily built, resembling in shape the northern bullfinch and found on handling to be far larger than a starling. The male is rose-red of body suffused with a blue-grey background shade on flank and rump. White wing bars are very conspicuous; the wings and tail are darkish but dull brown; the bill and legs are black. The female is more greenish but upon rump, head and upper breast shows a bronze shade instead of the male's red. Young of the year resemble the hen but have an overall greyish-green wash. The bill at this stage is slightly paler but reaches the same large proportions, stout as with the bullfinch and ideal for taking many buds and large seeds. The plumage is soft and downy not quite to the same extent as the waxwing (*Bombycilla garrulus*) but certainly sufficient to serve its purpose of protection against the bitter cold of their natural habitat. These finches are normally seen travelling in family parties.

Habitat
The subarctic birch woods and open pine forests of the Arctic circle and Siberia provide this bird of Northern Europe with its diet of seeds, buds, fruit and berries. Its true breeding range also takes in North America and Canada.

Aviary
Although a bird rather like the crossbill in its habit of eating and then sitting in the same position for long periods, thus acquiring a lazy reputation, the pine grosbeak in fact has to work hard foraging for food, and tends to conserve energy by sitting for a long while, slightly puffing out the feathers for insulation. They are strong fliers and require a good length to their enclosure with a minimum of four metres, though the ideal would be nearer six, and with a width of no less than three metres and a height of about two metres. Provide a small-roofed section at each end as a shield from driving rain with perhaps a little side shelter as well, for added comfort. They can of course put up with intense cold, but damp roosting conditions over a period invariably prove detrimental to general well-being. They readily take to new foods such as any of the brassicas, comfrey, sowthistle, dandelion, chickweed, dock seed, rhubarb seed, all fruits growing wild and apple. The rowan berry is a natural food for them as are buds of birch (*Betula*), willow (*Salix*) and the small young cones of most

conifers. Bearing these foods in mind one should plant an aviary to include many. Although the planning of an aviary need never be too complicated, it should allow for natural growth of as many basic foods as it will comfortably hold.

Food

The basic diet can be of the larger seeds, as one would use for hawfinch or crossbill: sunflower, a good quality pigeon conditioning seed, a little each of wheat, groats, safflower, mixed millets, buckwheat, rape and niger can be soaked as usual and given strained. Fruit is essential: give apple all the time, a few soaked household currants, wild berries when available and almost any of the greenfoods collected for our more common finches. This bird seems quite willing to experiment where softfood is offered and will invariably accept a baby food which has been mixed with milk and lightly sprinkled with one of its favourite seeds.

The inclusion of fresh fir branches whenever possible will help in eliminating boredom and encourage this bird to actively search for choice items. These branches must be fresh and not dry withered specimens where the sap has disappeared.

Insects are a valuable part of the daily food intake: mealworms are taken avidly along with many other easily cultured specimens. These birds quite often take flies on the wing, just as they would mosquito or may-fly in the wild. Insect life is essential if one is to breed from these birds: the young will not fledge without a large supply of animal protein in the diet.

Breeding

The condition necessary for these birds to breed can only be achieved by providing plenty of livefood and a good varied diet, not just prior to their usual month of May for nesting, but throughout the winter. They are slow to respond and a whole season can so easily drift by with negative results unless real efforts are made in respect of their diet and the inclusion of rich, stimulating, but non-fattening items; the extra long flight will help and with the feeding area sited in the centre, a maximum of exercise will be taken. Provide shelf-type nesting sites, made from branches of conifers lying on a stout, horizontally erected framework securely fixed at each end and spaced about twenty or twenty-five centimetres apart. These birds nest in similarly well-splayed branches when at liberty and only once have I ever had them nest in a large wicker nest basket, many years ago. Offer a few handfuls of twigs, mosses, rootlets, fine grasses and animal hair such as dog hair combings, cow hair and horse hair cut in lengths of no longer than ten centimetres; do not be surprised by the amount of twigs they expect. These are used to form a basal platform and outer walls and even in captivity the birds will persist in taking these vital precautions against cold reaching their nest contents. On to this base is then built the nest itself which resembles a larger version of the bullfinch nest, but is lined with grasses, moss and lichen, with rootlets and hair forming the inner lining. This nest is normally built very near the trunk of the tree on a strong branch.

The clutch of eggs rarely exceeds four: they are deep greenish-blue with dark purplish-brown blotches and spots and smaller, even darker, markings between. The female does all or most incubating whilst the male brings her food to the nest; incubation takes the usual fourteen days but, as with a number of birds in the far North, this can vary about a day either way depending upon weather conditions at the time.

Although such a remarkably tame bird, (mine would take meal-worms from me whilst incubating) as much privacy as one can allow at this time should help towards success. I find that some birds, even very tame ones, can feel reluctant to share nesting knowledge, and tend to sit too tightly on young, with adverse results from the lack of feeding that occurs.

If fortunate enough to have young hatch—and the eggs should be fertile if the pair have been allowed an aviary to themselves—offer as many types of livefood as can be obtained. It will soon be noticed which is their favourite for rearing purposes. The large wax-moth larvae of the American species were the favourite of mine; mealworms came second and after they had all been eaten, the birds would accept almost anything. At this time seed will also be given to nestlings, but many buds would normally be given and so cut the seed intake during the first eight days or so of the nestlings' existence. The best seed at this time is sunflower, soaked and just commencing to sprout. My birds took large amounts of sowthistle and comfrey, a lot of apple, Farlene baby food to which had been added soya bean meal, ants 'eggs', Abidec multivitamin drops, calcium lactate and milk, but they would eat it without additives, just mixed with milk.

I failed to rear the young of these birds and have no hesitation in accepting the blame for this as I had foolishly allowed them to remain in a large aviary holding a mixed collection of birds instead of removing them with the first signs of carrying nest materials. This is one of the few regrets I have over my years of bird study and I cannot overstress the importance of breeding from some of these rarities whenever such opportunities arise.

Scarlet Grosbeak (*Carpodacus erythrinus*)****
(greenfinch reared)
General Description
Sometimes called the rosefinch, this bird is about the same size as the greenfinch (fifteen centimetres). The adult male is brownish on back and sides but a rich crimson about the head, breast and rump. There are two pale wing bars. The bill is conical but thick as with most bud eaters and similar to the bill of the greenfinch but not so pointed. A juvenile male lacks the red in the plumage, being more grey-brown, whilst the female is even more dull, being totally brown, a pale soft colour slightly striated; there are many members to this genus in both the Old and New World.

Habitat
This finch occurs throughout most of the Palaearctic region and seems to thrive equally in mountainous regions and lowland reaching as far North in Scandinavia and Russia as 68° N. On the whole, one can say that they nest more in wooded areas of willow, poplar and alder than in coniferous forests, unless the latter are rather open. The feeding habits always remind me of the bullfinch with their taste for buds of fruit trees. Wild apple, rowan, willow and birch supply this bird with bud sustenance. The seeds taken are more in line with those of the goldfinch (dandelion, sowthistle, grasses, etc.) but its choice of fruit and berries again resembles the bullfinch's with rowan seeming the favourite. Much insect life is also consumed but these appear to be taken from trees and shrubs, rarely from the ground and so it seems that caterpillars are the main source of animal protein. This is rather a slow and late moulting bird, invariably retaining the old plumage until it has migrated south.

Aviary
An active bird but neither wild nor over nervous when housed in an aviary; due to the flight and constant movement, the enclosure should be longer than average, say three or four metres; two metres high and requiring one-metre width as a minimum.

Remembering this bird's fondness for buds, we must consider planting the ground with a wide range of greenfoods; brassicas, comfrey, spinach and dandelion are most suitable. Include a few conifers if possible to give a natural and attractive setting. The roof should include a slight sheltered portion at each end. Place the food in the central area in a cleared space so as not to impair the flying facilities. As with almost all northern birds these can stand cold frosty weather but are not too happy when subjected to excessively damp conditions.

Food
Screenings can form the base of the seed mixture. To this add sunflower in small quantities, wheat, kibbled groats, niger, rape, linseed, small millets, maw and gold of pleasure. Fruit in the form of apple should always be available and as wild fruits such as hawthorn, rowan and blackberries become ripe offer these in abundance otherwise a certain amount of the red on the plumage will disappear. Buds can be given as for other bud-eating species: hawthorn, birch, willow, wild apple, domestic fruit tree prunings (unless sprayed), conifer branches fresh from the tree will be stripped of the fleshy buds and help maintain these birds in good health. The regular provision of a daily livefood quota will advance the birds' condition until the arrival of the breeding season. May is normally the month when nesting takes place; the male should then be singing, and courting the hen.

Breeding
In the wild the scarlet grosbeak nests in a similar site to that of the yellowhammer, in a low bush well grown with tall grasses; in captivity, there is a tendency for higher siting of the nest, but low sites will not always be ignored. Try to grow a dense bush (juniper seems a good site) in the aviary with plenty of tallish grass or reeds surrounding it; if this is not practical then fabricate one low against the side of the enclosure with another similar site at about eye level. The nesting materials will be dry grasses, rootlets, coconut fibre, teased out string in short lengths, dog hair or similar materials. Vegetable down or hair will form the final inner lining.

The eggs are a deep bright shade of blue with a few dark squiggles and spots marking their rather striking colour.

When housed on their own these birds seem quite reliable yet in the company of a mixed collection they seem nervous when breeding. In all probability the finches to be found in most aviary collections are either rivals for the site or rather fierce strangers compared with the quiet nature of this bird, so docile in its behaviour that I have seen siskins and redpolls chase them away. Due to an unexpectedly short period of incubation, a mere twelve days, I lost a nest of young before I realised they had hatched; now as I write, I have a pair of these birds nesting again.

For the rearing of young a good regular supply of livefood is essential: mealworms will usually form the basic food but do try to provide a wide variety. Although I seldom recommend maggots, due to the ever possible danger of botulism, they can be used if they have been kept in clean bran for a period of five days and the black digestive tract is cleared.

Hawfinch (*Coccothraustes coccothraustes*)****

General Description

The second largest of our finches, measuring some eighteen to nineteen centimetres depending upon which area it hails from, it is rather top-heavy in appearance. Its very large bill and head are set upon rather thick-looking shoulders and it tapers conically to a short tail. The overall impression is of a strong bill and powerful body. The colouring is predominantly orange-brown and it has blackish wings, a rich dark brown back, white shoulder patches, chestnut head and face, and greyish nape; it has a black bib with the breast pinkish-brown fading to white at the ventral area through a most attractive range of browns. The four inner primaries and secondaries are curiously shaped, being curved at the ends and exhibiting a small notch at each side; the bill which is bone-pink during the winter months gradually changes to gunmetal blue with the advancing of breeding fitness. The female is paler and more of a dull brown. Young hawfinches do not acquire the black bib until their first moult. Before this, although rather resembling the hens in dullness, they have a distinct suggestion of breast bars and are yellowish in general appearance; the young can be sexed in nest feather by the amount of black around a young male's bill and his darker underparts. Regardless of any other characteristic the bill alone will identify these birds from all other finches.

Habitat

The beech and hornbeam woods, forests and spinneys are the usual haunt of this bird and only in the far North where conifers abound do they have difficulty in finding such vegetation: there they make full use of broad-leaved trees on the lower edges of the conifer forests. A shy retiring bird in the wild, it is one which can become extremely confiding in captivity, once it acquires a taste for mealworms and the knowledge that the keeper is the source of supply. In the wild they are far more common than one would imagine as they do tend to avoid humans. Evidence of their presence can, however, frequently be seen by lines of neatly shelled garden peas. Cherry orchards in late summer hold a fascination for them as, with their powerful bills internally shaped to grip the cherry stone, and with extra strong muscles in head and face, they are well able to break open the hard stones. Occasionally even a suburban garden will hold a pair or see a visiting family but more often it is a sudden 'tzik' which identifies them as being nearby. The nest is usually in a wood, a yew tree, or even a thick neglected fruit tree. I have seen them high in hawthorn hedges with just the steely blue bill and a pair of eyes watching me over the rim of a rather untidy nest. Since the breeding range of this bird covers so many countries, reaching fairly far into Scandinavia and Russia, there is the usual size variation between northern and southern birds; sometimes it is not so very noticeable with live birds, but found when comparing skeletons.

Aviary

From personal choice I try to use an enclosure which runs lengthwise parallel with a well-used garden path; in this way the birds tend to get more used to human movement and gradually become more confiding. Aviary bred specimens or hand-raised birds, however, have little fear of the humans they know. The enclosure should be at least three metres long, at least one metre wide and two metres high. This is adequate for breeding and since the male or female can become aggressive when nearing this period, the length does serve a very useful purpose in allowing evasive action by the less dominant bird. Providing a small-roofed shelter at each end of the aviary to cover a few conifer branches will provide a little seclusion when required; although these birds will quite readily make nests in branches prepared to form an attractive site, I have always offered large wicker nest baskets in an effort to ensure the safety of eggs and young. I do this because I have known free-standing nests to tilt badly when built on a branch site.

The aviary can be planted with conifers or elder: if other trees or shrubs are used, be ready for the buds to disappear at the first hungry onslaught. A background can be provided by hops on a frame or wire: these grow quite densely and although many buds will be pruned, they will still encourage spiders and many insects for the hawfinches: the seeds will also be taken if allowed to mature. Although this bird has a fondness for garden peas, I do not advise that these are included in the aviary as they are seldom given an opportunity to flower and grow the pods. It is usually far more rewarding to keep to the usual brassica or comfrey growth.

The winter months need cause no discomfort to this species: they are hardy, strong birds and so long as they are given a dry, draught-proof roost, and fed properly, they will come through in excellent condition.

Food

The sunflower, safflower, buckwheat and groats can form the bulk of the seed intake, the first three items in equal proportions and the last in a half proportion. These should then be mixed half and half with a good quality pigeon conditioning mixture and a small amount of commercially mixed finch seed. Livefood will be taken all the year round, but becomes the main item of the diet when any rearing is in progress: mealworms, locusts, wax-moth larvae, earwigs, well-cleaned maggots, the latter slightly dusted with Vionate can prove most beneficial. Ripe apple should be available at all times and with the arrival of garden fruit such as currants and raspberries these also can be added to their diet. Later when rowan and hawthorn berries become plentiful they will appreciate a daily supply of these foods. Rarely will the hawfinch, other than a hand-raised specimen, take a softfood. If one can coax them to use such a valuable source of nutrition then it does simplify the period when they have newly hatched chicks.

As previously mentioned green garden peas have a strong fascination for our subject and many I have known blasted out of existence in some countries by irate gardeners. I have not advised the use of cherry stones: I find that where these birds are supplied with enough of the above foods, they tend in captivity to ignore this fruit stone; offer fruits of hornbeam, sycamore, beech and wych elm.

Breeding

Compared to other members of the finch family the hawfinch can prove a little difficult to breed, but I would hasten to make clear that the problem can be overcome if one is willing to specialise and cater for this event. One can either culture or buy insects suitable for their use. Whichever is decided upon, they will require large amounts if they are to rear a full nest of young to maturity. A sudden change of diet to almost a hundred per cent mealworm can upset the parent birds with sometimes fatal results so the introduction must be gradual. Maggots are safe if well cleaned, but will require some form of multivitamin additive, either dusted on them in powder form or supplied as a few drops of concentrated vitamin liquid. Whatever is intended for the birds' use, do introduce it well in advance of the nesting season. The natural food of these birds when rearing is the green caterpillar of the oak tree; I know well from personal experience just how hard the collection of this creature is, but if one does take the trouble to obtain them they will be found to be full of vegetable matter, mostly in a part digested state. We could offer locusts which are fed almost entirely on grass. It is rare for hawfinches to offer nestlings any seed whatsoever until the young are at least eight to ten days old and I have on crop examinations found the remains of surprisingly large beetles in quite small nestlings.

The nesting site need be only a largish wicker basket lightly surrounded by conifer branches. Once breeding condition is reached they seem to throw all caution to the winds and will incubate in full view of their keepers. Supply a few fine twigs, plenty of coconut matting or strong bristly string teased out to individual strands and given in a moist condition; horse, cow or dog hair will be taken for the lining and a little moss is sometimes used in the wall construction. Offer a limited amount of grasses; strong rootlets will usually be used to bind this flimsy affair together.

Linnet (*Acanthis cannabina*)†****‡

General Description

The length of this bird varies between thirteen and fifteen centimetres depending upon whether from the northern or southerly area of the range. It is predominantly brown with a streaked chestnut back in the male. There are white feather edges in flights and outer-tail and the underparts are buffish but streaked with darker brown. The male will, in the spring, acquire through the feather tips wearing off a crimson marked breast and forehead. The female lacks the red and is much paler brown, often greyish brown in the head and nape, and is also just a little smaller. In the breeding season the bills will turn a dark bluish-black and the song take on an almost continuous sound; the crimson markings of the chest will appear on males only in spacious aviaries where they have been fed wisely on a well-mixed seed diet, wildfoods and insects and where they have been used to much flying.

Habitat
The northern range is almost to the Arctic circle and they cover most of Europe, reaching Africa and Asia Minor on their southern fringe. Although largely a bird of the common scrub-like lands, they do also visit gardens, open park land, railway embankments, etc. Wherever one finds gorse and similar vegetation the linnet is not too far off; low seeding weeds such as brassicas, chickweed and persicaria form the bulk of the diet, each one as it crops forming the main constituent. A farmland area may be the main source for a few weeks and then open moorland with the ripening of other plant seeds.

Aviary
Despite their shyness (less so with northern birds) they are easily accommodated. A two- by one-metre length enclosure will house a pair or even a trio, a male and two females. For winter shelter they need only the barest of roofed areas, with a little shelter from driving rain around the edges of this roofed section.

   Their aviary can be safely planted with a number of shrubs and flowering vegetation. Include a few brassicas, such as rape, cabbage and kale: they will provide all necessary greenfood, and later the seeds will be greatly appreciated by linnets. This bird seldom does the amount of damage to growing shrubs for which most finches are notorious. The inclusion of such natural items as gorse, broom and perhaps hops on a rear trellis against the furthest wall will encourage them to nest in spring.

   Bathing facilities should always be available, as for all the finch family.

Food

Screenings with an extra mixture of rape seeds and a little hemp would prove ideal for most of the year, with linseed added during the winter months and the hemp increased a little during this cold spell. Screenings, however, are becoming a scarce item these days and it may well be necessary to mix one's own linnet seed mixture: for this use equal parts of canary, grass (rye), small millets, red and black rape, turnip, linseed and a small amount each of gold of pleasure, lettuce, maw and niger. Sweet apple will be eaten by some and ignored by others; berries are rarely taken though I have in the far North occasionally seen linnets eat the flesh of rowan fruit. Persicaria and all the wild growing seeds such as chickweed are avidly taken as will be the seeds of Michaelmas daisy, forget-me-not and pansy from the garden beds. Sowthistle will always be found a valuable addition to any finch diet when rearing is in progress; linnets may not take this so much in the wild but when kept under controlled conditions they give it in quantity to their young. As with many of the finch family, acceptance of a softfood is an individual thing: some readily eat such foods as Farlene (Glaxo), moistened with milk and sprinkled with maw seed; others will take a prepared finch rearing food, whilst there are many which seldom take such items yet eat readily all the aphids available and rear their young on these with only soaked mixtures as mentioned above as a supplement.

Breeding

Rarely is a nest basket or fabricated site necessary if linnets are given a naturally planted aviary. They will make do with a few branches of broom, conifer, gorse or similar growth and build a nest securely fastened in this. They invariably make a strong nest of grasses, moss, thin twigs and rootlets, lined with fine hair and wool. If providing cotton wool do tease this out into small tufts to avoid leg entanglement. They will normally require only very small pieces of such material.

Three or four broods are often raised, depending upon the availability of suitable food: quite often if the supply of wildfood ceases then so too does their inclination to breed. The young of this species is noted for its wildness when first leaving the nest: even in a cage, if fostered out to a canary pair, they will run around the floor like mice. They do become tame very quickly in an aviary providing their parents are not over wild and as long as they do not have to be caught up and separated.

Give as many wild seeding plants as can be gathered and make sure a good and varied soaked mixture is always available. Aphids will frequently be taken from growing vegetation such as hops or even roses in their enclosure. This is one of the oldest of birds caged by man and the song alone makes it a very worthwhile addition to a garden aviary.

Lesser Redpoll (*Acanthis flammea disruptes*)****†
and (*A. f. cabaret*)**** ‡

General Description
The former is a resident of the British Isles and the latter of Europe as a whole: vast varieties of the redpoll group exist although all are about eleven and a half centimetres in length. In this lesser race there are those with a pale, almost white, breast showing a pinkish-rose tinge and others which are a rich rose-red from throat to deep in the chest. The variety is due to a certain amount of natural hybridisation occurring in the wild along with the normal tendency for southern birds to be darker than northern varieties. There is red on the forehead of all redpolls although a bad moult may result in only a yellowish-gold being present: this is rare and occurs only as a result of bad management and feeding, or illness during the time of the moult. The male lesser redpoll should be a rich dark brown-backed bird, striated upon flanks and rump and with a red forehead and chest; the small, delicate bill is of yellowish-bone, tipped black; the female lacks the red breast, showing far more brown in this area.

Habitat
Common throughout Europe in woody areas, in Britain it often nests in orchards, in small trees and even bushes; in some countries it prefers hilly terrain where birch scrub and conifers abound. Thickets of alder and overgrown hawthorn are popular sites for nesting and their untidy nest, rather like the greenfinches' at first glance, seems far too large for this very dainty and diminutive bird.

Aviary
If being bred merely for research or study of any particular phase of behaviour, these birds can be kept in a colony: they all tend to roost in one area, feed together, and eventually breed quite

amicably in fairly small enclosures without undue fighting or any damage. For this reason one may house a number of pairs or a few males with a larger number of females in one aviary. For the best results and also to enable any student the fullest advantages of observation, give a pair or a trio an aviary as recommended for the linnet. For more than this number of birds, one should add the volume of half that aviary size for each additional pair. Only a small portion of the roof need be sheltered and this proves most useful when spread around the full outer edges of the roof and slightly down the sides, leaving the centre and greater part of the roof open to rain and sun.

Growing conifers look attractive and provide a natural setting for this bird. As it damages growing vegetation there should also be much in the way of food growing at ground level: comfrey and a variety of the brassicas will prove ideal and will tend to keep the birds' destructiveness channelled to a food subject; hops against a rear wall of the enclosure will provide roosting area and also food from the ripening seeds and from the aphids it encourages, useful when rearing is in progress.

Food
A staple diet should be that advised for the linnet, but without any of the hemp or rape. Chickweed, dandelion, sowthistle, meadowsweet, grasses of all kinds and seeds from birch, larch and alder will all be taken in season; few fruits or berries are taken but redpolls are often seen removing apple pips from a core. I have had redpolls which take softfood, but in most cases it was where these birds had been foster reared by other finches, such as greenfinches brought up on such foods. This bird when housed on the colony system should be provided with a neutral feeding area with no nest sites in the immediate vicinity; one of the most pleasant ways of observing them is to hang large bunches of seeding grasses at eye level; they will then grip the fine stalks, feeding in groups and displaying their colouring and agility to their best advantage.

Breeding
This is one of the first birds that I ever bred and I am sure that most people who keep native European birds would find them one of the easiest and most entertaining to keep and breed in an aviary. Nest baskets, natural densely-growing shrubs, clumps of conifer branches fixed securely in almost any sheltered site, even

bunches of dry bracken, picked and bundled whilst still green the previous autumn, will be used for nesting. Offer mosses, dry fine grasses, fine twigs, rootlets and animal hair. The nest will be lined with vegetable-down, fine hair and feathers, even small tufts of cotton wool will be used but offer very little of this material and always in a well teased out condition as redpolls are prone to leg entanglement and similar accidents.

When the young hatch, the parent birds will take many aphids and other very small insects and although caterpillars and wax-moth larvae will be fed to nestlings at this time, very few birds will accept mealworms. The soaked seed mixture will be a great asset as too will soaked and sprouting teazle. Almost all wild seeding grasses and weeds will be eaten and the leaves turned for further supplies of insect life. The young upon leaving the nest are most attractive, smaller versions of the parents, minus the red. They often sit in a row upon a branch near the now discarded nest making a charming sight for any bird lover.

Mealy Redpoll (*Acanthis flammea flammea*)****,
Hoary Redpoll (*A. h. exilipes*)****, Greenland Redpoll
(*A. f. rostrata*)****‡, Iceland Redpoll (*A. f. islandica*)****
and Hornemann's Redpoll (*A. hornemanni hornemanni*)****
General Description
With the vast and subtle variations to be found within this group, one cannot be very sure of the correct race unless absolutely certain of the birds' origin. On occasions I have handled birds taken in Korea, others from Russia and still more from Canada and Iceland and there have been specimens in each group which were hard to pinpoint. Measurements can be deceptive, as too can weights, and even visual colour variation; I have seen large brown-backed birds, for example, from the least likely of areas. Gradually, with the hybridisation which is taking place in such diverse areas as Canada and Scandinavia, identification can be quite difficult. Aviculture has not helped in any way, since there is a tendency to breed from two large birds or two small specimens with a total disregard of the true races involved.

I have grouped together all the large races of Redpoll to prevent too much duplication in advising their requirements. There are Hoary or Coue's Redpoll from Northern Europe, Siberia, North America and Canada; Greenland Redpoll from

Greenland and Baffin Island; Iceland Redpoll from Iceland, and Hornemann's Redpoll from Greenland.

Some birds which have spent their existence in coniferous areas have slightly longer bills adapted to their feeding habits than others who feed more upon birch or those such as the two lesser races. These larger birds are in general much paler than the lesser redpoll, though much depends on the area of origin: the red of the breast area is replaced with anything from a pale, washed-out pink to deep pink, and apart from this colouring the breast is almost white. The *hornemanni* races have an overall silver appearance as compared to the *flammea*'s greyish-brown: the former have fewer striations on flank and rump and each is far paler than the lesser forms: some of the *hornemanni* seem almost as though they are covered with frost, they are so silver looking. The further north the bird comes from the more it tends to have a softer downy-like plumage. The foreheads are still rose-red in these northern varieties. In length they range from nearly thirteen to fifteen centimetres as compared with the less than twelve centimetres of the lesser redpoll. They vary in body weight and in the general impression they give of their body width and bulk.

Habitat
Those from the regions providing thick conifer forests will invariably prefer such areas in captivity and feed from the available sources of food, but others such as the *hornemanni* nest in conifer scrubland which means the nest may be sited less than a metre from the ground. During its migration to North America and Canada and its occasional visit to Northern Europe even the latter race heads for the coniferous areas.

Aviary
In the wild this bird will have to work hard and forage for sustenance. Such a Spartan life ensures that those which survive to reach breeding condition really are fit examples. Bear this in mind when planning an aviary to house them and endeavour to provide extra length for flight exercise. A three- or four-metre length enclosure by one or two metres wide and two metres in height would be suitable. Place the feeding tray centrally so that as much flight as possible is necessary from their roosting and perching areas at each end of the aviary to this central feeding area. One must ensure that these birds take adequate exercise as in captivity they do tend to become lazy, eating and then sitting

in one place for a longish while: this results all too frequently in obesity and deterioration of condition. Roosting areas should be sheltered and dry, one at each end of the long aviary. Plant these ends thickly with conifer, and the floor between with comfrey, dandelion and brassicas. As is often the case with the northern bird species, they can be remarkably tame.

Food
I would recommend that where screenings are obtainable, these are used as a base for the seed mixture. In its absence make up a mix comprising equal parts of small millets, plain canary, grass (rye), teazle, and smaller amounts of maw, linseed, niger, gold of pleasure and lettuce. Almost all wild seeding weeds can be given along with lettuce going to seed and near its ripened stage, seeding rhubarb, dock, sowthistle and dandelion. Bunches of seeding grasses will give hours of enjoyment and good food value to the birds. I would emphasise the need to use many of the various millets in aviary mixtures; they are good value for money and the millet sprays can be soaked for birds with nestlings. Few of these redpolls take mealworms unless gradually introduced to them first by having them cut into pieces on their daily seed. Their bills are really not made for this but they are all exceedingly fond of small caterpillars and soft grubs such as the wax-moth larvae; when rearing, some of these birds will feed their nestlings with large amounts of aphids. Sweet apple is occasionally taken (certainly the pips) but fruit in general is not bothered with a great deal. A good conditioning seed mixture can be very helpful if included in their diet, as one often finds seeds in this which are never sold commercially on their own.

Breeding
These are normally late breeders, but after a few seasons in more southerly latitudes they often make a start before their normal late June. Give plenty of conifer sites; wicker baskets can be placed here and there with perhaps a little moss in the bases to give the hens the right idea. Materials can vary slightly with the races' habitat but generally if one provides rootlets, mosses, fine grasses, fine twigs such as dead heather, lichen, animal hair (cow and horse hair are ideal with dog combings for the lining) and a little teased out cotton wool and small feathers, they will build their untidy nest, large naturally to insulate against cold. When providing the twigs, moss and rootlets make sure they are soft

123

and pliable by soaking overnight in water: this is wise with all the finches and though more important for the larger specimens, it will be appreciated by all as the materials are then more easily woven into position and set-dry in the shape chosen.

Nestlings will need many small live insects if they are to progress as in the wild. When supplying moth larvae, sprinkle a little calcium lactate and Vionate in the dish first; if one can get the parent birds to pass such useful extras on to their nestlings, the growth rate is increased, important during this period when basic bone structures are formed.

Long-Tailed Rosefinch (*Uragus sibiricus*)***
General Description
This most attractive species is, sadly, but rarely today. The body is the size of a large pale redpoll—*A. h. hornemanni* would be very near in size—and even the colouring is similar with a silver wash over the whole bird. It has a long tail similar to that of the long-tailed tits'. The forehead and lores are rich rose-red and the rest of the head is silvery-brown, just faintly tinted with rose; the back is brownish with the silver finish again with a pinkish flush; the wings show the same hues but the flights have whitish margins; rump and tail coverts are rich rosy-red; throat is silver and this extends to the ventral area, with a rose-pink flush on the breast. The bill is bone colour, short but not pointed, and is in fact typical of a bud-eater. It is like a bullfinch's but smaller and neater. The female is similar in colour but lacks the rich colouring of the male, showing a pink wash only on rump, upper tail coverts and flanks. The juvenile has no pink or rose until the moult and is predominantly a silver-ash colour. The tail alone measures nine centimetres, the total overall length being fifteen centimetres.

Habitat
The open bush-covered areas adjoining mountain forests are the favourite areas. It does not appear to be very fond of the forests, remaining on the mountain slopes where a wide range of plants grows. The seeds of these form its diet together with buds and small berries. Its region is Siberia and the Ural range where it roams in family groups.

Aviary
I have little doubt that the standard minimum would suffice for a

pair of these birds: my own were certainly in a far larger enclosure the first time they nested but I do not feel that this is necessary. A larger aviary would, however, enable one to test it for colony breeding. Mine were all very docile and I had about a dozen of them in all.

Food
If screenings are obtainable, use them as a base and add various other seeds to it. Hemp should be kept to a minimum. Grasses of all kinds, plain canary seed, the small brassicas, maw, gold of pleasure, millets, teazle, niger and many from the garden such as marigold, forget-me-not, pansy and Michaelmas daisy can be given. Offer all wild seeding weeds and grasses—sowthistle, probably a favourite in the wild, is taken greedily. Chickweed and persicaria are other seeds of which it seems extremely fond. Sunflower seed if soaked will be taken, as too will chopped-up mealworms from the surface of the seed mixture: many insects are eaten when visiting clusters of wild seeding plants. A rearing food such as Farlene, generously sprinkled with maw seed will be taken, particularly if housed with some other small bird that eats this food: the Farlene should be mixed with milk to provide extra animal protein. Quite apart from its usefulness as a food and perhaps in rearing, it is a valuable medium for introducing a little colouring matter should this be considered necessary.

Breeding
If elder, willow and hops are growing profusely in the rosefinches aviary, nesting sites such as those fabricated from clusters of birch twigs and conifer or even conifer on its own, wired securely and fixed amid the growing vegetation will encourage nesting.

Three pairs of mine nested, laid eggs and hatched young and each nest was constructed of identical materials: bents, rootlets, moss, vegetable down, animal hair, both horse and dog hair and a few small tufts of cotton wool. The length of the tail always tends to make one forget how small the true body size is, and the nest is therefore surprisingly neat and small. The eggs are a rather bright blue with sparse small black spots on the larger end.

When rearing is in progress many aphids are taken; mealworms when cut in small pieces and laid on their food are eaten or quickly passed to the young. The seed consumption of the young seems rather low and the crop shows very dark with green food.

Serin (*Serinus serinus*)****

General Description

For those who are familiar with the Border variety of canary I would say that the serin resembles a small chubby version of this, about eleven and a half centimetres long from bill to tail. If one visualises a green border canary then thinks of darker striations on it, one has an almost perfect picture of the serin. Predominantly green with small neat bill, the male has forehead, breast, rump, nape and an eye stripe of yellow; female colouring is more dull with far less yellow in the plumage. The young can be duller still, being slightly brown-green with even more striations than the female. The song is a very sweet little melody with perhaps not much variation, but so continuous and happy sounding that I always find it a pleasure to hear. It is normally a lively little bird, seemingly fit and happy in warmer dry weather.

Habitat

Gradually becoming more common throughout Europe, this bird now reaches Sweden in its northerly range and breeds in Poland and Russia. It is a woodland bird by choice, but where this ends and cultivation begins, their nests can be found in vineyards, olive groves, garden hedges and parks. Although becoming widespread it is still very much a Mediterranean bird.

Aviary

The minimum-sized aviary is ideal for a pair of these birds, and even with this size two females can be included with the one male if so wished. I have never yet known any real aggression show itself with these birds. Give plenty of winter shelter: although I would not recommend artificial warmth, they are better for having a small shed-type shelter attached to their outdoor aviary. In this manner they may take advantage of sunny winter days yet remain out of the damp when necessary. Construct this shelter so that plenty of natural light enters and clearly illuminates the interior. Where possible place the food inside. I would not advise closing these birds inside for the duration of the winter as they are early nesters, often undertaking nesting operations in March, and if shut indoors for all the winter their condition is not at its hardiest just when it needs to be. If it is not possible to build a shelter, then ensure a dry draughtproof roost.

The aviary can be well planted with conifers with plenty of

ground cover of food value: dandelion, brassicas and rye grass will provide a natural diet.

Food

A seed mixture should contain plain canary seed, mixed small millets, grasses, lettuce, and red and black rape. Very little niger or linseed need be included but a canary conditioning seed should assist in providing some of the small seeds so enjoyed by this bird. Do endeavour to obtain screenings for this bird thus giving it a free choice of wild seeds. Dandelion, chickweed, shepherd's purse, persicaria and clusters of seeding grasses suspended from the aviary roof can be continually pecked over and the fallen seeds gathered from the floor.

Softfoods will be taken if gently introduced. One of the favourites for rearing has been Farlene (Glaxo) baby food, mixed with milk; in the early stages of rearing one can always mix extra calcium lactate in such a food to improve the bird's bone structure and forestall any danger of rickets.

Insect life will be given to nestlings if available in the nature of aphids and such like. I have had one or two birds take maggot chrysalids, opening one end and drawing out the contents as goldfinches do, but this is rare in serins.

Breeding

This bird can be kept in a manner almost identical to the siskin. Small wicker nest baskets will be accepted and used readily. Natural nests may also be made in almost any growing vegetation or suitably fabricated site. Preference is always shown for conifer sites. Materials should include mosses, fine grasses, lichens and rootlets: the birds will require above average amounts of hair and feathers for lining this structure and the whole thing is a very warm little nest; in the wild, serins' nests are very well concealed.

Soaked seed, wildfoods and aphids all contribute towards successful rearing and the young, attractive little creatures, are well worth any effort.

Serin (*Serinus canaria*)****

General Description

Apart from being a little larger than *Serinus serinus* and showing more grey on the back and a little less yellow elsewhere, these birds are very similar. In an aviary they behave in much the same way. The surprising thing is how man has managed to change this bird to the domesticated canaries of today; the length is twelve and a half centimetres.

Habitat
The Canary Islands, Azores and Madeira form the home of this rather dull little bird. It frequents woods, orchards and gardens where the song can be heard from the perch and as it flies overhead.

Aviary
Provide a similar structure to that advised for this bird's close relative the *Serinus serinus* and treat in a like manner in all ways.

Food
Feed as for the serin or domesticated canary but tend to offer more grass seed than for the latter.

Breeding
I may seem a little uninspired by this bird but so much has been written on the domesticated canary that when a wildling of the species does occur in captivity, one can add only a minimal amount of advice. I would merely suggest that one treats a freshly taken specimen not as a canary but as a wild bird, in particular the *Serinus serinus*. These birds will nest quite readily once acclimatised and used to aviary life: they adapt to their surroundings quickly and soon begin to rear successfully. However, at an early stage they should be treated as wildlings and be given all assistance in rearing, with the provision of wildfoods and grasses; although a canary by name, they are in need of specialised treatment at first such as one always gives a newly taken bird.

Red-Fronted Serin (*Serinus pusillus*)***
General Description
The male is of a striking appearance with the fiery-red forehead contrasting against the black of nape, side face and breast; the chest fades to yellowish-green on the lower belly, and the wings although mainly blackish are streaked with a tawny rufous shade which extends to the tail; the ventral area is yellowish-white; the wings have yellow patches and, there are yellow feathers too at the side of the tail. A female is more dull and lacks the red forehead; the juvenile of this species is paler on the lower belly than the parents, very dull and blackish around head, nape, back

and breast, showing merely a little of a yellowish shade on wing butts and chest.

Habitat

A high altitude bird of coniferous forest, a species I have kept on a number of occasions but never studied in the wild. Mine came from Russia but their usual habitat is the high mountainous areas of the Turkish–Russian borders.

Aviary

When siting the enclosure for these birds, give a little thought to their natural environment, the altitude in particular, and erect the aviary in a cool site, one where perhaps the sun only filters through to the enclosure. I recommend this because when my own birds have nested and sun has struck the enclosure, the hens have looked most uncomfortable, raising themselves from the nests with bills open. Although there is certainly no scarcity of sun in their natural habitat, the high altitude does provide very pure thin air. Living lower, at sea level or thereabouts, they may not feel at their best. A dry roosting area is essential if they are to live a normal lifespan. They seem to detest dampness although they are frequent bathers. No heating is required in the winter roosting shelter.

The minimum size enclosure should be in the region of two metres square with a similar height. They are very active fliers, circling and diving at high speeds so one should give ample space for their manoeuvres. Conifers can form the background providing that they do not cause obstruction: they should be kept to corner sites and perimeter; the shelter need not be a very large one, merely enough for roosting and avoiding excessive dampness.

Food

Here we have a bird which in the wild eats large quantities of seeding grasses and other typical serin foods. Feed as you would *Serinus serinus*. Do not give too much niger as this bird very quickly becomes addicted to it and will make it its sole diet if allowed to. Small insect life is taken and when rearing there is a continual search for aphids and other insect pests among growing vegetation; with this in mind it is advisable to plant hops along one side of their aviary. They seem to take dandelion, sowthistle and seeding brassicas in large amounts. Hemp should be omitted from their diet. There are many wild foods to select from including the numerous seeding grasses which form their natural wild diet. The use of a commercial wild seed mixture or screenings will greatly assist their general health.

Breeding
These birds take to wicker baskets or conifer sites with little concern for nearness of humans. None of my birds has ever seemed at all shy at this time. One can leave them to build a nest in conifer shelves or growing vegetation once the materials have been provided: mosses, rootlets, dry grasses, lichens, hair and feathers should be made available.

Give soaked seeds at all times after the frosts of the winter have ceased right through the spring, summer and autumn, until after completion of the moulting season. Then over a period of a week or two, hard seed should be resumed mixed half and half with the soaked.

Siskin (*Carduelis spinus*)****‡

General Description
This bird is often considered to be one of the smallest of the finch family but it does vary in size depending on its region of origin. As is usual those from the far North are longer and also slightly bigger in body bulk. The length ranges from eleven to twelve centimetres. The variation is not noticeable in the field and indeed the larger of the specimens are found as residents only on the birds' very northern limits. An adult male is an all over green and very yellowish around face, rump and breast with large yellow wing bars and yellow also at the sides of the tail. The crown should be black, darker and more glossy with age and there is also often, but not always, a black bib just below the bill, but this varies from one male to another in size and depth of colour. The back is striated with black; wings and tail also show dark almost black feathers. The lower belly is unstreaked with the yellow fading out to white in the ventral area. The hen is paler, more greyish-green and lacking the black on crown and the bib marking; the wings also are greyish-green but do show the wing bar though in a paler shade of yellow: the whole body is more streaked except for lower belly to vent. A juvenile resembles the female somewhat but is even more streaked than she is. With

their first moult the young males will acquire a pale black flecked crown.

Habitat
They reach almost to the Arctic Circle in Scandinavia and Russia. Some are resident all the year round in their breeding grounds though the vast majority spread during winter over the whole of Europe. The conifer forests are the favourite haunts, a great deal of food being taken from trees. These same conifers provide the nesting sites for their small compact nests which are usually constructed on a high horizontal branch.

Aviary
Here again we have a small finch which adapts well to colony breeding. A surplus of hens should always be present where this method is operated. The enclosure for one pair will need to be two metres long by the same height and one metre wide. Perches should be provided by growing conifers at each end, and the feeding area must be situated centrally. The ground should be densely planted with comfrey, brassicas and dandelion. A small sheltered portion at each end should cover a few bunches of heather and this roofed section should extend downwards a little at both ends to provide an ample and dry roosting area. Keeping the main perching areas well apart to enforce exercise is beneficial to a bird such as this, which tends to overeat oily fattening foods. The deterioration in general condition, which occurs as a result of too little exercise, is reflected in that fewer hens will nest and rear successfully. An aviary double the above recommended dimensions would house up to three pairs and, providing the inmates are fed wisely, breeding attempts ought to result favourably.

Food
Very often I have fed siskins during the non-breeding seasons with the left-over seed mixture from other birds, such as that from the goldfinch enclosure. Any signs of obesity have thus been avoided. When breeding and rearing are in progress I increase the mixture to include soaked teazle, small sunflower, extra millets and niger. The ideal basis for their seed mixture is screenings or a commercially sold wild seed but if these are unavailable one can mix the smaller millets, rye grass, plain canary and teazle with half amounts of linseed, maw, gold of pleasure, lettuce and, if it can be collected during the winter months, dock seed. These will

add up to a varied and nutritious standard diet. As for all finches I would advise soaking the seed for at least twenty-four hours and straining it for a short period before offering it to the birds. It is vital that one feeds in such a manner until after all the birds have completed their moult. Once having started this method of feeding, there should be no changing in mid-season. Where space permits it, I would advise the inclusion of thick hop growth at the rear of the siskins' aviary: apart from the enormous quantities of aphids this will supply, the birds enjoy roosting in this plant. When collecting wild foods, remember that in the wild siskins will eat seeds from trees like larch, pine, spruce, alder, elm and birch. The favourite foods at ground level are dandelion, chickweed, sowthistle, persicaria, meadowsweet, fat-hen and dock.

Breeding
Almost all siskin hens will build a natural nest in conifer branches. It is ideal to have such vegetation of the right height growing in their enclosure. Until these are established, however, and the top growth pruned to thicken lower growth, it may be necessary to provide and fix conifer branches in the required nesting site areas. Nest baskets should also be fixed in position amid these branches, fairly high but sheltered from heavy rainfall. Once these baskets are established, it matters little if the conifer turns brown and drops needles: the aviary need not be entered again. Branches alone will soon turn brown and become unsightly, and they are of little use for nesting in. The nest itself is a neat cosy little thing, well woven together and comprising mosses, lichens, very fine rootlets and grasses: it is thickly lined with animal hair and feathers; resulting young make an attractive sight when fledging, perching in a row. They are diminutive creatures frequently leaving the nest at fourteen days or shortly afterwards.

Aviary bred strains of siskin usually take some softfood when rearing and many will eat it all the year round. Try them on Farlene (Glaxo) moistened with milk and sprinkled with maw and a little niger; once birds are using such foods for rearing there is seldom a case of rickets or any undernourished specimens among newly fledged young. During the breeding season when pairs are feeding young, provide as much as possible of aphids, gentle chrysalids, wax-moth larvae or even cut up mealworms: the latter should be placed on top of the daily seed mixture.

Twite (*Acanthis flavirostris*)****

General Description
This is a brown bird, very similar to the linnet at first glance and although the same length, a little over thirteen centimetres, gives the impression of being longer as it is slightly slimmer. It is easily discernible at close quarters by the orange-biscuit throat and long pronounced forked tail. The male has a rosy-pink rump and a bill yellow during summer and greyish in winter; the white in the wing is not quite so clearly defined as in a male linnet. The overall appearance is of warm brown streaked with darker brown, and lighter on the belly; the female is more striated, particularly on the chest and the young even more so on throat and breast. They are also greyer in head and nape.

Habitat
Considered the northern counterpart of the linnet, this bird inhabits the wild barren tundra areas and mountainous regions of the far North. However, it does breed in lesser numbers in northern parts of the British Isles, in hilly moorland terrain among heathers.

Aviary
Provide for this bird as for the linnet. It is not quite so nervous as its close relative but requires an aviary of about the same size with a conifer growing at each end. This shows them to their best advantage. Clusters of heather arranged from ground level to roof will cater for their roosting and nesting needs. Winter shelter can be of the barest minimum with a simple roof and vertical wind and rain break; the wild seeds of moor and cultivated land provide much of the food required and with this in mind one should grow brassicas and dandelion in the aviary.

Food
Feed exactly as for the linnet. A coarse feeder due to its environment, this bird will eat almost any wild seeding weed or herb. The seed mixture if given as recommended will keep them in excellent condition for many years; rarely have I known twites other than hand-reared specimens to eat softfoods, but I have seen them take aphids and other insect life.

Breeding
In an aviary this bird will often nest in a high site, differing

considerably from the wild, where it nests at ground level in heather and rock crevice. The clusters of heather as advised for its roosting facilities will also provide ideal nesting sites; twites will use wicker baskets but all the natural nests I have seen in aviaries were strong structures not requiring the support of a basket. The materials to offer are fine twigs—heather is perfect for this—or even birch or beech twigs, grasses, moss, all kinds of animal hair and small tufts of wool, and finally feathers for the warm lining.

This bird will definitely use small soft insects when rearing but the bulk of the nestling food intake is soft pulpy ripe seeds. When it is not possible to collect such foods, soaked seeds including rape, charlock, radish and turnip can be added to the normal mixture.

WARBLERS, GOLDCREST AND FIRECREST

If I appear to generalise on the subject of warblers it is with good reason as their needs are very similar although their habitats are widely dispersed and variable. As a general guide they all tend to require slightly more fruit and vegetable matter in their diet than do most softbills. They need bathing facilities more than any other birds.

The basic food is as described in Part One for insectivorous species: if a proprietary food is used, insist on having an analysis of its contents and you will be able to fill any gaps with fresh food of your own choosing.

It can be most helpful to use a baby food as a base for a supplementary diet, to which one can add a variety of items which must be included in a bird's daily intake: multivitamins, calcium lactate, colouring matter, extra protein of a particular kind, experimental additions to the diet can all be mixed in such a food which itself is moistened with milk. A few species are slow in accepting a further such food when already eating a man-made preparation, but natural inquisitiveness usually prevails and a tentative taste will normally ensure future acceptance along with that of the additions one wishes to introduce to them. Such additives as liquid multivitamins could always be included in the drinking water, but there is a great wastage in this method when changing drinking water daily. Then, too, one must consider the small percentage of water taken during twenty-four hours and the subsequent minute dose of the vitaminised product taken in this manner.

Ripe fruit such as apple, pear, grapes, peach, avocado pear, date, banana and fig should all be included in a warbler diet, as can soaked household currants, or even fresh or defrosted black-currants, blackberries and elderberries. Livefood can consist of wax-moth larvae or wood ant larvae ('eggs'), the latter in either a fresh state or defrosted. A few cut up mealworms every other day, and locusts, shortly after hatching, will be taken by almost all warblers.

Where one uses gentles, ascertain before use that the digestive tract, the thin black line to be seen running through the insect, has vanished; this is a safeguard against passing on botulism to one's stock: five days in fresh bran will normally clear any matter from this tract. One could obviate this process by feeding the gentles on a mixture of Farlene mixed with milk, thus being sure of the contents, and knowing no harm can come to stock from eating them, but here we would have a problem to contend with in the form of wet maggots which have an ability to climb out of any container and escape. The value of these gentles, or fishing maggots, since this is their prime purpose in being bred, can be greatly increased by powdering them lightly with such products as Vionate (Squibbs), Casilan, Complan (Glaxo) or a few drops of Abidec (Parke-Davis).

Fresh greenfoods and root crops are also needed in the daily diet: grated carrot, finely chopped or minced watercress, whole dandelion (flower, leaves and root) spinach, comfrey or any brassica minced finely and mixed in the basic softfood can provide day to day variety.

Minced raw or steamed fish or crustaceans such as prawns and shrimps can be given in small quantities to the birds' advantage. Any of these may be mixed with the basic insectivorous mixture.

Just prior to the migration almost all warblers gain a great deal of body weight and under controlled conditions this persists even if they are being fed correctly. At the peak weight many such birds in aviaries go off their food when no long migratory flight is undertaken and they gradually slim back to normal. The use of plenty of fruit and vegetable matter in their diet at this time will aid this normal process. They need not be placed in the winter quarters at this time unless extremely cold weather is being experienced or forecast.

It always assists in providing variety of diet if high protein or valuable food matter is included in the actual culturing (at least during the last few days) of any livefood intended for one's stock. The little extra contained in each digestive tract is well worth the trouble. I am very much against providing livestock with insects which have been living on their own fat for a week or so prior to their use, with little or no additives. Every insect taken by a bird has certain foods in its digestive system and all these partly digested items of vegetable, cereal or animal protein matter provide, over a period of feeding in this way, a greater variety than in man-made mixtures.

Blackcap (*Sylvia atricapilla*)****
General Description
Migrant. The male with the black crown extending to just about half-way through the eyes but not below has a dark brown back and wings, greyish cheeks, breast of pale silver-grey fading to white on lower belly and ventral area. A female is slightly more dull, a little browner with a brown instead of black crown. Juveniles are rather like the female but young males achieve a brownish-black crown. They are fourteen centimetres when fully grown. It is noted for its song reminiscent of the garden warbler which it has a habit of mimicking.

Habitat
A forest and open woodland species, preferring spinneys, sparse tree area but with overgrown brambles and thickets of scrubland.

Aviary
The standard minimum as previously advised will suffice. It should be planted with hops at the rear trained on the wire which will provide extra livefood. A thick bush such as juniper or bramble will be required for nesting purposes; site this towards the rear and under a wire roof. The aviary needs a shelter attached which should be a shed type of building, not necessarily heated but closed all round with plenty of natural light entering; these details apply in a temperate zone and must be varied according to one's climatic conditions. Free entry may be allowed to shelter and outdoor flight all year round.

Food
Use the basic food mixture, with the addition of fruit at all times, livefood of a limited quantity daily, and attempt to provide a varied diet; include as an extra, milk moistened Farlene.

Breeding
A pair may be housed together at all times throughout the year but allow one pair only to an aviary. Increase livefood supplies with the nearing of the breeding season. Supply plenty of grasses, varying from thick and straw-like to fine, rootlets, all kinds of

animal hair for lining the nest. Expect this to be constructed in the thick low bush provided for this purpose. The pair will need large supplies of live insects for rearing, and in later stages will give the young softfood and fruit. Insects will form the bulk of the diet until fledging.

Chiffchaff (*Phylloscopus collybita*)†***

General Description
Migrant. This little leaf warbler looks remarkably like the willow warbler but the dark legs and the monotonous 'chiff chaff' song identify it immediately. It is, too, perhaps a little slimmer in the body with olive-green plumage, yellowish below and with the distinct yellow eye stripe. A Siberian race is far more grey but alike in other ways.

Habitat
The favoured living area is tall tree woodland spots where it will take insects from the trees, on the wing and from the ground or low vegetation. Most of the food, however, is gathered from the leaves of trees where it will be seen flitting daintily. They are not so dependent upon bushes as the willow warbler, except for nesting when they build their dome-roofed nest in low, thick, bramble-like undergrowth.

Aviary
Treat exactly as for the willow warbler: pairs can be kept together all the time but there should not be more than one pair to an aviary. Plant the aviary with a dense bramble over about a square metre of the floor area. This needs to be quite thick and well established, otherwise it is better to fabricate a near natural site for their nesting requirements.

Food
Feed on the same diet as the willow warbler but allow a little more livefood: this can be cut up mealworms, only two or three a day, or wax-moth larvae, or thawed-out or fresh ant larvae. Most livefoods can be given in great quantity but then one has the difficulty of a semi meating-off period when brought indoors for wintering; it is for this reason that I ensure that softfood is eaten daily.

Breeding
A low thicket of bramble, or hawthorn overgrown with bramble and tall grasses growing up through this in a tangled mass, will appeal to the chiffchaff as a nest site, but do leave this well alone: do not peep inquisitively when feeding. Give materials such as grasses, fine twigs, rootlets, mosses, dead leaves, hair and feathers; with the arrival of young one must remember that the parents will offer them only insects; occasionally a hand-raised specimen does offer nestlings whatever it was reared upon itself, if that food has been in daily use ever since.

Firecrest (*Regulus ignicapillus*)†
General Description
This is very like the goldcrest but has black and white eye-stripes, a crown more red than orange in the male and a bronze neck patch. The female has a far paler crown when the feathers are parted but it is visibly so even when observed closely; the length is nine centimetres.

Habitat
It prefers low bushes, ivy covered low walls, broom, gorse and vineyards. It does not seem to favour any particular tree but likes low vegetation and has no special preference for conifers as the goldcrest does.

Aviary
As for goldcrest.

Food
As for goldcrest.

Breeding
As for goldcrest.

Goldcrest (*Regulus regulus*)†*
General Description
This and the firecrest are the smallest birds common to Europe at nine centimetres long. They are dull green, the male goldcrest being just a shade greener than a female. This colour fades to a creamy-buff on the underparts; both sexes have two white wing bars. The bill is a delicate one ideally suited for taking the very small insects it lives on in the wild. The crown has no real crest

but a male has a brilliant orange line centrally from upper fore-head almost to the nape which is edged with black; in display the male will spread the black edging feathers sideways to reveal the vivid orange colour to such an extent that it almost covers the crown. There is no conspicuous raising of any crest. The female's crown is only palish-yellow.

Habitat
Woodland areas are favoured, with a preference being shown for conifers and especially for large gardens and churchyards that contain yew trees. In the winter months this bird will often enter suburban gardens where it will seek insect life in dense low foliage, bracken and ferns.

Aviary
The standard recommended minimum is ideally suited to a pair of these birds. It should have a frost-free shelter attached to it, in which the food is placed at all times. Extra feeding time during the winter promotes longevity and entices small moths and other insects into the enclosure. A yew tree at each end should be kept trimmed to well below the wire roof. This encourages the birds to enter the shelter for a higher roosting site which will show them off in a natural setting; a small boggy area near a very shallow pond, well planted with ferns should cover the majority of the aviary floor. Wild bracken, however, grows too high and prevents any sighting of the inmates most of the time.

Food
This will depend entirely upon whether the birds were taken under licence as adults, hand reared from the nestling stage or taken as fledged young. In the case of the first, a certain period of 'meating off' will be necessary: patience and leisure time are essential to successfully complete this operation. It will be neces-sary to have a finely ground insectivorous food, and finely grated cheese, with a few cut up mealworms and gentles on top. This should be placed high near a perch where it will be obvious to the freshly acquired stock. Prior to the actual taking of such birds one must have prepared other feed too: have a culture of fruit flies breeding near an electric light bulb in the intended shelter; also have a good supply of wax-moths and their larvae available. The new birds should be placed in the shed portion of their quarters

and the cut-up mealworms and gentles renewed five or six times a day; their water, placed in a very shallow dish, should contain the advised amount of a vitamin additive. The moths can be liberated, about twenty to a pair of birds each day and the larvae should be placed on the food. Wood ant larvae are very suitable for goldcrests. Do not over feed these as the general aim is to encourage the birds to take the insects from on top of the man-made food, acquiring a taste for the cheese initially and later the basic food. This 'meating off' of adult birds can take a week or two, and it is for this reason that I would advise would-be keepers of goldcrests to hand raise their stock from about eight days of age: freshly fledged young will go on to an insectivorous mixture sooner than adult birds. Where one is allowed by licence to take them, nestlings will prove far simpler to raise, since they will grow automatically to take the offered softfood; see section on hand raising.

Breeding

I do not know of anyone who has ever reared a full clutch to maturity under controlled conditions: the task to breed at all from birds taken as adults is very difficult. Young hand-raised specimens well used to the man-provided diet will more readily accept a basic livefood supply of moth and moth larvae. Remember that one should offer only items of livefood which can be continually supplied: one cannot hope to rear birds if changing half-way to another source of food; parents treated in this manner will often continue to search for the insects they are used to receiving.

The nest of the goldcrest is a work of art: normally suspended beneath a horizontal branch and the size of a well-developed orange, it has a small entrance in the upper half of the semi-domed structure. The materials needed to form the main structure are moss, spiders' webs and lichen: spiders' webs, indeed, are taken in such quantity that when a partly built frame was dissected for inspection, the webs were still tacky and along with moss formed the bulk of the material. Some goldcrests use animal hair and wool, as well as feathers, for lining whilst others use only the last: I think this depends to a great extent on local habitat.

All the small garden pests such as 'greenfly', and small spiders as well as the moths and moth larvae will become vital necessities if fortunate enough to have young bred in captivity. If one plans well in advance, the wax-moth larvae can be in almost unlimited supply when wanted most.

Barred Warbler (*Sylvia nisoria*)†***

General Description

Migrant. One of the largest of our warblers, this strikingly attractive bird is very shy in the wild. It is bulky of body and long-tailed. The main colouring of mantle and upper body is pale brownish-grey. The underparts are darker grey with heavy barring from throat to belly. There is very little difference between the sexes though the female is slightly less barred beneath. A female I kept always had grey irises, whereas the males' were all bright yellow. It may have been an isolated case. The length is fifteen centimetres.

Habitat

Thickets, scrub and open woodland with dense low undergrowth is typical residential and breeding area of this bird. It is rarely seen in the open: one may hear merely a warning cry and catch sight of it disappearing into the nearest low bush. The song is a melodious warbling very attractive to the ear, repeated in short bursts and often interspersed with a loud 'charr–charr–charr', quite a jarring call.

Aviary

The minimum standard size aviary can be used for this species but I have always given far larger quarters during the breeding season. These birds will need a warm winter flight indoors; this can adjoin their enclosure or be separate; I have allowed them free access to all weathers but made certain that they fed and roosted inside during the winter.

Unless hand-raised specimens are kept, there will be much skulking in the undergrowth which is typical behaviour of the wild bird. However, once a rapport has been established between bird and keeper, they become very trusting. With their natural habits in mind, it is well to plant fairly dense undergrowth of raspberry canes, hawthorn and bracken over half of the enclosure area, leaving the balance clear and weed free. The use of some flowering ground cover can help and add to the aviary's attractiveness. My own aviaries have often held hops covering one or more of the wire sides. Quite apart from the amount of seclusion this offers, it has the usual benefit of providing an abundance of insect life.

Food

I would always advocate a high protein diet for these birds, but they must, too, have large amounts of fruit: this can be in the form of wild or cultivated berries according to the seasons, but sweet apple should always be available, with pear being given once or twice weekly. Soaked household currants will be greedily taken when berries are unobtainable; chopped figs and dates, if diced small, can be added to their basic food, as can most brassicas, dandelion and spinach, if well minced or chopped fine. Do not forget the daily supplies of grated cheese on their softfood. Where livefood is concerned, most species of the usual insects given to birds will be accepted, young locusts, cut-up mealworms and wax-moth larvae being favourites, together with wood ant larvae when available.

Breeding

The nest is rather like a larger version of the whitethroats', made of grasses and bents and lined with hair. It will usually be built in a dense part of the hedge well hidden by undergrowth but I have had them build in a large square biscuit tin into which had been pushed bunches of heather and bracken.

With the arrival of young, the usual large quantities of insect life must be supplied. Little fruit, if any, is given to very young nestlings but all manner of soft-skinned insects will be offered, even quite large locusts are smashed to bits, wings removed and frighteningly large pieces rammed down the nestlings' throats. When we have hand raised these birds, almost from the egg, or where parent specimens have been feeding young in the nest, we have used as the basic livefood wax-moth larvae and small daily supplies of wood ant larvae; one must be careful to ensure that a continuing supply of wood ant larvae will be available: I have found the birds so addicted to it that they search continually for it if it abruptly goes missing from their everyday diet. It is good to store it in the fridge or freezer and give a small daily ration. Odd as it may seem, these birds eat more of their man-made insectivorous mixture if it contains steamed fish or fish roe, yet they still like to remove the grated cheese piece by piece before taking the food in bulk.

My first barred warblers, hand raised, were from Italy. My

father many years before had spoken of their singing and mimicking qualities and so I decided to collect them: the less said about the cost the better, but for many weeks I speedily turned all thoughts of finances from my mind. No picture I have ever seen really does these birds justice. We had three nests from one pair in one year; they were found at the end of the season, within inches of each other, low in a hawthorn; egg shells in the enclosure indicated that hatching had occurred, but we did not rear any young. This happened for two years and I was rather over-stocked at the time of the next breeding season. I discussed with old friends, both leading ornithologists, what I should do and the birds were subsequently liberated in an area of Berkshire called Maidenhead Thicket, a dense mass of bramble. Studying them gave me much pleasure and invaluable information, and, I hope they, in return, received a not too unhappy existence at the hands of man.

Cetti's Warbler (*Cettia cetti*)†
General Description
Migrant. A frequent skulker unless hand raised, this bird is rarely sighted in the wild. In aviaries it becomes quite fearless when well accustomed to the keeper, but reverts to its skulking habits with the arrival of strangers. It is fourteen centimetres long with a tail wide and rounded at the end. The overall colour is a dark rufous brown; it has light grey underparts and a reddish tail; a white stripe above the eyes is very conspicuous. The sexes are very much alike but the hen appears a shade duller; the male is whiter on the throat. The song is of outstanding qualities, the rich and extremely melodious notes being rendered from a well hidden site in the undergrowth which it prefers.

Habitat
Generally a resident of marshy or nearby marshy areas, it hides in dense vegetation and bushy thickets not too far from reed beds. The nest may be found at the base of thick reed clumps on the ground or in dense nearby undergrowth.

Aviary
Although having given these birds, wild taken and hand-raised specimens, large aviaries with marshy areas, dense vegetation and overgrown conditions they never nested in my possession. Yet

after wintering a pair and then passing them to a friend, not an experienced bird keeper, who wished to record their song, a pair nested within a fortnight of being placed in an aviary similar in size to that recommended as the minimum suitable enclosure for housing birds. Nevertheless, I would still recommend a larger enclosure if one is to appreciate the general behaviour, including the sudden outpouring of song from one point, then sudden quiet, with the song coming from an entirely different direction within a few moments. The warm shelter or indoor flight for winter use is essential. It need not adjoin the outdoor breeding enclosure, but should it do so, make certain the birds roost indoors during the winter months.

Food
As for most birds frequenting marshy areas or the water's edge, I have always included shrimp meal in their softbill mixture, as well as steamed fish, and roe when possible, to replace the many small crustaceans taken in the wild. This basic food mixture should be rich in animal protein. Fruit can be kept to small amounts but vegetation in the form of dandelion and comfrey should be finely chopped or minced and included in their food daily as it will replace the undigested vegetable matter of insects which would be taken in the wild. Grated cheese is a favourite addition to the softfood and should be given daily. A very paste-like food can be offered to hand-raised specimens in addition to the drier mixture; it can be based on Farlene mixed with milk, and a wide variety of vitamin or mineral additives can be stirred into it.

Breeding
The provision of dense vegetation should encourage nesting. Reeds are a simple matter to grow and a bushy hawthorn, surrounded by a bed of raspberry canes and reeds would seem ideal surroundings. These birds build a base of vegetation and plant stems, and the nest itself is very deep cupped and constructed from leaves, grasses and rootlets. It is lined with finer grasses, feathers, hair and vegetable down.

Should young result, then offer as wide a variety of insects as is possible. When hand raised the nestlings have readily accepted almost any insects as have the adult birds kept. With this readiness to partake of most livefoods, nestlings stand an excellent chance of being reared.

Dartford Warbler (*Sylvia undata*)†

General Description
This bird has a dark brown mantle, gradually changing to slate-grey on the head. The long fanned tail is white tipped and this is flicked constantly whenever perched. The underparts are pinkish-chestnut to purplish-brown, and the throat is flecked with white, with the ventral area white. Length is twelve and a half centimetres.

Habitat
Wild open country, heath and moorland with low bramble-covered shrubs, are favoured. Heather or gorse forms a favourite song perch from which it will dance its courtship serenade, rising almost vertically in the air, then descending delivering the mating song. The alarm or scolding note will be heard more often than a good sighting. One is lucky to see its disappearing shape as it makes for the cover of a low gorse patch.

Aviary
When serious thought is given to breeding these birds, and to honestly justify their being kept when they are so prone in the wild to decline in numbers, I would suggest a minimum aviary of three or four metres square by two metres high. The ground should be densely planted with such natural items as gorse, heather, and a variety of ferns and bracken, with an area of sandy shingle left in the centre. A non-heated but artificially lighted winter shed or indoor flight should be available to them, where their food should be placed to encourage their voluntary entry. Quite often they will roost low in dead bracken or other growth, but the opportunity to retire to warmer roosting sites indoors will not often be ignored. If each corner of the outdoor aviary also has a small roofed section to shield them from heavy downpours of rain and they are fed on a suitable diet, these are quite long-lived specimens.

Food
As a resident warbler of England they must be fairly coarse eaters, at least during the colder months. They are simple to feed and will accept almost any small live insect, in addition to the basic insectivorous mixture. Small quantities of soft fruit and minced vegetable can be given with the grated cheese which they will take in preference to most other items offered. Wax-moth and wood

ant larvae are accepted and will be fed to the young. One nest taken in Europe together with their almost fledged nestlings reared the young almost entirely on these insects and cut up mealworms in a small indoor flight. Both adult and young took readily to the softfood and cheese provided. I have used small locusts (newly hatched) and a wide variety of insects, and rarely has anything ever been ignored: even minute striped snails have been eaten. Farlene or similar baby foods, mixed with milk, are also well accepted.

Breeding
My own birds have all been the subject of feeding experiments: in England this species has been almost lost on a few occasions and consideration of the food taken in winter time in the wild has always held a strong fascination for me, continually pondering the question of whether one can assist in any way by contributing towards their diet during the harder weather when so many losses occur. In the wild the nest is constructed of small particles, leaves, grass, moss, vegetable down, animal wool and hair. Very often the outer walls are decorated with spiders' webs and cocoons. The lining is of fine hair and down. This nest is usually placed very near the ground in overgrown heather, gorse or bramble but sometimes up to a metre high in the same type of vegetation.

Garden Warbler (*Sylvia borin*)†****
General Description
Migrant. Fourteen centimetres in length, this is a rather undistinctive bird in appearance yet a remarkably fine songster. It is the dullest of our warblers, greyish-brown with darker brown wings, paler throat, breast and underparts fading to white at vent, with a dark tail and grey-brown legs. The hen is slightly duller and browner. The song is a mellow repertoire of longer duration than most.

Habitat
Rarely if ever seen in gardens except perhaps during migration, it prefers dense bushy vegetation beneath trees; wooded areas; heaths and well-brambled moorland.

Aviary

A two-metre long aviary, by the same height and half this measurement in width, will comfortably house a pair of garden warblers. They should have a frost-free enclosure attached and they can be allowed to come and go from the enclosure to the outdoor aviary as they choose, all through the winter months; the placing of their food and water supplies in the indoor enclosure will almost certainly guarantee that they make full use of it. The aviary should include a densely planted area of hawthorn and raspberry cane, into which long grasses are allowed to intermingle. This should cover at least a third of the enclosure's area, and the addition of hops growing at the rear will give extra food supplies natural to their requirements.

Food

At times other than the breeding season, a good insectivorous food supply with a generous amount of fruit—fig, date, banana, apple, pear, grape, all soft fruits, wild or cultured and wild berries such as elderberries—with a minimum of live insects will keep these birds in excellent condition. Give also a paste-like food as recommended and include plenty of vegetable matter in their diet. The occasional mealworm cut-up on their food mixture will assist in advancing breeding condition. If a plentiful supply of livefood is available, mealworms need not be increased in quantity but variety can be provided in the form of soft-skinned items such as wax-moth larvae.

Breeding

I would venture to state that the garden warbler is one of the easiest birds of its type to keep in good condition and to breed from. Provide as natural a nest site as possible and offer moss, grasses, fine to coarse, rootlets and all animal hairs. Apart from the daily feeding and the occasional offering of insects when in the aviary's vicinity, leave these birds well alone.

Do not be surprised if more than one nest appears, as the male often makes several: whether these are to secure his mate's approval or merely a form of breeding display I do not know. With the arrival of young birds the diet must include a wide variety of insect life; very little fruit will be taken during rearing and indeed the intake of all softfood except the pastes previously mentioned fall to a minimum. As the young leave the nest they will automatically take the paste and other softfoods offered as well as much fruit. With the arrival of the migration time it is very surprising how much weight can be put on although the fruit intake does seem to grow beyond belief.

Grasshopper Warbler (*Locustella naevia*)†
General Description
Migrant. This bird is thirteen centimetres long and of an olive-brown and sombre appearance. It has a well rounded tail and wings of darker brown; it is streaked darkly on the mantle; the underparts are lightish brown. It is the song, or grasshopper-like 'reeling', that reveals its presence more than the rather rare sighting.

Habitat
Very secretive movements characterise this bird in open woodland, scrub, grassland with overgrown vegetation, low grassy bushes and even heath and moorland.

Aviary
Provide an enclosure of double the minimum recommended aviary size. Plant two sides densely with thickly growing vegetation and low bushy-type hawthorns through which grasses can grow; to the rear plant hops for seclusion as well as a source of food. Leave a path inbetween the two beds of vegetation and cover this with gravel as a barrier to weed growth. My own aviary which housed these birds was planted with junipers, spreading horizontally, a buddleia, honeysuckle, and ground covered with Rose of Sharon (*Hypericum calycinum*). Winter quarters are essential; extra feeding hours are vital and a little gentle warmth keeps these birds in good overall condition. Such quarters can easily adjoin the summer aviary but if the birds are allowed out during the day, one should ensure that they roost indoors at night during the colder months when frosts are possible.

Food
Fruit can be kept to a minimum but minced vegetable matter must be added to the basic diet which can be a high protein softbill food. Grated cheese should be given liberally and a few cut-up mealworms placed on top of their softfood daily. These birds will eat very young striped snails, smaller than an apple pip; they manage to get the flesh and leave the shells. Ants larvae, the large race preferably, from pine woods or beech plantations are

eagerly taken if provided on the aviary floor. The inclusion of plenty of insects in their diet is necessary and culturing one's own supplies makes their upkeep more economical. Elderberries and soft fruits will be taken more in the autumn than at other times as is usual with migrating warblers.

Breeding
An exceedingly rich animal protein content in the diet is vital for this bird to achieve breeding condition which is often illustrated by the quivering wings and tail of the male as he proffers a leaf or other small gift to his mate.

If the aviary is well planted so that these birds can travel, rodent-like, in the undergrowth, they will feel at home. Nesting materials to offer are dead leaves, grasses, a little moss, rootlets, bents, and a variety of animal hair, fine to coarse. To rear successfully much livefood is required by the parents. The young are fed solely on insects and their larvae; many of the insects can be cultured for this purpose in adequate quantities. When suddenly increasing the quantity of mealworms with the arrival of newly hatched nestlings, do always ensure they are cut-up upon the daily food mixture and not thrown alive and whole to the birds.

Icterine Warbler (*Hippolais icterina*)†
General Description
Migrant. Very like a large wood warbler, the icterine warbler is stockily built. It has yellow underparts and olive-green on mantle and wings although these and the tail are a shade browner; the legs are bluish-grey, the inside of the bill is red and most noticeable when taking food from the hand. It has a habit of raising the crown feathers when inquisitive. It is a very lively bird flitting among tree foliage in its search for insects. The song is rather a discordant jumble of notes, sometimes liquid sounding and sweet to the ear and at other times quite harsh. The length is thirteen and a half centimetres.

Habitat
Never very far from human habitation, this bird is found along river banks among the tall trees, on the edge of woodland, in orchards, tall hedge-rows and even gardens where fruit trees and bushes abound.

Aviary
An enclosure of three to four metres long by one or two wide and two metres high would suit this energetic warbler. Plant it with hops along one long side and grow a thick hawthorn hedge at one end: into this let plenty of raspberry canes grow. Provide a roofed portion over the top of the hedge, just large enough to shield a nest from the main force rainfall but allowing adequate water to reach the growing vegetation and the birds will be encouraged to use the hedge for nesting. I have always found this bird to like a little gentle heat during winter months in addition to extra feeding time, so the shed-shelter or indoor flight, perhaps attached to the outdoor aviary, should be equipped with some type of heating apparatus.

Food
A high protein insectivorous mixture, with plenty of both fruit and vegetable in the diet should be supplied. These birds seemed so very fond of eating butterfly eggs that I mixed fish roe in their food, this being the nearest in likeness and an extremely high protein content food. Farlene will also be taken as will almost any small insect; wax-moth larvae, which quite possibly resemble a natural food of theirs, is a firm favourite at all times. When mealworms are fed, ensure they are cut up and never given alive. Elderberry and a number of other wild and garden grown soft fruit are eaten and in fact I have frozen supplies during the summer and autumn to be given later when they were out of season.

Breeding
Normally nesting in the fork of bush or tree, the recommended site described under the aviary heading should prove suitable. It is an attractive nest composed of grasses and rootlets all tightly interwoven with a final lining of fine grass and animal hair. Rearing of any young will depend entirely upon the ability of the bird keeper to provide ample small insect life.

Orphean Warbler (*Sylvia hortensis*)
General Description
Migrant. A rather large bird, fuller in the body than the blackcap, the male has the jet black crown but the black extends down to well below the eye, giving it black cheeks. The throat is a conspicuous white, as are the outer tail feathers. The mantle is grey-

151

ish. Its length is fifteen centimetres. It has a rather repetitive song. The female of this species is similar in appearance to the male but without the density of black about the head and face, being more dull in this area, the breast too is slightly paler on the whole.

Habitat

Open woodland, orchard, park, scrub, olive groves and even gardens are visited by this bird. It spends much of its time flitting through the trees taking insects from foliage and while on the wing.

Aviary

This member of the warbler family requires a maximum of flying space. Aim for a length of four metres with a minimum of one metre width and two metres height. In the wild this bird will nest up to well over this height in tree or thick bush. Cultivate a thick hawthorn bush in the rear of the enclosure with a dense mass of raspberry canes growing up through it. I have kept these birds only for experimental feeding purposes, never with the intention of trying to breed from them; however, having seen them nesting in the wild, I would think this type of site should be acceptable. Separate warm winter quarters are necessary.

Food

I have kept freshly taken adult specimens and also hand raised this species and they seem extremely simple to cater for. Offer the usual insectivorous mixture and grated cheese, with plenty of fruit and vegetable matter, the latter being minced in the softfood. This is another bird which readily takes Farlene mixed with milk. The fruit can consist of ripe apple, pear or almost any soft fruit will be taken. With late summer, elderberries and blackberries will be appreciated. Cut up mealworms in limited quantities can be given along with most small soft insects: flies, moths and larvae will be accepted but mine were never very keen on locusts.

Breeding

A tall thickly growing hedge in the aviary will provide a similar nest site to that chosen in the wild and when looking for these birds I have found nests in branches between two and three metres from the ground. These nests are made from grasses, weed stems, fine twigs and rootlets, decorated externally with spiders' webs and cocoons and lined with hair.

When watching a pair feed their young in the wild I saw a vast number of unidentifiable small caterpillars being given. When keeping them I have tried them with both wax-moth and wood ant larvae: these were taken in very large quantities and I imagine they would be able to rear young on these as other warblers in my possession have done.

Reed Warbler (*Acrocephalus scirpaceus*)†****

General Description
Migrant. This bird has a rather erect stance with a slightly raised crown. It has a rufous brown back, a tail of darkish brown and a crown of brown with distinguishable rufous wash; the rump too bears this same shade; throat, breast and belly to vent are much paler, a soft beige-biscuit colour. It is, therefore, not by any means a colourful species but the male is one of the noisiest of birds during the courtship with a continuous and rather monotonous song. Sometimes it barely ceases throughout the day and is broken occasionally only by a few 'chuckling' notes. The song is often the only means by which the sexes can be told apart. It is twelve and a half centimetres in length.

Habitat
It is rarely found very far from reed beds or smaller ditches with sufficient reed growth to provide a nesting site. At times it is forced to congregate in small areas due to a shortage of nest sites.

Aviary
On the only occasions that I have known these birds to nest and rear successfully, their aviary included a pond and small reed bed: the sinking of plastic buckets, an old type square earthenware sink or even garden fish pond incorporated in the enclosure will give plenty of reed growth to cover their needs. The aviary itself can be as small as the minimum standard breeding unit. The inclusion of willow, planted at each end, gives a near natural setting and ensures a maximum of flight. One of the vantage-points provided by this vegetation will become a favourite singing site where the male will carry out his courtship song, fluffing out his feathers and fanning his tail. During the winter months these birds will require a shed-type shelter to which they can retire when too cold outside. Extra feeding time with the provision of artificial light is a more vital factor for good general health than extra warmth. Instead of this type of shelter one can remove them

to indoor flights. They may normally be housed together all the year round but to house two pairs of these birds an aviary would have to be at least seven metres long with a pond in the centre and a feeding area at each side. There would be an osier bed at each end of the enclosure. A little outdoor roofed shelter is needed to cover a few of the rear willow branches.

Food
A good quality insectivorous mixture must form the basis of the diet and to this can be added a few cut up mealworms, and grated cheese (Cheddar-type consistency). Free access to the pond will ensure that a number of natural insect foods are taken.

Breeding
The nest of this bird is a wonderful piece of engineering: it is slung between growing reeds often only just above the water surface: it is cup shaped and made from grasses, moss, reed flowers, and then lined with feathers, hair and wool or vegetable down. Quite frequently the hen will slide off the nest and the male will take her place without any indication other than the song going silent. When rearing the parents will need much livefood.

Great Reed Warbler (*Acrocephalus arundinaceus*)**
General Description
Migrant. Resembling a giant reed warbler, this bird measures nineteen centimetres. It has a conspicuous eye stripe, a far stronger bill and although the song is similar it is far louder, and seems almost as loud as that of the thrush when one is standing near the aviary. As the song includes many coarse grating and croaking notes, one can be thankful that it does not continue to the same extent as that of the smaller birds. Nevertheless it is a fascinating bird to keep, becoming delightfully tame in a very short while with such confidence that it will follow one about to obtain the luxury of a mealworm from the hand. The sexing of these birds can be difficult, but the noisy specimen is invariably the male.

Habitat
This bird frequents freshwater margins, predominantly reed-bed areas throughout the European mainland.

Aviary
During the out of breeding season months I have housed three
pairs together with only the slightest of bickering. As with its close
relative it requires extra feeding time and a draughtproof indoor
flight or shelter. The aviary should be similar in all respects to that of
the smaller bird.

Food
I have seen adult specimens of this bird take a ten-centimetre
locust and hammer it until limp and fit to swallow. They will
readily kill and dismember mealworm beetles after their egg laying usefulness is finished and from this one can appreciate that
they have a taste for livefood of many kinds. A good insectivorous
mixture is taken freely, along with grated cheese. Many angling
friends used to pass over their catches to me so that we could
steam and mince the fish and include this in our softbill foods.

Breeding
I can really add little to that already advised for the more common reed warbler. This larger member of the warbler family can
be treated in an identical manner at all times.

Sardinian Warbler (*Sylvia melanocephala*)†
General Description
Migrant. The actions are very like the lesser whitethroat, and the
underparts resemble this bird but here the likeness ends. It has a
conspicuous eye and eye-ring of red; the back, wings and tail are
grey; the dark, almost black, tail is graduated at the sides with
white outer feathers; the head of the male is black, this extending
below the eye to the cheeks. The female is less dark with no black
cap and she too closely resembles the female lesser whitethroat.
The male has a dancing display flight. The song, otherwise very
whitethroat-like, is carried on over longer periods and is perhaps
a little more liquid in its rendering.

Habitat
A woodland bird, it frequently skulks in densely growing vegetation, bramble or bush, but tends towards more open park-type
country. It is often seen for a few moments in country lanes in
Mediterranean countries before diving for cover with its scolding,
rather wren-like chattering.

Aviary

If half of the aviary is densely covered with such vegetation as raspberry canes, honeysuckle, bracken, or dense evergreen shrubs, the standard minimum type will suffice; leave the rest of the floor area bare or with low growing heathers, rockery plants and such like. Winter quarters will be necessary, frost-proof and possibly warmed, but remember that more important is the extra feeding time made available by the use of artificial lighting. This can be operated simply by using a timeswitch so that the birds' light comes on at 7 am until daylight then again later in the day until 8 or 9 pm. Where the winter housing does not adjoin the aviary, the aviary will need to have a small roofed portion providing shelter from heavy rainfall.

Food

A good softbill mixture should be the base to which one adds grated cheese, fruit of all kinds, and some vegetable matter. I have witnessed these birds taking small buds from nettles and even tearing a leaf of chickweed to pieces in their feeding habits. Fruit is essential, so always keep ripe apple available; wild items such as elderberry, blackberries, etc. will be readily accepted. In fact when fresh elderberries are made available very little else is taken.

Breeding

These birds normally nest very low, almost at ground level, in the wild but where the natural vegetation of the area does not allow this, I have seen nests as high as two metres and more. They prefer a dense mass of growth; honeysuckle was selected by my birds on two occasions, despite a wide variety of other vegetation being present. Materials needed are bents, coarse and fine grasses, rootlets, plant down, and hair; externally the nest looks untidy but the inner cup is beautifully finished; the outsides are often decorated with spiders' webs, some even being used on the internal structure.

   I cannot over-emphasise the value of the larvae of both wood ant and wax-moth at the time of newly hatched young; one is obtainable in the wild in great numbers and the other very easily cultured for this specific purpose. Even newly hatched locusts will be taken but whatever is offered as the basic livefood should be persevered with throughout the rearing: continuity of rearing foods is very important.

Sedge Warbler (*Acrocephalus schoenobaenus*)†***

General Description

Migrant. The song alone makes this bird a welcome addition to many a collection. A healthy contented male with a mate somewhere in the background will sing almost from dawn to dusk from his choice of perch. Although it can be described as brown, this does not do justice to the feather pattern: it is of a warm brown, darkly streaked on crown and back; it has a broad whitish eye stripe; the rump is rufous; the tail is dark brown; the breast and underparts are a creamy hue, darkening on the flanks; it is grey legged. It measures about thirteen centimetres.

Habitat

Lakes, ponds, rivers and streams attract this bird, the vegetation on the bank or nearby low hedgerow providing its nesting site. It is seldom visible for more than a moment or two as it flies from one song position to another and disappears in the reeds. Its flight is low and of rather a jerky nature.

Aviary

Use the standard minimum-sized aviary. Include a pond to grow reeds and provide a clear area of water. If possible obtain two or three large clumps of sedge and plant this around the pond in such a manner that it keeps moist: the over-flow from rainfall will suffice to keep this grass growing and it will usually form into at least one nest site; a couple of teazle plants with long grasses growing between them will give some attractive song perches and nest sites, adding eye-catching vegetation to the enclosure with its blooms. A warm shed-like shelter or indoor flight is necessary, together with a few hours of artificial lighting during the darker days of winter enabling later feeding. The maximum hours of darkness I allow my stock, even in an unheated indoor flight is ten, but for some this may be too long, as with a nursery-type light in use I have witnessed small insectivorous species eating at midnight.

Food

For most of the aquatic warblers I often include a little minced small crustacean foods such as prawns and shrimps in their diets to replace some of the small crustaceans that they obviously take in the wild. The basic diet is still an insectivorous food of high protein value. To this is added the usual grated cheese. I give these birds very little fruit, but increase the vegetable matter such as minced dandelion, comfrey, carrot and brassica. Sedge warblers will take almost any small insects, from ants' larvae to locusts. This is another bird that I partially feed on Farlene. For many of the smaller warblers I include a few drops of Abidec or similar multivitamin liquids.

Breeding
One can offer nesting sites as mentioned under the heading of aviary. Feed the stock well and hope that they will nest and rear. Offer materials such as weed stalks, moss, grasses, hair, vegetable-down (willow) and feathers. Any young will require much livefood so plan well beforehand, perhaps by culturing various insect food items. I know a bird keeper who grows a variety of vegetables for his own use in his aviaries, firmly convinced that since they encourage aphids the birds will keep his plants insect free and benefit at the same time.

Subalpine Warbler (*Sylvia cantillans*)
General Description
Migrant. Resembling rather a paler version of the Dartford warbler, the male bird has a white moustachial stripe. His shorter tail has white outer feathers and his overall length is twelve centimetres. The upper parts and mantle are pale grey; wings and tail are considerably darker and the breast is rufous pink. The female is far more dull in appearance, predominantly greys and light browns.

Habitat
Thick vegetation and scrub form the most favoured habitat, the choice being very similar to that of the whitethroat. Its movements too are very whitethroat-like, as is the dancing song-flight display.

Aviary
The minimum standard enclosure is large enough for a pair of these birds. Plant life should be as for whitethroats or Sardinian warblers. Winter housing needs to be warmed and frost-free, and extra feeding hours are vitally important.

Food
A rich protein food should have grated cheese, fruit and vegetable such as dandelion grated finely and added. The whole should be

rather dry, not too moist. These birds will, however, accept a supplement dish, consisting of Farlene baby food moistened with milk to a wet paste.

Breeding
This bird will often nest in creepers as well as low dense shrub-like vegetation. Materials to provide are coarse and fine grasses, animal hair and plant down. The male will frequently be seen displaying to the hen whilst holding plant down in his bill.

Any young will need much small livefood, as with the Sardinian warbler: they readily accept almost any soft-skinned insect for rearing purposes, certainly showing a preference for moth larvae, wood ant larvae and young newly hatched locusts.

Willow Warbler (*Phylloscopus trochilus*)†****
General Description
Migrant. This bird is greenish above and more yellow beneath; the legs are light brown to flesh coloured. The length is eleven centimetres. It can easily be confused with a number of other warblers, the most common being the chiffchaff, though the legs of the latter bird are always dark. The eye stripe in both birds is yellowish; alike also are the call and alarm notes but the song is totally dissimilar. Young willow warblers are very yellow and in the wild can be easily mistaken for wood warblers.

Habitat
Scattered trees, woodland dells, quiet secluded gardens with trees, bushes and fruit canes all provide our subject with the small insects which form its diet. I would hazard a guess that of the warbler family it is our most common summer visitor.

Aviary
Use the standard minimum-sized enclosure and house the pair on their own but together all the year round. Willow warblers will need to be either wintered indoors in a flight or have a shelter attached to their aviary: they will frequently venture out during colder months, but with their food placed in the shelter and extra feeding time given, they will rarely attempt roosting outside. If the shed is illuminated they will enter with the dusk and remain in its draughtproof safety overnight. Give thick bramble-like bushes.

Food

An insectivorous mixture, grated cheese, ripe apple, pear, peach, fig, or avocado pear should be offered; some fruit should always be present. A little Farlene may be given daily mixed with milk to which can be added vegetable matter. Larvae of the wax-moth so easily cultured and given in addition to the above foods will keep these birds healthy for a number of years: mine rarely saw a mealworm, and seemed not to suffer from its exclusion from their diet.

Breeding

The aviary in which I bred these birds was densely overgrown. The bulk of the aphids they took whilst rearing came from a hop plant that covered the rear of their enclosure but since it contained so many plants and flowers there were probably many types of insects I was unaware of. Provide grasses, dead leaves, mosses, fine rootlets and twigs with hair and feathers for lining; my own birds even used skin from honeysuckle and what appeared to be dried leaves from garden iris. On the occasion when these birds reared successfully in my aviaries I was able to provide wood ant larvae together with wax-moth larvae; these with the vast amount of aphids present gave the parents most of the insect life needed.

Wood Warbler (*Phylloscopus sibilatrix*)***

General Description

Migrant. This bird has a more distinct yellow eyestripe than either the willow warbler or chiffchaff, and is also larger, measuring nearly thirteen centimetres. In body bulk, too, one can notice the difference. It can sometimes be confused with a young willow warbler due to the similar amount of yellow exhibited: the legs are yellow and the breast, also of this colour, is very noticeable; the mantle is yellow-brown with an olive-green wash to it. Underparts are white. The wings are longish making the tail appear shorter than it is.

Habitat

Beech woods and open forest areas are the favourite haunts, and although in some parts of Europe quite common, it is often not seen and one is only aware of the bird's presence by the song or catching sight of the frequent aerial excursions after insects. One might see the attractive mating display, where the male will behave like a large dragon-fly, vibrating the wings in a blur of speed ending in a spiral descent in his wooing of the female. These birds nest in woodlands amid overgrown brambles and the dead branches from the overhead trees, in thick dead bracken newly surrounded by the current year's growth. Sometimes they make use of a depression in the ground. The nest iself is made of dead bracken fronds, leaves, grass and bents and lined with hair.

Aviary

A little above average height should be the aim for an enclosure to house these birds. Without this one cannot really appreciate the full beauty of their movements during the breeding season. The absence of the extra height may also limit the display which is needed to trigger-off the hen's response. Just over two metres in height or an apex-type roof of this maximum should suffice. A length of two metres and a width of certainly no less than one metre would be required, the width being increased to two metres if possible.

Plant the aviary thickly at one end, or the rear, with both brambles and bracken; if brambles are considered too unpleasant for one's own entry into the enclosure, substitute raspberry canes as thickly as can be managed; these will hold their own with the bracken and provide near ideal conditions. When planting the aviary in this manner, leave half of the floor area peat and shingle covered with heathers to restrict weed growth. A frost-proof winter enclosure will be needed, and a little gentle warmth may be required if the birds seem to feel the cold. Extra feeding time provided by artificial light is a necessity for general good health and longevity.

Food

A good quality softbill food containing a high percentage of animal protein should form the basic diet. One should add plenty of grated cheese, sweet apple or pear and finely minced greenfood; mine received daily rations of both wax-moth larvae and cut up mealworms on their food. The former were given alive to them. During the autumn months there is an abundance of wild berries to be taken; such fruit as elderberries, raspberries, blackberries and even the soft fruit part of rowan, can be given; I have seen these birds eat the flesh of rowan that has been lying beneath the trees after finches and the like had removed the pips and discarded the soft flesh.

Breeding

As mentioned in the section on habitat a natural site would be dense bracken and undergrowth; almost any similar type of site will be accepted by these birds once in peak breeding condition. Much of their nesting material will be collected from the surrounding site: dog hair or other suitable lining material will have to be added.

Since much of their food is caught on the wing when at liberty, I used to liberate a daily supply of wax-moths into their enclosure. Remember that the fly resulting from the fishing maggot is little else than roughage unless it has been specially fed. If feeding this insect in any bulk at all firstly ensure that they have access to honey-water to which has been added a vitamin supplement. When rearing is in progress they will take small locusts, grasshoppers, moth larvae, cut up mealworms, maggots treated with Vionate or similar additive, earwigs, and wasp or bee pupae. The young we hatched were reared for the first week upon wax-moth larvae and wood ant larvae, and as the adult pair had been reared by hand on a Farlene-based food mixed with milk, they did at this time offer their young a certain amount of this valuable food.

Lesser Whitethroat (*Sylvia curruca*)***

General Description

Migrant. This bird has light, silvery-grey upper parts, darker ear coverts and cheeks, snow-white throat but pale pearl-grey on chest and belly fading to white at vent. The outer tail feathers are white. The length is thirteen and a half centimetres.

Habitat

Open woodland with plenty of dense undergrowth, brambles, and nettles are particularly attractive to this bird, along with orchard areas which have been neglected over the years. Nests are about a metre from the ground in dense bush or bramble.

Aviary

These birds can be housed together all the year: the standard recommended minimum is ideal for one pair of these birds. Ensure that a shelter is attached or available for winter use; a little gentle warmth will be required at that time as well as additional feeding time. The aviary should be planted thickly at one end with a densely growing hawthorn; beneath this and growing in and around it plant plenty of raspberry canes; clusters of dead bracken can be attached in the corners at varying heights. There should be a small roofed section at each end. Supply a small shallow pond as they are fond of bathing often. Keep the ground growth low, apart from in the rear nesting section.

Food
As for the willow warbler, but include more fruit in diet.

Breeding
Materials such as fine twigs, grasses, rootlets, dead leaves, spiders' webs, vegetable down, animal hair and sometimes small pieces of fluff rather like tiny pieces of cotton wool should all be offered.

When the eggs hatch the young are small and therefore their requirements are correspondingly so. It is no use at this time offering maggots; later at the eight-day stage they will be taken; now they need aphids, wood ant larvae, moth larvae and a supply of mealworms, increased daily, to cope with the urgent need of the nestlings. Large transparent plastic sacks can be very useful at this time: whereas in the old days we used an upturned umbrella to collect insects from tree branches, one can now put small branches of beech or birch almost fully into these transparent sacks and shake the branch well, collecting over a short period a horde of minute insects to release in the breeding pen or freeze for later use.

Whitethroat (*Sylvia communis*)****

General Description
Migrant. This bird has a rufous-brown back and wings; the head is greyish-brown; the underparts are light buff and delicately tinged with pink; the throat is very white as with the lesser whitethroat; the tail's outer feathers are white. The length of this bird is fourteen centimetres. The sexes are very similar; if anything the female is browner on the head and a little more dull in the body, with no pink tinge.

Habitat
Dense nettles, brambles and other undergrowth attract the whitethroat. It is not so skulking of habit as the lesser race. The nest is usually placed low in thick hedge, bramble or plant.

Aviary
As for the lesser whitethroat.

Food
As for the willow warbler but include more fruit in diet.

Breeding
As for the lesser whitethroat.

FLYCATCHERS, TITS, BEARDED REEDLING, WREN

Of the other small insectivorous species grouped here the birds in the first family are altogether more delicate, and difficult to maintain in the best of condition over many years. Very serious consideration must be given as to whether one can devote the time and energy which will be required to look after these birds properly. The spotted flycatcher is really no more troublesome to care for than most insectivorous species, however the other races mentioned are very much more difficult to keep.

Whereas livefood is almost vital for all these birds in rearing young when in the wild, one can hand raise excellent specimens without it, replacing with other easily procurable animal protein the small insects given by parent birds in the wild. Some hand-reared birds, if kept on the same (or similar) diet as that on which they were raised, will in turn offer such food to their own offspring, but unfortunately this is not a frequent occurrence. We tend in general to offer a softfood, and then do everything possible to keep the birds away from it by providing much livefood elsewhere in their aviary.

It is far better to have one food dish only and into this should go the cut-up mealworms, wood ant pupae and wax-moth larvae all mixed well into the basic food. The provision of growing hops or other vegetation in the outdoor breeding enclosure will already offer a wide alternative variety of insect life. A wide deep dish which requires a covering of food so shallow that there is little need for the birds to throw it over the sides will be found very much better than deep food vessels, in which the bottom layers of food will remain untouched.

We must offer a rich diet to flycatchers, equivalent to that of their wild insect food intake: we should pause and dwell for a moment on just how wide the variety of insect life is and what the undigested matter in them is likely to be: pollen, liquids, unlaid eggs or even smaller insects. Although we may not be able to equal this variety we can ensure quite simply that the basic soft-food is fresh, nutritious and wholesome and, a most important point, a palatable mixture. They will need a small amount of fruit and fresh vegetable matter but for these birds it is more important to include steamed fish, fish roe, ox heart and liver, shrimps and prawns, all minced. If very small fish such as minnows are available they can be killed and passed through a mincer before being stirred into the basic mixture. A man-made softfood can be excellent as a basic food, but fresh items cannot be stored for long and it is in the provision of these that the main care is needed for these birds. The softfood is a basic requirement and although it should be adequate for a bird to live on temporarily, it was never intended as the sole source of each and every body need.

It is not essential for every bird keeper to also be a budding nutrition chemist or even to study this sphere in any depth. As long as he knows which foods supply suitable protein, vitamins, mineral salts, fuel foods for slow and quick body absorption and roughage, he should be able to supply all birds' needs. Fresh water is one of the most vital in addition to the many liquids available in the solids as moisture content. The recommended items are not intended to be fed in large quantities: small amounts over a long period are far more beneficial. The only item that I always use regularly is grated Cheddar cheese: if one or two other items are missed from the diet for a day it then matters little.

A healthy bird is one that clears the food dish daily, taking the various foods as they come and not forever searching for an item that is in short supply or not present: the extra livefood taken from the wild by a bird such as this will not deter him from taking the basic diet.

The other birds in this group *need* not be fed in quite so specialised a manner, although personally I like to standardise when I can and treat most of my small insectivorous birds in this way: the larger have a slightly more coarse diet.

Red-Breasted Flycatcher (*Ficedula parva*)
General Description
Migrant. A mere eleven and a half centimetres long, rather like a slim robin, this bird has an ever flicking tail which exhibits to

advantage the white patches beneath which are just visible from the side view. It is mainly brown above and white below: the male only, has the red breast, his mate being more of a pinkish-biscuit shade but pale in this area. The song is a chattering, wren-like warbling.

Habitat
Woodlands, broad-leaved forestation, parkland are its haunts. It is rarely seen except when it leaves the cover of foliage to take insects on the wing; then the white under-tail patches are conspicuous.

Aviary
I would never consider an enclosure smaller than a two-metre cubed structure suitable for this species. My own birds were hand raised and consequently tame but even so nervousness showed itself when strangers came to view these birds. Apart from this, the beauty of their flight could not be seen or the necessary exercise taken in a smaller aviary. Plant with beech along two sides and keep this stunted by cutting the tap-root for the first few years. Winter quarters of a warm nature should either be attached or at their disposal for the cold months, but I have allowed them free use of outdoor aviaries, making certain that they roosted indoors at night; these birds often retire to the seclusion of an attached shed with the first signs of strangers approaching, even in the summer.

Food
With some flycatchers including this one I like to add steamed ox heart and liver to a good basic softfood: still provide the grated cheese, miss out the fruit except when fresh elderberries are available, add some finely minced or chopped vegetables, and on top of the food put four chopped-up mealworms per bird per day. Wax-moth larvae should be given in small quantities but it is essential that one does not over-do the livefood intake to the point where the birds do not take the insectivorous mixture. I have seen some inexperienced bird keepers hatch out half a gallon of maggots into flies and proudly exclaim how their flycatchers are living on them; it has often been too late to rectify the damage done. Although they are not normally fish-eaters, I have included steamed fish roe in their food with excellent results; this roe of course resembles the eggs of a number of insects and as such

looks like a natural food. Very often it is the sudden increase in livefood availability that upsets rearing birds: this sudden change of diet is not necessary with hatching of nestlings. For the first day of their lives they require little insect life. Having reared from the egg by hand, I am well aware that the first few hours are essentially a drying-off period where warmth is the vital ingredient to success; the food intake at this time is of the barest minimum.

Breeding

These birds usually nest in the hole of a tree, or a brick wall but their nests have been found against the bole of a tree upon small twigs or branches holding the structure in position. Offer a variety of nest boxes, facing in differing directions. They can be of two distinct types either half open fronted or having just an entrance hole: if using the latter make sure that the hole is a very large one; strangely these birds seem to avoid the smaller-type entrances. The nesting materials are quite varied: moss, lichen, fine twigs, dead leaves, plant down, animal hair and spiders' webs will be used during the initial building.

The larvae of the wood ant, wax-moth, or any other small moth acceptable to them, day-old locusts, wasp and bee grubs, should be offered. Supply as wide a variety as possible and see which are used most for feeding their offspring. Whereas the pied variety or the collared flycatcher can often be seen taking small beetles, the red-breasted variety seldom if ever seems to eat them: they certainly have a more delicate-looking bill and like the spotted flycatcher spend much time picking-off flying insects, flying from a favourite perch and returning with their prey. Unless one manages to obtain hand-raised specimens, I doubt if these birds will take to the baby food paste, previously recommended as a nutritious supplement to their diet: those which have been raised by hand usually retain a taste for such things as were introduced during their rearing.

Spotted Flycatcher (*Muscicapa striata*)***

General Description

Migrant. It has a grey-brown mantle, wings and tail darkly striated; the breast is paler but dark streaks cover the upper chest fading to white underparts; the bill is greyish-brown and legs black. The sexes are alike except for a slight difference of the throat marking; a male has a larger white area here.

Habitat
Sparse woodland areas, orchards, parks, gardens, a few trees in a group, or a country lane edged by them will attract a pair for their short breeding season. They will be seen to fly out from the foliage, catch some flying insect and return to their selected perch: they spend hours in this method of feeding, rarely feeding at ground level

Aviary
The minimum recommended enclosure will house a pair of these birds. There is no great need for a lot of vegetation, except perhaps for that which encourages insect life. I have known them to nest in dense-growing hops covering the side of their aviary, but equally they are capable of choosing a shelf or open-fronted nest box as a site. Their winter quarters must be frost free and can either be attached to the outdoor breeding pen or a separate building to which they must be moved: the former is always to be preferred. A little gentle warmth may be necessary if they show signs of feeling the cold. If the shelter for winter use is not attached, during inclement weather some form of roofing will be a necessity.

Food
A good insectivorous mixture must form the base with various additions such as grated cheese, a little finely minced or grated vegetables, a few cut-up mealworms daily and even freshly killed beetles. Where flies are added to the diet, keep the numbers down or make sure that a dish or saucer of honey-water is available for flies to drink from, otherwise they are mere roughage, with little in the way of any nutritional content.

Breeding
Usually the nest is to be found at a height of two or three metres, so a high nesting site in the aviary will normally be preferred. The materials required will be moss, grass, rootlets, fine twigs, fibrous plant skins, spiders' webs, plant down, feathers and hair.
These birds are most obliging in that they accept most insects when rearing: however, if supplying maggots then a dusting of Vionate and extra calcium lactate will be required. Still provide

cut-up mealworms on the food, and the larvae of ants and moths if possible.

Pied Flycatcher (*Ficedula hypoleuca*)†**

General Description
Migrant. The male is strikingly black and white during the breeding season but the female is at all times far duller of plumage, merely a grey version of him although retaining the white wing bar. During the winter months a male will very much resemble the female but he still exhibits a slight whitish forehead, and upon really close inspection, a little more white in the wing bar. This pied variety of the flycatchers can be hardly distinguishable from the collared-bird after the autumn moult though at close quarters one can just make out the dull remains of the conspicuous collar of the latter bird and what is left of the white rump, both being faintly visible as grey-white when compared with the true grey of the pied flycatcher in these areas; this is of course only during the 'eclipse' plumage. We have during the breeding season a male with black crown, cheeks, mantle, back and tail, with white wing bar, forehead, breast and belly: the female exhibits grey where the male is black, with her wings slightly darker than her mantle but retaining a white wing bar; the length of this bird is thirteen centimetres.

Habitat
Forests, woods, orchards, and anywhere with an abundance of trees will attract this bird. Unlike the red-breasted or spotted varieties, this bird often feeds upon the ground; fallen caterpillars and small beetles are more often than not the food taken in this manner. The nest is usually made in the hole of a tree, or even a nest box provided by man. Many birds build their nests in holes in building walls, the materials used being moss, grasses, dead leaves and hair.

Aviary
Make an effort to provide a large enclosure, the least possible being a two-metre cubed outdoor enclosure with a shed-type shelter attached; the latter will require a little warmth during the winter when these birds should remain inside. The outdoor floor should be of a sandy, gravel-like finish, clear in patches but planted with heathers, lavender, rosemary and such like. A rear side can be covered with a strong growth of hops. Few perches

are needed but a little roofed area outdoors is helpful to cover
nesting boxes and provide a dry roosting place when weather is
wet or chill winds blow.

Food
This is one of the hardest birds to keep in top condition over a
full active lifetime. When I know that a bird keeper is capable of
moulting this bird into and out of colour year after year then I
have real faith in his proficiency in bird management.

The diet must be rich yet not fattening. If it is over-rich the
kidneys may suffer; if lacking in nutrition the eyes soon exhibit
sticky, watering edges, then a closing of the nictitating membrane, badly limiting the sight, with further deterioration. Even
at this stage one can 'bring back' these birds; the daily use of such
vitamin supplements as Abidec and a complete change of food to
an improved diet can slowly set about an improvement. To take
on the management of these birds if not fully capable of caring
for them is not justifiable, and one embarking upon this move
should firstly acquire the necessary experience or be in the position where he may call upon, and receive, continual advice from
more experienced people.

Give a well-balanced insectivorous mixture, dampened with
milk in preference to water, but serve in a dry or fine crumbly
condition: to this add finely grated cheese, steamed and finely
minced ox heart, liver, fish and roe; the addition of minced
shrimps or prawns now and again is acceptable. Add the usual
chopped or minced dandelion or comfrey and fresh elderberries
when available; a small number, say three per bird, of mealworms, each cut into about six pieces and well mixed into the
food; give two or three very young locusts, or moth or wood ant
larvae per day per bird.

Rarely will these birds unless hand reared take a paste as
previously mentioned, to which could be added an assortment of
items, as and when one wishes. If they can be persuaded to take
such a food as a supplement so much the better: use a small
amount daily and use it to introduce variety.

If these birds are housed in pairs instead of singly, and one sees
a bird suddenly attack another, keep the aggressive one under
observation. It is normally a very placid bird with a strong pair-
bond, but they can become rather spiteful when the diet is
unsuitable and they are being 'starved' of something needed. If

the bird makes a habit of attacking the other, particularly when about to be fed or whilst searching for something in the food dish, house it on its own for a few weeks, offering a course of a reliable vitamin additive, perhaps in the drinking water, and leaving the bath out of their enclosure until later in the day, when one is sure the drinking facilities have been made full use of. As an alternative one can add such a vitamin preparation to the milk which moistens the softfood. The need to do this should never become continuous: look upon a course of these supplements as a remedy whenever there is a strain upon the bird, or something seems not quite right. The diet needs to be checked carefully if the above occurrence does crop up in one's stock.

Although the provision of insect life is important, the softfood is the basic ingredient for good health; it is no good feeding solely on the insects which are available to man, without fully investigating the diet in the wild and varying it accordingly. To give insect life in quantity is not a good thing under controlled conditions as even when offering half a dozen different insects, one is not providing the equivalent of the wild and varied intake. Far better to ensure the provision of a well-balanced basic diet of man-made food and, more important, that it is being eaten daily by the bird. The insects included in the food then become an inducement to eat more of the basic mixture. When young are being fed, either by parents, or if raised by hand, always cut many insects into small pieces and mix into the food, no matter whether mealworms, moth larvae or locusts. Mealworms of course should always be offered in this state, never alive or whole.

Breeding

I must admit that I have never yet bred this bird to maturity under its natural parents though I have hand raised it on numerous occasions. When I have had pairs in the past, something else always seemed to crop up, more important than my pairs of pied flycatchers, or they had to share an aviary with non-breeding spare birds. They have got as far as laying eggs on a few rare occasions, having nested in a variety of box-type sites: the provision of these, facing in a number of directions, should be made early in the autumn in their breeding area and left to weather outdoors over the winter. They seem to take to these more readily than to the freshly installed site. Provide mosses, grasses, dead leaves and as many different kinds of animal hair as can be gathered, fine dog hair, horse hair cut into short lengths, and a few feathers. These birds seem to vary widely in their needs for nesting material and some nests have contained totally different items to others, such as spiders' webs and lichen. It is better to give a little of each and observe which materials the individual birds select, then supply accordingly.

The foods used when hand-raising birds can be so vastly different to that given by the true parents, that one cannot really compare them. I have used wax-moth larvae and a paste of our own softbill mixture with various additives such as calcium lactate, greenfoods, fish roe steamed and crumbled, the whole being moistened with milk. When the parents are rearing they use many caterpillars and other small soft-skinned insects. The safest diet for success is of wax-moth larvae, wood ant larvae, freshly hatched locusts and two dozen or so finely cut-up mealworms mixed into the basic food mixture four or five times a day; only the mealworms and large locusts need be cut up.

White Collared Flycatcher (*Ficedula albicollis*)**
General Description
Migrant. Very like the pied flycatcher except for a white rump, a full white collar around the neck and slightly more white upon the forehead. The song too varies slightly, being softer and more liquid. The male is totally black and white during the breeding season whilst the female is grey, rather more so than a pied female, and shows upon close inspection a slight lightish grey patch on the rump and around the neck where her mate is white. There is a little more white on the wing of the collared bird in both sexes but one needs to have examples of both varieties in front of one to compare such differences. The length is again thirteen centimetres or just a fraction below.

Habitat
Although overlapping the area of the pied flycatcher, they are a more southerly race in general but have a like choice of habitat.

Aviary
Treat exactly as the pied flycatcher.

Food
Their dietetical requirements are the same as that of the pied flycatcher.

173

Breeding
Treat as the pied flycatcher.

Azure Tit (*Parus cyanus*)
General Description
This is longer than the blue tit, measuring some thirteen centimetres. The extra length is not in the body but taken up by the
slender tail which is blue, edged and tipped with white. The eye
stripe is bluish-black and there is a small patch of the same colour
in the centre of the breast; the crown, cheeks and under-body are
white; the wings and mantle bluish-grey, but the wings have a
brownish wash. The outer feathers are more blue and edged with
white.

Habitat
This bird frequents the banks of streams and broad-leafed woods
rather than dense forests, invariably keeping to the fringes in such
places as willow thickets and birch groves.

Aviary
This is a very active and restless member of the tit family, used to
fairly strong flight and it should therefore be provided with an
aviary of more than the usual length, perhaps three metres long
by one metre wide and two metres high. A small roofed section at
each end should shelter hole entrance-type nest boxes left in
position all the year round. One side of the enclosure should have
a thick creeper such as hops to encourage insects. The ground
should be mainly gravel and sand with possibly rockery plants for
decorative purposes; include two cotoneaster (*Rosaceae horizon-
talis*) as the berries will be appreciated in the autumn, and will
also serve as the bulk of the perching needs. A further perch at
each end beneath the sheltered sections will suit their requirements. Never house more than a pair together.

Food
A good insectivorous mixture should be given with grated cheese,
two or three cut-up mealworms daily, steamed fish, or fish roe
occasionally, mixed well into the food. Any small insects can be
offered in limited quantities; always bear in mind that the birds
should be encouraged to eat plenty of softfood, so the livefood
should be added as an attraction. Some of these birds peck at a
slice of sweet apple while others seem to completely ignore it; a

little could be minced in their food together with small quantities of greenfood. Peanuts will be taken in moderation as too will sunflower seeds. There is no need to hang a piece of suet or beef fat in their aviary, as with a well-balanced diet there should be no call for it.

Breeding

These birds should prove no more difficult to breed than the near relative, the blue tit. Log-type nest boxes can be used, either home-made ones, or natural ones in the form of an old birch tree bole, rotten and fallen, but having numerous old excavations by woodpeckers. The latter can look quite attractive when an enclosure is planted naturally. For the first five days after young have hatched offer small soft-skinned insects: aphids are ideal but difficult to collect in bulk; the hop plant should provide many if included in the aviary plant-life. One can give ant and moth larvae, and increase the number of mealworms during this time to fifty cut up in their food. Give these night and morning. As the young get older so the insects can be increased in size and quantity. When over five days maggots can be given by the dishful; add a few drops of cod-liver oil, no more than ten drops to a half pint of maggots, and then powder them well with Vionate.

The nesting materials are mainly moss and various kinds of hair; it is all so closely woven that it becomes almost like felt to the touch. The eggs are very similar to those of the blue tit, being white and spotted with dull red. The young also resemble their near kin in leaving the nest at about eighteen days. With freshly hatched young, it is always advisable to use calcium lactate for dusting livefood. Maggots in particular hold this powder very well if first moistened with a few drops of cod-liver or olive oil; all such oil should be used very sparingly, one is aiming only to equip the insect with the slightest film of oil for adhesion of additives, although using a beneficial item for doing so.

Blue Tit (*Parus caeruleus*)****‡

General Description

This is a remarkably well-coloured creature and measures eleven and a half centimetres. It is blue capped, yellow breasted, with greenish mantle, and blue wings and tail. It has white cheeks and blue legs and a blue-black line through the eye to the nape, descending beneath the cheeks to join under the bill covering the throat. It is very active.

Habitat
It frequents almost any park, garden, orchard, or olive grove, almost always near human habitation, but in the main avoids coniferous areas.

Aviary
A two-metre long aviary, by the same height and one metre wide, as advised as the barest minimum for breeding birds, will certainly house a pair of blue tits. The vegetation growing in this enclosure should be as for the previous bird as should the nest boxes which will often be used for roosting during inclement weather. Keep one pair strictly on their own; do not mix them.

Breeding
The biggest problem is not in getting these birds to nest, but in finding sufficient food to keep up to a dozen youngsters alive whilst being reared. Provide a box-type nesting site, log or man made; the hole would naturally be small but this matters little when housed on their own, as they should be. Nesting materials such as moss, fine grasses, wool, vegetable down, carpet sweepings, animal hair and fur, feathers, leaves, spiders' webs, even pieces of decorative wrapping are often used. So many unexpected materials turn up in their nest boxes that they must be the most unfussy of birds in this respect. The nest is a warm felt-like cup surrounded by a wide variety of materials and contains white eggs marked with fine spots and smudges of dark brownish-red to purple-red.

The feeding of young should be as for the previous bird, the azure tit, a close relative, to which all this bird's needs may be likened.

Coal Tit (*Parus ater*)**

General Description
It is of a similar length to the blue tit, eleven and a half centimetres, but slimmer in appearance. It is black capped with a white nape patch and cheeks; it has a black throat; the upper parts are slate blue; underparts are white; flanks are smokey-buff, and wings and tail almost black. As are most of the tit family, it is an active little creature.

Habitat
Although it is more inclined towards coniferous areas than the
blue tit it is still a frequent visitor to parks and large gardens. It
nests in holes in banks, trees and walls.

Aviary
The minimum-sized aviary will adequately provide a comfortable
residence for a pair of these birds. Fix log type or box nest sites
in position beneath a roofed portion of the enclosure. Plant out
the aviary as for the azure tit with perhaps the addition of a larch
at each end situated not too far from the next boxes: this can
always be 'topped' and stunted to protect against wire netting
damage. House one pair only to an aviary.

Food
Provide a diet identical to that of the azure tit.

Breeding
These birds normally have fewer young than the blue tit, the
usual maximum being about seven or eight. The rearing task is
therefore slightly easier. This bird can be treated in a like manner
to the azure tit. Nesting materials vary little if at all so provide
moss, fine grasses, and a variety of animal hair, plant down,
feathers and spiders' webs.

Crested Tit (*Parus cristatus*)†
General Description
Crested with long upturning feathers of black but white flecked,
this bird's upper parts are greyish-brown, with a rufous shade to
the rump; the cheeks are white edged, and a black collar covers
the throat; a further black line runs back from the eye then curves
round behind the ear coverts; it is a rufous buff on the flanks; the
wings and tail are brown. The overall length is eleven and a half
centimetres. It is very active, feeding creeper fashion and on
ground.

Habitat
Frequenting coniferous woods and alders if nearby, not usually
too far from human habitation, it is to be found in Scotland, not
in England, but throughout Europe including Scandinavia, as far
as the Urals.

Aviary

The standard minimum will suffice as a home for a pair of these birds. A small section of the roof should be covered at each end of their enclosure; beneath these site a number of nest boxes. Since these birds often feed in a similar manner to the tree creeper, I have seen aviaries backed to advantage with vertical lengths of pine: these were split down centrally with a few branches left to protrude for perching. A few stunted pines in their aviary makes a natural and attractive setting. I would still suggest that one side be left for a climber such as the hop. I cannot emphasise too much the value of this in supplying aphids for the aviary inmates.

Food

Provide a diet as for the azure tit.

Breeding

Having watched many of these birds abroad, observed them rearing, hand raised them and kept them over a long period, I have little hesitation in proclaiming them to be no more difficult to breed than any other of the tit family so far dealt with. Treat in a manner identical to that suggested for the azure tit for all feeding requirements. These birds will often eat from rowan berries during the autumn. Nestlings' livefood must be varied. The nest materials are grasses, moss, feathers, wool and fine hair.

Great Tit (*Parus major*)

General Description

White cheeked, it has a contrasting black crown and neck-line joining with a bib and black throat, the black of which runs centrally down the bright yellow breast and belly; the back is yellowish-green; rump and upper tail coverts are slatish-grey; wings and tail are black edged with slate-blue. The length is fourteen centimetres. Its chief characteristic is its pugnacity.

Habitat

It is common almost everywhere within reach of human habitation, though more rare in thick conifer forest.

Aviary

Due to the pugnacious qualities of this bird, it should never be kept in a mixed collection. Even when an abundance of food is present, they invariably disgrace themselves. A standard minimum enclosure is large enough to breed this bird. Plant as for the azure tit but include *Pyracantha coccinea*, the berries of which it will take towards the end of the year. A small area of the roof at each end of the aviary should be covered to give some shelter. Nest boxes should be left throughout the year, just cleaned in early spring by scraping; if other treatment is attempted these tits can take offence and quite easily turn away from the sites.

Food
Provide a diet as for the azure tit.

Breeding
They are a very common bird, yet I have never attempted to breed them. I have hand raised them often, kept them for observation purposes and even had liberated pairs nesting at my door. They should present few if any problems. Offer such materials as dry grasses, moss, rootlets, animal fur and hair, feathers and spiders' webs.

The number of young produced can be up to fifteen but this number is rare; it usually is nearer eight or nine. Nevertheless one should be prepared. Food for rearing is as for the azure tit.

Long-Tailed Tit (*Aegithalos caudatus*)**
General Description
Over half of the fourteen–centimetre length is accounted for by a long slender tail. At first glance one sees a black, white and pink bird, usually in family groups, flitting among tall hedge-rows where they will be searching for insects or even berries during the winter months. The northern and eastern forms have clear white heads, while the western bird has a wide black stripe over the eye which joins the black of the mantle; the upper parts are dark with a pinkish wash; the rump and shoulders are rose pink; the wings and tail have white outer feathers. The sexes are very similar but with a number to compare one can sex the western form by the male's white line running from forehead to nape. If the heads are slightly greyish-tinged on the white, fading towards the black edge, they are fairly safely assumed to be female. The very white, wide, distinct division on the crown is the male. As with any such sexing, one can make an error through well-marked females or poorly marked males. Birds from the far north of Russia will be seen to have slightly longer tails than others.

Aviary

The standard minimum is just about adequate for a pair of long-tailed tits but an aviary constructed longer by at least another metre is far better. Plant densely on two sides with honeysuckle and hops. Into these climbers, which should be kept separate at opposite sides of the enclosure, or one end and one side, push a number of clumps of bracken either dead or growing. This aviary should have a small roofed portion at each end and a frost-free enclosure attached. It need not be heated in any way but it would greatly assist the birds' condition to provide extra feeding time at night during the winter months.

Food

A nutritious softfood mixture will be needed for the basic diet; to this add grated cheese, steamed and minced ox heart, liver, fish and fish roe; sweet apple and small amounts of vegetables, such as dandelion and brassicas, can be minced and mixed in the food. Mealworms must be kept to a minimum and whenever given be cut into small pieces then mixed well into the mixture. Encourage these birds to accept the Farlene paste; it may first need to have some grated cheese mixed with it, so that they recognise the flavour of a familiar food. Small insects can be given daily but not too many unless breeding and rearing young.

Breeding

With the arrival of spring check that the clusters of bracken are still in position in the climbing plants; these frequently help to form the foundation of a nest. The materials to offer are varied: as many spiders' webs as possible which can be collected on bent twigs, rounded as the frame of a tennis racquet; moss; lichen; feathers; animal hair, and even small lengths of teased-out soft fibrous string. No nest will be constructed properly without the spiders' webs as this binds the domed structure together, not only during construction, but also when decorating and weathering the exterior with lichen. Many years ago spiders' webs were used in medicine to stop bleeding of wounds; the long-tailed tit seems aware of the moisture barrier properties and covers the outside of the nest with this material, then camouflages it with a mass of lichen.

I have hand raised these birds on numerous occasions, using wax-moth larvae, ants' 'eggs', wasp and bee grubs and mealworms and a softfood paste. A number of these soft-skinned insects, with mealworms cut small, should be adequate for a pair to rear young satisfactorily and I have seen it done.

Marsh Tit (*Parus palustris*)†

General Description
Crown to nape is a glossy black and this extends below the bill to form a bib; upper mantle and back are greyish-brown washed with olive; this fades out towards the rump and the wings and tail are also this grey-brown shade; the lower belly is dull white, whilst the sides, breast and flanks are pale buff. Very like the willow tit but without the sooty matt-black crown. Juveniles however can easily be confused with one another. All have white cheeks and the sexes are alike. The length is eleven and a half centimetres.

Habitat
Woods, damp localities and orchards all seem to attract this bird but marsh seems to have no special attraction for it. Near broad-leaved trees and steep banked streams one can often hear his 'schup-p- schup-p- schup-p'.

Aviary
The standard minimum will again provide adequate space for this bird for breeding. Give hollow log-type sites, in nest boxes or old birch boles, which may have been found rotting on their sides in the woods; these if stood erect in an aviary corner form natural sites and an old woodpecker hole may soon be accepted. The aviary should have a roofed section at each end for cover and although a shed-type shelter is not vital, the provision of one allows extra feeding time to be given during short winter days.

Food
Feed as the azure tit.

Breeding
Twigs, grass, moss, wool, hair and feathers will often though not always be used. It is normal for this bird to nest low in the wild but in an aviary it may quite often choose a high nest box. These, with the alternative hollow logs, can be at various heights. Treat in all other respects as for the azure tit.

Willow Tit (*Parus montanus*)†

General Description

The description of the marsh tit also fits this bird except that the crown in this variety is more dull black. The bib, too, is a little larger and tends to fade out, rather than end abruptly as in the marsh tit. When handling it one can discern a pale buff patch on the secondaries of the willow tit's wing: length is eleven and a half centimetres.

Habitat

This is identical to that of the marsh tit.

Aviary

Treat as for the marsh tit, but since this bird very often excavates its own nest hole in rotting wood, tree boles of a soft crumbly consistency should be provided in addition to the usual boxes and hollow logs.

Food

As for the azure tit.

Breeding

Since this bird frequently excavates the nest cavity, the inner part is covered with wood chippings. Rarely in such a case does this bird build a nest, instead shaping these fragments to suit itself then lining the hollow with animal hair, vegetable down and sometimes feathers. There are occasions when they have been known to use old woodpecker excavations and other cavity sites and then quite often a little more nesting material is used. In other aspects we can treat this bird in the same manner as the marsh tit.

Bearded Reedling (*Panurus biarmicus*)****

General Description

The male head is a clear blue-grey; the 'moustaches' start at the lores, reach the eye, then turn in an abrupt and elongated downward sweep to each side of the upper breast; the back is a rich chestnut-fawn; it is black beneath the tail coverts, the tail itself being a rusty-red with the outer feathers edged and tipped with grey; the throat and upper breast are white with a greyish wash and flanks are a pinkish-rust. The female lacks the blue-grey on the head, hers being a pale buff; she has no black beneath the tail.

Both sexes have a long tail, well over eight and a half centimetres. The juvenile resembles the female but back and crown are thinly striated with black. They can be sexed at this stage, the male having an orange bill, whilst the female bill is bone colour: the male also has a small amount of black in the ventral area.

Habitat
Marshes and fen areas where large reed beds exist are favourite haunts. It is the seed of this common reed which forms the bulk of the food intake during winters in the wild; at other times aquatic insects are the source of the food supply.

Aviary
To breed this species, it is recommended that an aviary for each pair be at least three or four metres square and two metres high. One secluded corner should then be set up to resemble the birds' wild habitat: a small pond, even if only a metre square, in which can be grown a dense mass of reeds will suffice and long grasses should surround this area. Although it is not essential, I would suggest that some form of evergreen bush be planted very near and slightly overhanging the reed bed: this is for roosting purposes and also to shield any nesting site from heavy rainfall. Winter quarters should be attached to this aviary and although winter artificial heat need not be supplied, the extra hours of feeding from the use of electric lighting will prove beneficial. The birds may have free use of the outdoor aviary at all times.

Food
The basic insectivorous mixture should have minced grated cheese, minced steamed ox heart and liver, fish and fish roe all mixed well into it. A daily quota of mealworms can be given but these should be cut into small pieces at all times and well stirred into the food; live wax-moth larvae, ants 'eggs', day-old locusts all can be given sparingly in the food supply. No fruit need be included but some vegetable matter must be supplied; if hops are grown on a rear wire section of their aviary, they will provide a host of aphids which will be greedily taken. Many aquatic insects are high in calcium content, so if using maggots, remember to powder them well with Vionate and calcium lactate: this will help to replace items lost from their natural diet.

Breeding
The first breeding of these birds was from a pair that I passed to

a friend; the following year I managed it too, but whereas his pair had nested naturally in a reed bed, mine disregarded the offered natural sites and used a half open-fronted nest box about one and a half metres from the ground. So much for all my well intended efforts in reed planting. The rearing was not difficult as they found much in the way of insect life in the aviary, which contained a wide variety of plants and shrubs in addition to the reeds and dense undergrowth.

Whilst rearing is in progress offer all the insects possible including such things as ant and moth larvae, small locusts and caterpillars which can all be given alive. Mealworms as always must be cut into small pieces and mixed well into the softfood: this guarantees that a certain amount of the softfood is consumed. The free use of mealworms on their own can addict a bird to them to such an extent that they will eat little else and must then be 'meated off' before returning to a well-balanced diet again. If maggots are to be offered as a rearing food, hold this back until after the five-day stage; even then they should be treated with the additives previously mentioned. Before this 'risk period' is over, use all soft-skinned insects.

Wren (*Troglodytes troglodytes*)†****‡
General Description
This little creature of nine and a half centimetres long is a very popular and well-known species. Mere brown it may be, but the feather pattern when studied is very attractive; the barred plumage, rich chestnut brown shades with darker markings, the short rather stumpy cocked-up tail of rufous hue, the blurred flight and loud song endear it to all who know it.

Habitat
This bird ranges almost anywhere, from mountain to moorland, town park to country garden. The domed nest may be found in places as varied as an ivy-covered tree, a garden shed or may be built into a garden birch broom or the pocket of an old gardening jacket hanging in a shed.

Aviary
Certainly the standard minimum-sized enclosure will house a pair of these birds. Plant two sides with such creepers as honeysuckle or hops: the latter may not look quite so attractive but it does help with the natural food supply of aphids. Give a small roofed area

at each end of the enclosure. A shed would certainly be appreciated in cold winters but it is not vital if plenty of warm roosting sites are allowed to develop. Nest boxes could be sited amid the creepers which will act as a wind break.

Food

The usual basic food should be supplied, with grated cheese added. Give three mealworms per bird cut up small in the daily food. If there is a danger of one bird getting too many, provide two separate feeding areas and they will very soon get to know their purpose. A little soft fruit such as apple or pear, and some vegetable greenstuff, should be minced finely and given in the food. Insects such as moth and ant larvae, both storable in freezers, can be given all the year round: enough to keep them at the dish should be supplied. Softfood will always adhere to cut-up insects such as mealworms, and the live softer skinned creatures' movements in the food will attract birds to it.

If the birds do not seem to be reaching breeding condition in time, or you wish to make certain of their doing so, add the extra animal protein of ox heart, liver and perhaps fish roe to their diet. I like to do this as a matter of course with many species and I honestly believe that this is what has helped me to breed so many varieties over the years. The song of a male, or the absence of it, will soon let you know how your method of feeding is affecting the birds' general health.

Breeding

Nest boxes or natural sites may be used. At times two or three nests made by the male are ready for a female's inspection. Once a nest has been approved by her she sets about lining it; the materials one should offer are grasses, very fine short pieces, leaves, moss, animal hair and feathers. The birds will appreciate a wide variety of sites. Although the rule is one pair of birds to an aviary, any resulting young of this species can stay with the parents until early the following year. It is most likely that all will sleep together in an old nest that becomes the common roost and this is quite normal during cold weather.

Provide ample supplies of aphids, wax-moth larvae, cut-up mealworms in the softfood and even wasp or bee grubs if possible from the day the young hatch; since they are a resident species they have to be fairly 'coarse' feeders: earwigs and many other seemingly unlikely wren foods will be taken at all times.

THRUSHES, 'CHATS', 'STARTS', BLUETHROATS, NIGHTINGALES, SIBERIAN RUBYTHROAT, RED-FLANKED BLUETAIL, ROBIN, SIBERIAN BLUE ROBIN, WHEATEARS AND ACCENTORS

This is a large group of birds to describe in one chapter and diets do vary greatly in some instances, yet all are fairly coarse eaters. Not all, it must be emphasised, will survive on a like diet: in some cases the basic food may hold very similar ingredients, but where, for example, thrushes prefer a fairly coarsely ground mixture, such birds as bluethroat, dunnock or red-flanked bluetail would all prefer a finely ground basic food.

When not feeding young, all the birds of this group may have their livefood cut to a minimum as long as the basic softfood is adequately nourishing and the subjects are taking such food readily. During the moult a slight increase may be made in the daily intake of livefood and again during the partial spring moult when not only is there a plumage change of sorts, but the breeding condition is gradually being built up. Vast quantities of insect life, however, should never be necessary if the birds are wintered and fed correctly. The general management of stock will reflect in the exhibited condition of the birds.

Whereas for example a ripe apple with the skin broken can be thrown into the thrush family's compartment and will be consumed forthwith, such is not the case with all the birds covered here and fruit should in general be either grated or minced; the moisture in food mixtures should drop and be replaced with that from the pulped apple, pear, fig or other suitable fresh fruit. Diets for various birds may well remain similar but the preparation can be very different.

When considering coarse-feeding varieties of birds, one should be careful not to confuse coarse feeding with a dull boring mixture. This can never be described as good husbandry; this type of diet may well keep birds healthy for a short lifespan—a matter of months or even a year or so—but rarely will a bird keep in faultless condition or be capable of rearing full clutches, let alone of fertilising the eggs. A diet for a caged bird would not be expected to fill the requirements of one that has a large enclosure to exercise in, just as a manual labourer will require a higher calorific food intake than one in a sedentary position. We give here the amount of food needed by a bird living in an aviary; a caged specimen on a like diet could become fat, lethargic and probably develop an internal malfunction of one kind or another with eventual fatal results. Daily exercise over a large area promotes health and general fitness when taken in conjunction with a sensible diet.

The coarse feeders' main requirement is for a well-balanced protein–vitamin–mineral food form. Always give fresh vegetable matter, fruit and animal protein as well as farinaceous meals: it is a simple matter to include these if grated or minced finely. Forcing birds to take common earthworms, where it is not normally a part of their diet is unwise: bacteria can very easily be introduced in this manner. One bird may indeed have a built-in resistance to eating such items but another may well become infected with a serious disease through eating such microscopic unicellular organisms. Some vegetable growth such as comfrey is very high in mineral content and such foods should always be available. If there is a danger of mineral deficiency include a seaweed meal in the food mixture: if used as an additive of up to five per cent of the basic food any seaweed should supply adequate minerals and trace elements. During the autumn when wild berries are at their most plentiful, collect elderberries and rowan fruit. These will be eaten greedily whilst supplies last and such fruit can easily be frozen for later use and even continual feeding throughout the winter.

Wheatears, like redstarts, nightingales and a few other insectivorous species, can live together in pairs quite amicably in an indoor enclosure, only to fight when placed into a breeding pen outdoors in the spring. The introduction of such birds is recommended by using side by side enclosures with an adjoining door, then when it is considered peak condition has been reached by both birds and a response is observed, they can be 'paired' in their new joint enclosure.

187

Blackbird (*Turdus merula*)****‡

General Description

The male is totally black except for the bill, which is yellow for most of the year and changes to deep orange with the arrival of breeding condition. The length is twenty-five centimetres. The female is identical in size but has dark brown, verging on black, plumage. Young of the year are very rufous on upper chest, dark like the female but found upon close inspection to be densely striated. Partially albinistic specimens are common and this abnormality varies in extent from a feather or two, to complete wings or tail, or evenly or unevenly marked white patches on head or body. The bills of female and young are a bone-yellow.

Habitat

The blackbird is common everywhere as garden bird, frequenting orchards, forests and most woodland or agricultural areas.

Aviary

I would recommend an aviary of three metres in length, two metres high and at least one metre wide for a pair of these birds. Beneath the perches it will be found best to add peat so that it may be turned over when soiled, or shingle so that hosing or rain will remove any accumulation of droppings. Certainly a fairly large area should be left clear. In other areas where there is less chance of vegetation becoming unsightly through soiling, the inclusion of evergreens or even flowering shrubs will both provide cover and add to the attractiveness of the enclosure. The structure needs only very little shelter which should consist of a small section of roof at each end being covered, and perhaps a board or two of timber below this to prevent driving rain causing the inmates discomfort. Perches should be kept to a minimum, with one at each end beneath the roofed section for roosting and two lower if natural growth is not available to them for this purpose.

Food

Provide a coarsely ground insectivorous mixture. If on the fine side a little honey can be mixed with it. Include grated cheese, minced green and root vegetables, grated fruit or a few soaked household currants; three cut-up mealworms per bird daily stirred into the food will cover their livefood requirements during out of breeding season periods. I have always used steamed and minced ox heart and liver and also steamed fish when available: there is no need for large amounts of such foods and two teaspoonsful per pair is adequate when mixed well into the basic food. Fresh ripe soft fruit should always be available: I have always found many greengrocers most helpful in providing over-ripe fruit if one's purpose is explained to them.

Breeding

Where adequate growing shrubbery exists to provide suitable nesting sites one rarely need provide additional sites. Some birds like a cluster of branches surrounded by evergreen and others need nothing. I have usually offered a choice, natural site and half open-fronted box-type sites which were about twenty-five centimetres cubed, with a small board covering the lower half of the front. At other times they have used a box of the same area but only a third as deep and with no roof. Materials required will be a variety of coarse and fine grasses, dead leaves and weed stems: mud should be available for the lining of the inside of the outer shell; this can be from a small pond in their enclosure or a bowl holding mud and placed near their bathing facilities to keep it moist; the final lining will usually consist of fine dry grasses but depends entirely upon the native habitat of the birds: those in the far North use such materials as pine needles, whilst I have found some in Italy lined almost completely with leaves.

With the arrival of young increase the number of mealworms, cut-up, and mixed into the food: the first day of hatching cut a dozen or so into small pieces and add to the food, the next day this needs to be doubled and again on the fourth day. On the second day after hatching, give such items as young locusts, moth larvae, wood ant larvae and even a few well-cleaned maggots treated with a few drops of cod-liver oil (three or four drops to a two-ounce container): these additional insects should be in a separate dish so that one can tell at a glance how the foods are being taken. These supplies of live insects will have to be increased according to the number of growing young and their food consumption: as the birds increase in size so too can the insect life: fully grown locust will be broken up by parent birds and the softfood containing cut up mealworms will also be given: locusts are good value for money when well fed and an excellent rearing medium.

Occasionally, prior to pairing, one bird can be a little too aggressive: endeavour to learn which is less advanced and increase its daily mealworm quota, or offer a vitamin additive in its drinking water, before placing them together. Never house more than one pair in the same enclosure and avoid having pairs even next door to each other. Keep a totally different species between their aviaries if using rows of flights.

Fieldfare (*Turdus pilaris*)***

General Description
This bird resembles a mistle thrush in size, being just over twenty-six centimetres and thick set of build. It is very aggressive, and only amicable individuals should be kept together, since much damage can otherwise result. The sexes are very similar with bluish-grey head and rump, very noticeable white underwings, rich chestnut back and wings slightly browner, the breast is golden brown heavily spotted with black, and the underparts buffish.

Habitat
A bird of Scandinavia, it is found in open coniferous forests and broad-leaved tree areas; during the winter it travels south to wherever it can find wild berries or agricultural ground on which it survives during these hard months.

Aviary
As for the blackbird.

Food
As for the blackbird.

Breeding
As for the blackbird.

Ring Ouzel (*Turdus torquatus*)**

General Description
Twenty-four centimetres long, this bird resembles the blackbird in colour and size, but the large, almost half-moon shaped, gorget will immediately identify the male. Upon closer inspection one will also find that he has paler wings with a grey edging to them. The female also shows this gorget but it is far less marked. She is much browner in appearance with more conspicuous light edging to the wings. The song is wild and beautiful, perhaps not so

much so as that of the blackbird but it is louder, and when heard at night or in a quiet rocky area the clear pipe-like notes are very attractive.

Habitat
Mountainous rock-covered areas and wild moorland suit this bird very well: they will nest among the deep heather on the steep side of some ravine; beneath fallen branches or growing bush; in a hollow beneath jutting rocks, or occasionally low in tree or shrub.

Aviary
As for the blackbird.

Food
As for the blackbird.

Breeding
As for the blackbird but add moss to the nesting requirements and cut down on the quantity of mud. There is no lining of mud in the ring ouzels' nest but they often 'cement' the base to some solid foundation with it.

Redwing (*Turdus iliacus*)****

General Description
Although the smallest of our common thrushes at twenty-one centimetres long, it is by no means unattractive. The conspicuous white eye-stripe and the deep chestnut-red flanks quickly distinguish it from other thrushes though the spotted throat and breast are reminiscent of the song thrush.

Habitat
This is basically a Scandinavian birch forest and scrubland species, although now nesting over a slightly wider range, wintering in gardens and agricultural areas throughout Europe.

Aviary
This is the only member of the thrush family that will, in my experience, breed on the colony system but I am not advocating it, although very little bickering takes place in a large aviary containing a few pairs. For one pair provide an enclosure as recommended for the blackbird. Should one wish to house a family together, original parents and offspring, such an enclosure would have to be extended correspondingly.

Food
As for the blackbird.

Breeding
Supply all materials as for the blackbird but add mosses and lichen together with some rotting crumbling wood pulp; a decayed birch will normally provide ample. This bird will often use this with mud to line the outer cup frame; fine dry grasses will then form the inner lining. All other needs are as the blackbird's.

Mistle Thrush (*Turdus viscivorus*)†****

General Description
Measuring at least twenty-seven centimetres long, this bird is far more grey than the song thrush; the breast spots are larger and the face noticeably paler; the outer tail feathers are white tipped. The song although very loud lacks the musical qualities of both the blackbird and song thrush.

Habitat
This bird frequents well-wooded country but where trees, both coniferous and broad leaved, are not too dense. It often nests in trees adjoining agricultural land or parks, even large roomy gardens or orchards which will provide most of its needs.

Aviary
The enclosure as recommended for the blackbird would be considered the minimum size for this bird if it is hoped to breed from them.

Food
As for the blackbird.

Breeding
As for the blackbird.

Rock Thrush (*Monticola saxatilus*)***

General Description
Here we have a most strikingly attractive bird: the male is a wonderful sight when in breeding plumage with a Cambridge blue head, neck and throat; orange-chestnut breast with a crescent of this hue on each feather; a conspicuous white back patch seen more in flight than when at rest; the wings almost black, and

the tail rich chestnut. The female is much browner and is finely speckled without any of the male's brilliant hues. Young resemble the hen in every way, and are not easily sexed until the adult moult in the spring: on close observation one can tell the male by his white back patch which shows very slightly once out of nest feather. The length of this bird is nineteen centimetres.

Habitat
It inhabits the mountainous areas of Europe but is rarely seen because of its shyness and habit of 'freezing' into a watching position when spotting an intruder. It nests in a rock cavity.

Aviary
As for the blackbird.

Food
As for the blackbird.

Breeding
It readily accepts a half open-fronted nest box. In all other respects treat as a blackbird.

Song Thrush (*Turdus philomelos*)†****‡
General Description
The commonest of our thrushes, it is much appreciated for its song. The overall appearance is of a warm slightly olive-tinted brown; the underparts are white; the breast is covered with dark brown spots; there is a slight orange tinge to breast and flanks and the back always seems very nightingale-like. The length is twenty-three centimetres. The female is almost identical to the male though her breast spots may be larger and recede lower on the belly, whereas the male's stop short of the lower belly and he carries more white on the ventral area.

Habitat
It is common everywhere in field, orchard, sparse woodland, coniferous or broad-leaved tree forests and town or country garden. It is often chased away by blackbirds who also like to be near human habitation and the food that this proximity provides.

Aviary
As for the blackbird.

Food
As for the blackbird.

Breeding
As for the blackbird, but include wood pulp with nesting materials.

Whinchat (*Saxicola rubetra*)****

General Description
To say that the plumage is made up of various browns and black hardly seems to do this bird justice for it is a remarkably attractive chat in breeding plumage. The male has a black cheek patch; a very conspicuous white eye-stripe; a white wing bar with almost black shoulder patch and flights. The rich brown of the back and crown is evenly marked with a brown so dark it is almost black; the throat at the edge of the black cheek is white; then from here to the belly he is a warm orange-tan fading to white at the vent. The female is more brown all over and after the autumn moult both look very much alike. The young are similar to this eclipse plumage.

Habitat
Open ground and moorland provide favoured haunts where it nests beneath an overhanging tuft of grass.

Aviary
As long as one does not have to enter the enclosure to feed or water the birds, a three-metre by one-metre by two-metre high aviary would provide ample space for a breeding pair of these birds. Allow grass to cover half of the floor area and the remainder should be of shingle and peat with heathers and perhaps an evergreen or two. Winter quarters should be attached unless the birds are to be caught up in the autumn for transfer to warmer indoor flights. This bird can be allowed to leave such an indoor flight and use the outdoor aviary at all times, but ensure the food supply is indoors so that it is encouraged to enter for food and roost inside.

Food
As for the blackbird but use a finer ground basic food. Fruit can be grated fig only, with a supply of elderberries when they are ripe on the trees. Give grated or minced vegetable, brassicas,

comfrey and dandelion, plenty of grated cheese and steamed ox heart and liver. With insects kept to a minimum at all times other than when rearing is in progress, extra feeding time during winter is essential.

Breeding
Provide grasses, moss, and animal hair for nesting materials. As well as ensuring that natural grass sites form, hang one or two half open-fronted-type boxes at the rear. A biscuit tin loosely packed with dry bracken and grass can be erected on a post to stand about a metre from the ground; this type of site is often accepted in preference to others. All advice on rearing is as for the blackbird, except that small locusts rather than full grown ones should be given at all times.

Stonechat (*Saxicola torquata*)†***
General Description
In breeding plumage the male is predominantly black and chest-nut-brown though the white side neck patches and white in the wings are exploited in the mating display; so much white remains hidden at other times that the large areas of it bared at this time are almost unbelievable. The head, throat and back are black; the chest is chestnut fading downwards to buff. The female is browner on head and mantle at all times and the young resemble her. The length is twelve and a half centimetres.

Habitat
Gorse bushes seem the favourite of this bird and even if only one or two exist in otherwise open moorland the male will invariably choose one and keep to a particular perch for singing. He has a song flight, too, when he rises almost vertically, then rises and falls over a distance of three or four metres delivering his court-ship song.

Aviary
Because of this bird's shyness when nesting, try to give a large enclosure of three metres long, two metres high and two or three metres wide. If planting naturally with gorse, procure small bushes without damaging the tap-root; the larger ones often die when moved: heather is another useful plant for this species and if one can manage a mixture of the two, covering half the floor area, with sand and shingle for the rest, these birds will settle in

very quickly. For winter quarters there should be a frost-free enclosure attached where they can retire at night or during the colder weather. Extra feeding time is beneficial although this is a very late roosting species.

Food
As for the whinchat.

Breeding
As for the whinchat.

Black Redstart (*Phoenicurus ochruros*)†****
General Description
Migrant. The male in breeding plumage is blackish all over except for the rufous tail and white wing patch; the mantle is slightly more grey but the face and breast are true black. Some males do not reach this full adult plumage for two years; I have seen many breeding in what can only be called their juvenile plumage. The female is dark grey all over with the merest lightish-grey showing in lieu of the white wing patch. The young resemble the female. The length is fourteen centimetres. The song is rather like the noise of a small whistle when drenched with saliva, a kind of bubbly warble which is easily identifiable.

Habitat
The habitat varies greatly with the country of residence, ranging from ruined houses, large desolated buildings where structural steelwork or holes in the wall can provide nesting sites. Rocky hill country with nearby villages and farm outbuildings all provide for this preference towards rock or wall cavities.

Aviary
The most successful breedings have occurred in aviaries of at least two metres long; these need a width of at least one metre and a height of two metres. Since a pair of these birds rarely if ever squabbles, unlike its close relative the redstart, one can leave them together without fear of losses. A shed-type shelter should adjoin their aviary and they can be allowed to use both indoor and outdoor quarters during the colder months; extra lighting for longer feeding hours is an asset in keeping them in top condition and advancing it towards the spring when they should breed. Where no such shed exists, place them in a flight as large as possible but in an unheated birdroom: as long as they remain

frost free and are fed correctly they will remain fit throughout the winter.

Food

I like to keep these birds almost entirely on a good quality insectivorous mixture. When they do have mealworms, each insect is cut into small pieces and mixed well into the food; the only live insects I provide are wax-moths and their larvae. They receive a generous ration of grated cheese, steamed ox heart and liver which has been finely minced, vegetable matter, and a little fruit which has also been minced; now and again I give carrot and the roots of dandelions. Of course one can keep them on a far more austere diet but it is the variety which makes all the difference when breeding is top-most in the bird keeper's mind. I honestly believe that this extra attention to detail is responsible for many of my own first breedings and other successes.

Breeding

I could not even guess at how many pairs of these birds I have kept since a child, and I have never known a case of severe fighting between a true pair. One can, if not careful, mistake a young male for a female, but a true pair never have exhibited any bad feeling towards one another when in my care, and I have rarely been without them. This amity usually simplifies keeping, pairing and breeding in general but I have known two hens to go through the complete breeding ritual, one nesting, laying and brooding the useless clutch whilst the other female would sit on guard, frequently calling off the brooding hen upon the approach of humans: this well emphasises the importance of correctly sexing one's birds if in juvenile plumage.

Provide half open-fronted-type nest boxes: some need not even have the roofed section. The black redstart is very easily accommodated: I have had hens which used a shelf and built alongside a vertical post. The materials they will need for nesting are dry grasses, moss, fibrous plant skin which they will take from dead vegetation such as honeysuckle and iris, animal hair, feathers and small particles of wool. With the hatching of young do not overfeed with a sudden glut of livefood: a young bird is quickly satisfied at this stage and can easily cease to gape: this to a parent bird is a dead youngster and as such may be thrown out of the nest. It is far better to allow double the normal quantity of cut-up mealworms in the food mixture and just a small quantity of wood ant or wax-moth larvae in the initial first hatching period, increasing gradually from then on.

Redstart (*Phoenicurus phoenicurus*)†*****‡

General Description

A well-coloured male in breeding plumage is one of our more exotically coloured birds: he has a grey-blue mantle and crown; white forehead; black throat; brilliant chestnut breast and tail with the wings darker; the contrast where the black cheeks meet white, grey-blue and chestnut make him a most handsome specimen. The length is fourteen centimetres. The female and the young are dull brown but retain the red-chestnut tail. The youngsters are easily identifiable by their spotted general appearance.

Habitat

Oaks and beeches with nesting holes are great favourites, but this bird is found equally in coniferous and broad-leaved forest areas, and even open scrubland can attract them at breeding time. An old army petrol can lying on its side on a shooting range once proved to be the nesting site of a pair, and they reared a brood of five successfully. Well matured orchards may well hold a pair or two. On its northern limits, it has only to arrive a week later than usual and starlings or great tits will have taken over the usual sites.

Aviary

On rare occasions these birds have been known to breed in very small enclosures, even large flight cages when not placed outdoors soon enough after their winter housing. This is hardly the ideal method of breeding them, however, and unlikely to produce full nests of strong youngsters. The problem with these birds is pair acceptance, and I would advise the would-be breeder of this species to use two of the standard minimum-sized enclosures side by side with an adjoining door. Each of these aviaries should hold suitable nesting boxes, those with an entrance hole being most acceptable; the rear of each could have hop plants climbing the wire as an attraction to aphids thus providing a natural ready supply of food; the floor space can be planted with a variety of flowering shrubs and evergreens. A frost-free shed-type shelter should join on to this outdoor breeding pen or suitable indoor accommodation be available for wintering these birds separately.

Food
As for the black redstart.

Breeding
Some birds are always a problem to pair and the redstart can be one of these. To understand this one must consider their natural method of pairing. In the wild a male will return to a breeding area and take up a territory; he will sing and thus attract a female to this area; he will then hover butterfly-like in front of a chosen nest site and the female, if in the required condition, will follow him. Should she not do this, and remain aloof, he will invariably chase her from his territory. This procedure will carry on until the 'right' hen accepts both him and the nest site; she will enter and thereafter there will be no squabbling. We should bear this in mind when pairing our birds: we can hardly keep unlimited numbers of females to try with each male but by housing them in adjoining aviaries we will see when the female reaches breeding condition by observing her behaviour when the male tries to attract her to a nest site in his enclosure. As he hovers in front of the nest hole of a box near the dividing wire of their two aviaries, she will endeavour to investigate the site by flying to the nearest point of the division; let this carry on for a day—no longer—and whilst the male is going through his display, open the adjoining door; this can be managed with a length of string so that entry into the enclosure is not necessary. Keep the pair under observation and if he attempts to attack her and drive her off, separate the birds for a few more days. I have used this method with a hen on each side of a male and never yet known it to fail. Under the normal method of introducing a pair, many birds have been lost, both males and females, depending upon which bird was more dominant at the time.

When a very old friend of mine of days gone by, Mr Reggie Tout, was attempting to breed a hybrid from the robin (*Erithacus rubecula*) and the redstart, I fostered eggs of each species under the other: the young were reared satisfactorily but, as I feared, no hybrids resulted: the mating behavioural patterns are so different that in neither case did it trigger off the required response. We liberty bred redstarts also by this method, giving eggs from an aviary pair to wild robins for rearing, the robins having nested in an enclosure which had been left open and empty over winter. Such experiments are interesting but so much of the information

is difficult to generalise with when foster parents are used. The
risk of losing redstart pairs to predators when liberated in a
suburban garden was too great and whether they too would have
managed to rear the young on the livefood available in such an
area was one question which remained unanswered.

For information on rearing the young redstarts when hatched,
refer to black redstart and treat accordingly.

Red Spotted Bluethroat (*Luscinia svecica*)****
and
White Spotted Bluethroat (*Luscinia svecica cyanecula*)**
General Description

As they are so closely related we will deal with these two birds
under the same heading. They are both very robin-like in action.
The mantle and back are a rich dark brown and the tail is rufous,
there is a noticeable pale eye-stripe; the throat is blue and this
extends to the upper breast where it ends with a darker hue; there
is a thin, almost white, line here separating this blue from a rich
reddish-chestnut crescent across the width of his chest; beneath
this he is pale buffish, fading to almost white at the vent. The one
difference clearly visible in the throat markings of adult males is
the red spot in one and white in the other race. The females as
adults can also be identified in this same manner, the red-spotted
variety clearly exhibits a faded chestnut spot above a far paler
blue upper chest patch and white-spotted female shows little if
any blue with only a whitish spot to her throat. The moult in the
autumn brings a much paler plumage to the male: the blue
recedes lower; the throat barely shows a red spot and even the
chestnut band is duller in the red-spotted male. The male of the
white-spotted race fades correspondingly and is slightly paler
still. The young are heavily spotted rather robin-, redstart-, or
nightingale-like, resembling these birds also in that when they
leave the nest they invariably go to ground and can hardly fly at
this stage. The length is fourteen centimetres.

Habitat

The mountain bogs of Northern Europe, Scandinavia and Russia
are the usual breeding areas of the red-spotted race. The white-
spotted bird hails from Central and Southern Europe. Although
still preferring the same swampy ground and stubbly vegetation,

the bird from more southerly regions also frequents drier mountainous areas.

Aviary

A minimum of three metres long by two metres high and one metre wide does not really do justice to these birds: they are seen at their best in a largish enclosure, perhaps rather boggy from the over-flow of a pond. Try planting some evergreens and a wide variety of flowering shrubs. Even when hand-reared specimens, they are a little on the skulking side, sometimes confiding enough to take food from the hand, but just as frequently disappearing into the undergrowth. Winter quarters should be attached, to avoid chasing and having to catch up these birds annually. Provide extra lighting during the shorter days but heat is not required when allowing this additional feeding time; they may use an outdoor aviary daily just so long as they have the warmer shelter to retire to when needed. This is another bird which will benefit from having hops growing on one side of the enclosure: the hunting is good for them and ensures adequate exercise being taken by a bird which can otherwise become obese.

Food

Keep mealworm consumption to a minimum; encourage bulk feeding on an insectivorous mixture. This bird can easily become sore footed through too many mealworms in its daily intake; feed as for the black redstart. Bluethroats are very fond of elderberries during the moult.

Breeding

Although nesting on or very near the ground when at liberty, this bird in an aviary freely takes to a half open-fronted box or an easily assembled site such as a biscuit tin erected up to a metre from the ground on a mouse-proof post: this tin should be packed loosely with dry bracken and grasses. With the tin sited on one side so that the open top is facing away from full sunlight it becomes fully weather-proof. I have used this method many times for nest sites and in fact the white-spotted bluethroat was bred for the first time in this very manner, not in my aviaries on that occasion, although from birds which I had passed on. Nesting materials should include such items as dry grasses, ranging from fine to coarse, moss, animal hair and vegetable down.

When fortunate enough to have young hatch do not be too

liberal with mealworms and always cut them up small and mix well into the food. The larvae of the wax-moth are far less addictive and safer to feed in bulk. When rearing on wood ant larvae, gradually decrease the supply as the young get older, increasing moth larvae and young locust supplies daily. I find that the young more readily take to the insectivorous mixture from locusts and moth larvae than from mealworms or ant larvae. When mealworms are cut up small in softfood as advised, it will be seen that many feeding parent birds will take gradually increasing amounts of softfood to the young, the first smaller quantities having adhered to the pieces of mealworm.

Nightingale (*Luscinia megarhynchos*)†****
General Description
Migrant. From the rear view it is rather like a song thrush in both colour and shape; the tail is certainly more rust hued but the back colour can be very similar. Considering the amount of romantic poetry which has been written on this bird it is quite a dull specimen; so many disappointed spectators have remarked on its sombreness as compared to its wonderful reputation for song. The upper parts are a rich russet shade, deeper rufous on the tail and darker brown on the wings. The male is white at the throat and more greyish of chest fading again to white at the vent. The female is more of a creamy-pale brown on the chest, fading slightly at the throat, and white towards ventral area. The length is seventeen centimetres.

Habitat
I suppose I was about five years old when I hand reared my first nightingale; that bird later sang whenever his mealworm tin was placed in front of his flight: to this day I still have a fondness for this bird and its haunting song qualities when heard in the very early morning or breaking the stillness of night. The copses and spinneys, and broad-leaved woodlands where overgrown bramble and nettles exist are its favourite haunts. The nest is usually placed on a thick platform upon the ground, in very low bramble or nettles. It is made of a dead leaves foundation—oak are usual —and completed with more dead leaves, grasses and animal hair for the lining.

Aviary
Although the standard minimum will suffice once a pair have

accepted one another, this is another species which greatly benefits from having two adjoining aviaries with a door in the dividing partition. Keep them next door to each other until you see the female showing her acceptance by remaining close to the division on the ground. When the male sings and displays she should respond. These birds will need a frost-free shelter attached for their use in winter. Heat is not necessary so long as extra lighting enables them to feed late into the evening and in the early morning.

Food
As for the black redstart, but include more fruit in the diet and Farex.

Breeding
The base of the aviary for nightingales' use should have a shallow pond, as they are frequent bathers. The rear half of the floor should hold two rhododendrons or similar evergreens; beneath these should be a dense mass, at ground level, of honeysuckle, periwinkle and strawberry: these plants form just about the right density without having to resort to brambles and their unpleasantness. A trip into some woods will normally provide a good-sized bag of old oak leaves; offer these, grasses and animal hair, and cow hair or dog combings prove acceptable to the nightingales.

On the last occasion on which I bred these birds we had a crowd of friends gather at my home prior to a meeting in a nearby hall, the hen nightingale had young and I believe every one of the visitors peeped at her; they can become very tame at this time in an aviary and that particular hen took a number of insects from offering hands that afternoon.

When young hatch, increase the supply of cut-up mealworms and continue to do so gradually, all the time offering large quantities of other insects: they will accept small locusts, moth larvae and ants 'eggs' without any hesitation.

Thrush-Nightingale or Sprosser (*Luscinia luscinia*)**
General Description
This bird is darker brown than the ordinary nightingale and lacks the rufous shades of that bird; it also has a lightly spotted breast and is noticeably thicker set: this stouter appearance gives the impression that it is far larger but the length is the same at

seventeen centimetres; the song lacks liquidity of the ordinary nightingale's. The young are even more heavily spotted than its near relative.

Habitat
This is much the same as that of the nightingale which is known in Britain, but, hailing from Eastern Europe, Russia and Siberia, it has also a tendency to frequent more boggy, moist areas. They nest in the same manner with more or less similar materials.

Aviary
As for the nightingale.

Food
As for the black redstart, but include more fruit in the diet and Farex.

Breeding
I would treat as for the nightingale, although my experience is limited to one pair of these birds.

Siberian Rubythroat (*Luscinia calliope*)**
General Description
Migrant. At first glance, from the rear this bird will resemble the nightingale, but seen from the front the throat will immediately identify it, or, from the side, it will be seen to be shorter and less of a typical thrush shape. The length is fourteen centimetres and the overall colour a dark wood-brown with an olive wash; the throat of the male during the breeding season is bright red; there is a white stripe above the eye from the forehead and a further moustachial stripe of white; the lores are black; the scarlet of the throat is edged with deep slate-grey, fading to brownish grey, to buff, then white at the vent. In the autumn the red throat of the male fades. The female has no red throat at any time, and the eye and moustachial stripes hardly show at all: her throat is white. The juvenile bird resembles very much a young robin or redstart being very spotted and an all over brown.

Habitat
A bird of wooded marshy areas, it tends to skulk in dense thickets. It is found as far north as the Arctic Circle, feeding mainly on the ground. It nests in the shelter of a bush, upon

the ground, or perhaps in densely growing plants. The nest is an untidy structure of grasses, a little moss, some rootlets and hair.

Aviary
Provide a two-metre cubed structure with a frost-free shelter attached: the latter would need to have electric lighting during the winter months for extended feeding hours and possibly a little gentle warmth during the hardest of the weather. The outdoor aviary in which it could be allowed daily, even in winter, should contain a small pond and a rather damp area surrounding it, with moss and a few rocks. If this is in the foreground and the near vegetation kept short, then the rear of the aviary could be allowed to grow fairly wild with decorative grasses and hops on the aviary sides. The section between the pond and the overgrown portion could contain a mixture of rhododendrons and azaleas for added seclusion and shelter. The part of the aviary joining the shelter should have a section of the roof covered to shield any nesting site from heavy and driving rain.

Food
As for the black redstart.

Breeding
The song of the male when he is courting the female is very sweet and melodious, not as loud as a nightingale; it is rather soft, but somewhat unvaried. I have never seen any bickering between pairs of this species and have housed them together, but I have known other bird keepers to have trouble pairing them: for this reason perhaps for the first attempt it would be prudent to pair them using two adjoining aviaries until the temperaments are known. Offer the nesting materials as recommended above and watch for some response from the female, usually a following of the male backwards and forwards along the dividing partition. My own birds got on remarkably well together, nesting took place almost as soon as I liberated them into a breeding enclosure from an indoor flight where I had wintered them. The eggs are a greenish-blue with pale reddish-brown spots on the larger end. For feeding during rearing treat as for nightingale.

Red-Flanked Bluetail (*Tarsiger cyanurus*)*
General Description
Migrant. This is the size and shape of a redstart, measuring in

length fourteen centimetres. Head, cheeks, mantle, back and tail are all bright blue, with lighter eye-stripe, shoulder patch and rump; the throat is white; the breast is greyish fading to white at the vent; the flanks show a rufous patch reaching half-way along the wing. A female is very nightingale-like in general coloration but she has the rufous flanks and blue on her upper tail. The juveniles are very like the young of robins, redstarts or nightingales and heavily speckled but with upper tail blue.

Habitat
This bird breeds mainly in Russia, frequenting the swamps of coniferous forests or boggy areas of birch wood. It is fond of low cover. The nest is usually similarly placed to that of the robin in bank cavities or a root of a fallen tree.

Aviary
My experience with this bird is rather limited and may not be typical: but I have found it as troublesome as the redstart during pairing. To prevent a threatened loss I felt compelled to use two adjoining aviaries with a door built into the wire division: using this system one has control, which is always wise with so rare a subject. Plant as for the bluethroat, allowing a pond to overflow on to surrounding soft soil. I allowed my birds the use of outdoor quarters during the winter but provided them with extra feeding time by using a time-switch on the shelter lighting circuit: this shelter was not heated but seldom dropped much in temperature during the coldest of nights due to its good insulation.

Food
These birds enjoy taking mosquitoes when having a pond in their enclosure; these are taken on the wing in a manner reminiscent of that of a flycatcher feeding. Provide a diet as for the bluethroat, rich in animal protein, by adding the ox heart, liver and possibly steamed fish and fish roe. Keeping mealworms to a minimum, those that are given always being cut into several pieces and well mixed into the food. Elderberries are taken when fully ripe.

Breeding
Provide the biscuit-tin-type nest site, securely fixed on its side to a low pole and fill the tin loosely with bracken. As an alternative offer a half open-fronted nest box. It is all very well to build natural sites into a decorative bank or rockery, but with the difficulty of keeping naturally planted enclosures totally free of

mice it never seemed to be worth risking with such a rare bird. The male will attempt to attract the female to a site in much the same way as the robin and although the male will carry nesting material to the site it would appear that the nest is made entirely by the female using moss, grass, rootlets, animal hair and wool.

In the event of any young being obtained, feed as for the black redstart.

Robin (*Erithacus rubecula*)****‡

General Description

For anyone who may be unfamiliar with this bird, it measures fourteen centimetres in length. Its distinctive orange-red face and breast, white belly and vent, olive-brown upper parts, erect stout-looking stance, its confiding manner in visiting gardens during the winter should help even the complete stranger to European birds identify it. It can be very pugnacious when guarding its territory and will not even tolerate the opposite sex during out of breeding season times; two males will fight to the death over a mutually chosen territory: I have personally separated two by hand, when the uppermost was pecking at the head of the trespassing bird and I was compelled to keep the attacked specimen until the head healed over before I released him in the country.

Habitat

Woodland, park, garden or hedgerow, the robin is common in most places, nesting in a bank cavity, a shelf in a garage where free entry can be obtained at all times, the root of an upturned tree; I have even known them to nest in an empty open aviary.

Aviary

Due to their pugnacity towards even their opposite sex, this is another bird which I would recommend be housed in adjoining aviaries prior to peak condition being reached. Each need be the standard minimum size only. There is no need for anything but the open-fronted type of shelter joining the aviary at one end as these birds will winter out quite well. In fact they will arrive into condition earlier than when housed indoors during the colder months. A perch should be at each end of the enclosure, with two more in the shelter situated fairly high. The food tray should be in an easily accessible position so that later when they are breeding one does not need to enter the aviary. A small pool will be welcome since these birds will bathe even when snow is on the ground. Apart from this, it will encourage insects to visit their enclosures.

Food
As for the black redstart.

Breeding
Place a nest box, of the half open-fronted type, in each aviary with both sited as near to the dividing partition as is possible; if well roofed and covered it will not matter if they are in the open: I would suggest they are placed at a height of a metre from the ground. The male, upon reaching breeding condition, will sing constantly and display to the female; until she responds they must not be placed together; when she reaches the required condition and she sees the male fly to the nest box in his enclosure and enter it, she will then try to follow him by clinging to the wire division as near as she is able. The second day they will do this again and one or both may carry a dead leaf or some other piece of nesting material; when this occurs open the dividing door and keep a watchful eye on their general behaviour. All should be well from this point onwards and even more so if a wild pair are in the vicinity. The male under controlled conditions will then challenge the wildling and quite possibly have a daily fight through the wire with him; this is a very natural event and would be happening in the wild; it deflects much of his aggression, and channels it in the right direction, towards any interloper.

I would think that the robin is one of the simplest of insectivorous birds to breed, in that where the provision of suitable rearing food is concerned they make devoted parents. Once the young become self-supporting, however, make every haste to remove the young birds as at that time it is quite natural in the wild for the male to drive them out of the territory so that his mate can nest and rear another brood. Many birds among the softbill species have this tendency, and it will be found necessary to carry out this procedure in the majority of breedings. Feed as for the nightingale when the young hatch.

Siberian Blue Robin (*Luscinia cyane*)
General Description
A very rare bird to find in aviculture today, the upper parts are dark blue, rather matt in appearance; the forehead is far brighter; the tail, wings and crown are brown but washed with blue; the

underparts are white; the flanks are rufous flushed. The female is more olive-brown, with a slight rufous tint showing in the wings and tail; the underparts are white. The length of this bird is fourteen centimetres.

Habitat
It frequents dense bushes and undergrowth where it creeps and skulks in Siberia. It sings well, from a low tree or bush, nesting upon the ground in dense vegetation.

Aviary
As for the rubythroat.

Food
As for the black redstart.

Breeding
The only two birds I ever had caused considerable worry if placed together during the winter months. To avoid disappointment with such a rarity, I would advise pairing them by using adjoining aviaries as described for the robin.

Wheatear (*Oenanthe oenanthe*)†**
General Description
In breeding plumage the male can be a strikingly attractive bird with pale powder-grey crown and mantle, black cheeks beneath a white eye-stripe, throat white, and upper breast a warm buff fading to white at the vent; he has black wings and tail with white rump and tail coverts. The female is much browner and paler, more of a sandy-buff, but retaining the white rump; in winter the male resembles the female. The length is fourteen and a half centimetres.

Habitat
The wheatear inhabits open country, uncultivated areas and moorland.

Aviary
With the knowledge that the pairing of these birds can sometimes cause problems, one should be prepared for such eventualities; it is far better to use two enclosures side by side with an adjoining door, than place two birds together and hope for the best results to occur. I would suggest as a minimum for the breeding aviary a two-metre cubed enclosure; the adjoining one for the use of the

female until breeding condition and pair acceptance is reached need be only half this size. Since these birds will use rock crevices, rabbit holes, drainage pipes, cavities in heaps of rubble and the like, it is not taxing to fabricate a site to suit their needs. Make certain that the site will be on ground not likely to become water-logged or in the path of heavy downpours of rain. Construct a main nest chamber of bricks or fairly thick timber, without a top and one side. Run to this a piece of earthenware pipe, approximately twelve to fifteen centimetres in diameter and about thirty centimetres long. Cement all this in position then cover with soil except for the roof of the nest chamber; for this one should construct a lid with a rim, as with a biscuit tin lid; make it of timber and cover it with roofing felt; make it in such a way that one can raise it easily for inspection at a later date. Wheatears will benefit from having an enclosure they can retire to during winter months though they may be allowed the freedom of the outdoor enclosure. Make sure their aviary floor is well drained; the use of plenty of sand, shingle and gravel during the preparation for them will ensure a maximum of dryness. With the addition of heathers, rock plants, and a song post at each end all will be ready for the occupants.

Food

A good insectivorous mixture with grated cheese, steamed ox heart and the usual minced vegetable matter will form the basis. Give very little fruit other than in autumn when elderberries will be taken. Include a small daily quota of cut-up mealworms in the food; items such as wax-moth larvae and particularly locusts, of which they are extremely fond, can be given daily in small quantities, naturally increased when the rearing of young is expected.

Breeding

As the male advances in condition so he will come into song and try to call the female to one of his selected sites. When, and only when, she is observed making a response and trying to reach the nest site, open the dividing door. When paired in this manner things should progress satisfactorily. Many birds, males and females are lost through being introduced before they are in peak condition. The materials they will require for nesting are grasses, moss, rootlets, dead leaves, small tufts of wool and animal hair; dog brushings are ideal.

With the hatching of eggs, increase the chopped-up mealworms in the food; double will suffice at the first stage. Offer ant larvae if obtainable, newly hatched locusts, wax-moth larvae and greenfly; almost any small garden insect, woodlice and earwigs will all find a ready welcome.

Greenland Wheatear (*Oenanthe oenanthe leucorrhoa*)***
General Description
I have measured these birds at times and found them well over the expected length, at sixteen and a half centimetres: this is considerably more than the more common bird. In the field it can look very similar, but close by it is found to be far more bulky of build. It is altogether a darker bird with a darker and richer grey on the mantle, the wings too are blacker, and the breast is almost tan compared with the buff of the smaller race. The plumage is far paler during the out of season months, but even at this time differs considerably from the common bird.

Habitat
Although called the Greenland wheatear, this bird nests over a vast area of Greenland, Iceland and North-East Canada, tundra areas and open wastes being its haunts.

Aviary
As for the wheatear.

Food
As for the wheatear.

Breeding
As for the wheatear.

Black-Eared Wheatear (*Oenanthe hispanica*)
General Description
When in breeding plumage the male is very attractively coloured; the wings and tail are typical of this family, black but with the usual white coverts and rump; the ear coverts are black; the black commences at the bill and a black line runs through the eye, in much the same manner as the cheek patch of the common race but here it extends further back. The body colour is a creamy-buff and the crown at times is almost creamy-white. The female is pale brown almost like the common female. There is also an eastern race which has a black throat. The length is the same as the common race at fourteen and a half centimetres.

Habitat
Barren dry open country is the favourite terrain as well as vine-yards particularly those with stone walls.

Aviary
As for the wheatear.

Food
As for the wheatear.

Breeding
If a wall can be constructed with natural-looking holes, perhaps formed by a terracotta flower-pot cemented into position with a jutting slate over-hang for protection from rain, these birds can be persuaded to use them. Although these birds tend to nest at ground level, even beneath dense shrub or vegetation, many will still take to hole sites and thus keep better out of the way of mice. For all other details consult the wheatear entry.

Alpine Accentor (*Prunella collaris*)****

General Description
This attractive specimen is far larger than the hedge accentor and more brightly coloured, and although predominantly brown, grey and chestnut, its markings are beautifully uniform in appearance. The throat is dappled white and black and flanks are chestnut streaked in a rich rufous shade. The song is sweet sounding and constant, a continuous musical warbling, the first few notes reminiscent of a piece from the woodlark's song. The sexes are very much alike, in fact I have mistaken one for the other quite often. The juvenile shows far less of the rich colours and is more greyish, having no throat markings or rufous on flanks. The length of this bird is eighteen centimetres.

Habitat
A bird of the high European mountains, when seen, and this is only rarely, it is usually on some rocky slope among juniper bushes and stunted conifers where other vegetation grows thinly. It nests in a low bush or rock crevice beneath such growth.

Aviary
I would like to think that a minimum of three metres long by at least half that in width and two metres high would be given as an enclosure for a pair of these birds. They can live together all the

year round and need no shelter other than a small-roofed area at each end, this dropping downwards around the sides for more complete weather proofing. They seem to greatly appreciate rocks, so the base can be decorated in many ways using this material and also suitable plants; a juniper or two and conifers will give them a perfect setting. Bathing facilities such as a shallow pool will be made full use of.

Food
The food should include both seeds and softfood together with some insects. I use threshings plus rape, panicum millet, maw and gold of pleasure; they enjoy the grasses as much as anything. An insectivorous mixture with a little grated cheese and a few cut-up mealworms should be given daily; often the use of this during the winter months drops considerably but the consumption increases again with the arrival of spring, summer and autumn, then lessens again. Mealworms will be eaten during the winter period.

Breeding
Against all expectations and despite specially prepared rock crevices and nest boxes ours nested low in a dense buddleia bush and reared successfully there. They do not seem very territorially minded and when I had two pairs together at one time, there was little bickering.

The nest looks rather like a dunnock's but is larger and made of grasses, a little moss and lined with animal hair. It was sited about thirty centimetres above the ground. The eggs are light blue but with a matt greyish wash.

If they gave any seed to their young I never witnessed it, but they did regurgitate when the young were very small. They certainly collected aphids. The young were out of the nest well over a week before they were seen picking up food which in this case quite likely included seeds, but I could not be sure. They resemble the hedge accentor in the feeding habits and make one wonder at the actual food intake. We gave a wide range of livefood when the young were in the nest: wax-moth larvae, mealworms, caterpillars, in fact anything found crawling, was usually offered. There was a continuously running stream in their enclosure, and young and old were often to be seen at the edge, eating something either from the moss there or from the water itself.

Black-Throated Accentor (*Prunella atrogularis*)†****‡
General Description
This is a rather sombrely clad bird of black, brown and a light shade of mushroom; the head is black with a clearly defined light brown eye-stripe and moustachial stripe, the throat-marking ending abruptly on the chest of light mushroom. After the breeding season the black tends to fade quite a lot. Very typical of the accentor in behaviour and movements, it has a quick, flitting, flight and is always on the move in undergrowth and at ground level; the length is fourteen centimetres.

Habitat
Another bird of the high mountainous regions, mine came from Russia, where stunted conifers and juniper grow. Nesting takes place almost at ground level in a dense bush.

Aviary
The standard recommended minimum enclosure should be sufficient for these birds: it can be planted out rockery style with the junipers and conifers around the edges. A small shallow pond is used daily when available.

Food
As for the Alpine accentor.

Breeding
The nest which was discovered after the young bird had fledged was found deeply set in a cluster of dead bracken: clumps had been fastened at intervals almost from ground to roof on one side of the aviary. It was about thirty centimetres from the ground and made of dry grass and chickweed, then lined with animal hair. Two broken egg shells were found, the colour seeming very like a hedge accentor's but perhaps more glossy. In all respects treat as for Alpine accentor.

Hedge Accentor or Dunnock (*Prunella modularis*)*****
General Description
Of a skulking nature, with quite attractive song, this bird is always tight of feather when all else in the depth of winter looks forlorn. Active and lively it is a brown bird with greyish head and the male has grey underparts. He has an even more slate-grey

head during the breeding season. The length is fourteen and a half centimetres.

Habitat
It is found almost anywhere in gardens, woodland, country lane, vineyard, farm, even town park and any open space cultivated or wild, throughout Europe.

Aviary
The standard minimum is sufficient, planted with bushes at the rear. Include a shallow pond for bathing and to attract livefood. The merest of roofed sections will be sufficient against rainy days or winter shelter.

Food
As for the Alpine accentor.

Breeding
Probably one of the simplest of native birds to breed in captivity, although common, it makes a pleasant bird to study. Often the male will complete a further nest whilst his mate is still feeding the first lot of young; I have known a male build five nests in one season in this manner and the female laid in each as her young of the previous nest fledged, the male taking over parental duties in respect of the fledglings. One bad point with accentors is that the male will resent the presence of the young and continually chase them: they should therefore be removed early so that fatalities do not occur. These birds will nest in almost any small bush, hedge, shrub or climbing honeysuckle. The nest is made of twigs, grass, leaves and moss with a lining of animal hair. The eggs are glossy bright blue.

LARKS, PIPITS, WAGTAILS

Here we have a group of fairly coarse feeders, all spending much of their time upon the ground where they search for insect life. Larks will take a number of small seeds during the winter months. Although aphids and small insects will be greedily taken whenever the opportunity arises, these birds are well able to take far larger insects and I have seen them all tackle almost fully grown locusts: the young of these insects are certainly acceptable to this group for feeding their young. Many wagtails in captivity have been reared, for example, on small fish fry: I mention this so that the reader will experiment and investigate further possibilities; the fish mentioned above were placed in shallow containers holding a small amount of water.

The basic food should be a nourishing man-made insectivorous mixture, with the additives mentioned in Part One on feeding. The mealworms can be increased slightly in number but still cut into small pieces and mixed with the food.

With this group of birds, due to their habits of ground feeding and running around hunting, one has a wonderful excuse to make the aviary look a real show-piece: small ponds, rockery plants, decorative stone and rocks, clear areas of flat shingle and sand, mossy banks to the pond and flowering shrubs will help in bringing to life what is far too often a mere dead area of wire and soil. Some of the aviaries I have seen holding the wagtail family have included waterfalls, running streams, much semi-tropical vegetation and even fish pools; apart from the visual pleasure one can obtain from such garden surroundings, the natural insect life is an added bonus for the inmates.

Providing that larks have been housed together all the winter, they can be introduced to a breeding pen together. With pipits, a certain amount of rather hectic chasing is quite normal so do not be too distressed when observing a male singing violently and chasing a female back and forth in their enclosure: they too can be wintered together and introduced to the outdoor breeding aviary at the same time.

Shore Lark (*Eremophila alpestris*)***
General Description
One of our most attractive larks, it measures sixteen and a half centimetres long and is distinguishable from all others by the yellow fore-throat and patch to the rear of the black cheeks, also by the black 'horns' rising up from each side of the head, above the yellow of the forehead receding over the eye and down behind the cheek patch to link up with the throat; it has a black crescent on the upper chest. The over-all appearance elsewhere is of warm brown with perhaps a slight pinkish wash, the upper parts being more noticeably so; the underparts are much paler. The female shows less black and upon close inspection will be found a little smaller.

Habitat
It is a bird of the Arctic Circle where it breeds in the mountainous alpine regions, wintering south on salt marshes and beaches.

Aviary
I have kept many of these birds and each one has become tame to the point of foolishness, walking over and around my feet in their enclosure; yet despite this fearless and tame attitude in captivity, the mating display flight does require a larger area than may be considered necessary. Make an effort to provide at least a three-metre length by two-metres width and height. Such an enclosure can be made most attractive and provide ample space for their mating and breeding needs. A small roofed-in section at each end with one or two downward fixed boards will keep them dry in the wettest of weather and provide a reasonably draught-proof roost. There need be no special winter shelter but if one can be attached then I feel sure it must contribute to longevity. Our birds nested beneath a tuft of coarse grass growing under, and up through, a small conifer, so keep the aviary base a mixture of peat and shingle with heathers and a few small stunted or horizontally growing conifers.

Food

Provide a good softbill mixture, with the usual additions of grated cheese, vegetable and a few cut-up mealworms; although it is basically a softbill, screenings or small wild seeds can be strewn over a small section of the aviary floor; grass seed and the smaller of the brassicas will be pecked over during the winter months but these should be provided only as a supplement to the insectivorous food. Because of their taste for small crustaceans, I often minced up a few shrimps or prawns in their food and on such occasions it was noticeable that they were cleared completely by the next feeding time.

Breeding

In the wild this bird nests beneath a jutting rock, a cavity in the ground or some similar site that is usually shielded by a tuft of vegetation but I have never had one build other than on the ground. The materials were merely a variety of dry grasses, bents and a lining of vegetable down, a rather untidy structure.

Presumably foreign to them as an item of food, mine took fairly large quantities of young locusts, and wood ant larvae; fly maggots were given after being thoroughly cleaned and treated with cod-liver oil and Vionate. Handfuls of cocoon-like material that wax-moth larvae use for pupation were given and the birds would tear this silk-like material apart into shreds, to reach the insects inside.

Short-Toed Lark (*Calandrella cinerea*)***

General Description

Measuring fourteen centimetres in length, this lark is a sandy-brown in colour, lightly streaked with darker brown and with white underparts; it displays a small dark patch on each side of the breast. The sexes are very alike but the female is slightly smaller. Neither can be called stocky or thick set but she is certainly the slimmer of the two.

Habitat

It inhabits sandy wastes, dune-like areas and steppe country in Southern Europe.

Aviary

The minimum standard enclosure will house one pair comfortably. Keep the base well drained with a finish of fine shingle and sand. A few heathers and tufts of sedge or long grass will provide them with an ideal setting. A wintering shed should either be attached or available for their habitation during the colder months. Extra feeding time will greatly benefit them during such times.

Food
Feed as for the shore lark.

Breeding
Although the nest is apparently started in a hollow of the ground, it ends up looking as though on a platform of smaller stones; this is an illusion since the stones are piled up to the edge after the structure has been completed. At the foot of the clumps of grass make impressions in the shingle with the clenched fist, then hang the vegetation over to hide it. The materials this bird will need are mainly dry grasses but there is a soft lining made finally with animal hair, vegetable down and feathers. Any resulting young should be offered insects as for the shore lark.

Lesser Short-Toed Lark (*Calendrella rufescens*)

General Description
This resembles the short-toed lark to a great extent but is far greyer about the upper parts and also darkly streaked on the upper breast and without the dark chest patches. It is not crested in the true sense but does tend to raise its head feathers. The length is the same at fourteen centimetres. The sexes are alike but here again when one can compare a true pair, it will be seen that the female is slightly smaller.

Habitat
This is very similar to that of the short-toed lark but seems to show a preference for more damp vegetation and marshy areas adjoining water.

Aviary
As for the short-toed lark.

Food
As for the short-toed lark.

Breeding
As for the short-toed lark.

Wood Lark (*Lullula arborea*)†****

General Description
This bird is shorter than the skylark and lacks the white outer feathers in the tail; otherwise it is rather similar: the plumage is a rich brown; it has a whitish-buff eye-stripe running to the nape; the breast fades to white on the underparts, the head feathers are often raised in crest-like formation but not always so. The sexes are marked alike, the darker streaked back of the female being a little less broad in comparison. The length is fifteen centimetres.

Habitat
I prefer the song of this bird to most others I know, and when listening to it in wild open country, quiet orchard or on alpine summer farmland it has a wonderful quality hard to describe. One never quite knows how one may come across this bird, whether singly, in pairs or a family group in which they travel very often. They may be seen from the New Forest in England to the olive groves of Italy.

Aviary
Give one pair an enclosure of at least three metres long by two metres in width and height. Erect the male a song post where it may sing in the sun; this need be only a rustic pole standing a metre above the ground. The base of the aviary should be kept fairly clear; allow two corners to become a little overgrown with grass, but elsewhere it is better to have a hard shingle or gravel base, with perhaps a few heathers. As a wind break and to attract insects, plant hops at the rear of the aviary. This bird may be a resident in the winter, and I have seen them nest whilst there is snow on the ground, but a frost-proof shelter with extra light to extend the feeding hours should prevent any losses and enhance one's chances of breeding these larks.

Food
As for the shore lark.

Breeding
As for the shore lark. Nesting materials should comprise moss, coarse and fine grasses and animal hair.

Skylark (*Alauda arvensis*)****
General Description
In length the skylark is eighteen centimetres. The mantle is a more dull brown than the woodlark, and there is a far longer tail having white outer feathers. Here again the crest is not always raised but can be very conspicuous at times. Head and mantle bear dark streaks; the underparts are whitish with streaks on the upper breast; the eye stripe is a little more buff than in the woodlark when compared side by side. The sexes are alike except for the males' heavier build.

Habitat
Open country, cultivated or fallow, provides haunts for this bird: it may be alpine meadow or low heath or fen. On a warm summer's day one may be lucky to hear this bird's song somewhere in the vicinity.

Aviary
As for the shore lark.

Food
As for the shore lark.

Breeding
As for the shore lark.

Meadow Pipit (*Anthus pratensis*)***
General Description
Although dark brown it tends to be a greyish-brown as compared to the reddish-brown of the tree pipit; it is streaked with darker brown on head, mantle and upper chest; the underparts are whiter; the back claw is long and almost straight, far longer than that of the tree pipit which curves more for perching. The tail has white outer feathers which show very clearly in flight. The length of this bird is fourteen and a half centimetres.

Habitat
It frequents uncultivated country, dry or damp, sand or bog, and is always on the move in low pasture land. It is found along freshwater margins and is not dependent upon trees.

Aviary
A pair should have an enclosure of at least two metres length: the mating flight can be boisterous so if one can manage to build the

enclosure a metre longer it would be more suitable. Allow one and a half metres width and two metres in height. Include a shallow pond in their aviary and the remainder of the base can be grass, except for a small perimeter around the pool which should be shingle. Winter quarters should be attached, with lighting to assist extended feeding facilities.

Food
A basic insectivorous food, with added grated cheese, minced vegetable and root crop should be provided. A few mealworms cut into pieces and mixed well into the food will be appreciated. Give daily feeds of any available live insects but not in any great numbers unless with young.

Breeding
The nest will be made from various grasses and vegetable matter and then lined with animal hair. When young are being reared offer additional mealworms, cut up in the food, ants larvae, moth larvae and young locusts. Fly maggots can be used after treating as usual with a little oil and additives. The nests are sometimes so well hidden in the grass, just under an over-hanging tuft, that it can be exceedingly dangerous to enter the aviary when breeding is in progress.

Rock and Water Pipits (*Anthus spinoletta*)
General Description
Oddly the Latin name is shared in this instance. The water pipit tends to have a more southerly region; it is paler, rather more grey, and has white outer tail feathers; in these two factors it varies from the rock pipit, that bird having grey outer tail feathers and being a little more brownish, though less so than either the tree or meadow pipit. Of typical pipit appearance these races can at first be confused one for the other; the more one handles them, the greater seems the difference though the textbooks usually differentiate between them merely on habitation. The bird that frequents the mountainous areas is referred to as the water pipit, and the one inhabiting rocky coastal regions is the rock pipit. They are both streaked on the upper breast and mantle, the belly being whitish-buff and the water pipit having a distinctly notice-able white eye-stripe. These races are the largest of our European pipits, measuring sixteen and a half centimetres in length. The sexes are very much alike.

Habitat
The rock pipit is more or less confined to rocky stretches of coast, only in winter coming inland during the worst of the weather. The water pipit inhabits the mountainous areas of Europe.

Aviary
Both races use a rather hectic mating flight whilst chasing the female and for this reason a minimum of three metres in length should be planned for, with a width of two metres and an aviary height of the same measurement. A depression in the ground, hidden by vegetation is the normal nest site chosen, or perhaps a crevice but I have known these birds to nest in a half open-fronted nest box at varying heights from the ground. The ground should be shingled with a few decorative rocks and plants surrounding a shallow aviary pool, I have watched many times the small freshwater shrimps being taken by these birds whilst wading, long legged, in such pools.

Food
As for the meadow pipit.

Breeding
Offer coarse and fine grasses, moss, animal hair or fibrous string cut into short lengths and teased-out into single strands. In other respects as for the meadow pipit.

Tree Pipit (*Anthus trivialis*)†***
General Description
Migrant. A rich dark brown, this bird is darkly streaked on head, mantle and upper breast; the background on the breast is a buffish-tan which fades to a white ventral area; the throat is whitish. Sexes are very similar but it is normal for the female breast streaks to extend further down the belly, and the background colour of the upper breast to be paler; the hind claws of this bird are shorter than those of the meadow pipit and curved, making them more suited to its arboreal habits. The length of this bird is fifteen centimetres and it is stoutly built.

Habitat
It is found on woodland heaths, and commons with scattered trees. This is our arboreal member of the pipit family and it will have a favourite song point from which it begins its song; it will then rise steeply and quietly, bursting forth into full song as it

reaches the summit of the song-flight before plummeting earth-wards, singing the whole time, to land back on the same perch.

Aviary
Recalling the flight-song habits, and the mating-chase which precedes true pairing, a three-metre long enclosure should be allowed; this can be two metres wide and of the same height. This type of enclosure will take a stunted silver birch at each end: if the tap-root is cut three times over its first four or five years and it is wired in position it should remain well within the limits of the roof. A small shallow pool, with a sand and shingle bank and grass for the remainder of the base will take care of these birds' aviary requirements for the better part of the year. For the winter they should be given the use of a frost-free enclosure where they can venture outdoors as they wish. This shelter should be provided with artificial light, so enabling extra feeding time to be taken. In this manner and under such conditions tree pipits will live for many years.

Food
As for the meadow pipit.

Breeding
Supply with moss, dry grasses, bents and withered fibrous leaves such as iris, with finer grasses and animal hair for lining materials. In other respects treat as for the meadow pipit.

Grey Wagtail (*Motacilla cinerea*)†**
General Description
With blue-grey upper parts, the male has a black throat during the breeding season. Occasionally, too, I have known females to have this throat marking. The underparts are a brilliant yellow; the very dark wings are tipped with white; the tail also has white outer feathers and both above and below the eye is a white stripe. The female is a little more dull. The length of this bird is eighteen centimetres. The juvenile birds are duller and slightly brownish on the chest, showing bright yellow only on the under tail coverts; the young males are brighter than the young females and paler on the throat.

Habitat
Rarely do these birds wander far from water, streams and old country bridges; old rock walls near streams are all favoured. In

summer they frequent fast-running mountain and hilly rock-bound streams; during the winter they move to lower freshwater areas, even village parks where water exists. It nests in a wall cavity, where a brick may have fallen out, beneath a bridge, in a jutting waste water pipe, or along a steep bank in the roots of a tree overhanging the stream.

Aviary

An enclosure should be about three metres long by one or two metres wide and have an adjoining winter shelter where electric light may provide a little extra feeding time during the winter months. A shallow pond should be incorporated into this aviary, and very near this two or three near natural sites be built for their use; these can be constructed quite easily with water-proof inspection lids: make certain that the interior is dry and not subject to flooding by heavy rain. The inclusion of a few ornamental rocks, an evergreen, a few small flowering shrubs and plenty of moss planted around the edges of the pond should give a pleasant setting. These birds can be allowed to enter and leave the shelter all the year through.

Food

The basis will be the insectivorous mixture, and additions will be grated cheese, minced steamed ox heart and liver, fish and fish roe, cooked and minced in the same way, well mixed with the food. A few mealworms daily can be cut into small pieces and stirred into the mixture. The same treatment should be given to small locusts and moth larvae and any other insects given when no breeding is taking place. Supply daily small quantities of green-food, finely minced; but only occasionally does fruit need to be mixed with the food; they will, however, eat ripe elderberries during the autumn.

Breeding

These are fairly simple birds to breed from, and in fact most of the wagtails are ideally suited to somebody just embarking upon the keeping of insectivorous species. The nest materials to offer are fine twigs, rootlets, grasses, moss and animal hair; dog comb-ings are perfect for this use as they make a good nest lining.

With the arrival of young, double up on the number of cut-up mealworms on the first day they hatch; treble it on the third day, always cutting them into pieces and mixing into the food. At the same time as this increase in mealworms, supply large quantities of small locusts, moth larvae or wood ant 'eggs'. Feeding times now become necessary three or four times per day: as the insects are used, so the containers need replenishing. Maggots should not be used before the young birds are about five or six days of age: then be sure they have been cleaned thoroughly and supplemented with the recommended vitamin/protein/mineral additives.

Pied Wagtail (*Motacilla alba yarrelli*)****

General Description

The most common of our wagtails, the contrasting black and white makes it a most attractive bird to watch. The crown, breast, mantle, back and tail are all black, the more shining jet coloured it is, the better, normally, is the health of the specimen; the cheeks, forehead and underparts are white. The length is eighteen centimetres, and it is rather more stout than the white wagtail which it resembles so closely, though it has a black rump, rather than the grey of the white variety.

Habitat

They are never very far from water, but although often frequenting rivers and fast-flowing streams, they are seen as often on cultivated farm land near a pond or boggy area. During the winter they come into gardens and nearer human activity. It nests almost anywhere from a garden shed shelf, drain pipe, cavity or hole in bank or rock face, to an upturned root of tree, or thatched cow barn, in the thatch or inside.

Aviary

As for the grey wagtail, but offer half open-fronted nest boxes at varying heights.

Food

As for the grey wagtail.

Breeding

As for the grey wagtail.

White Wagtail (*Motacilla alba*)****

General Description
Apart from the grey rump of this bird and the mantle which is of the
same colour, there are few other striking differences between the
white race and the pied during the breeding season. The grey back
is the surest sign, whether in the field or aviary, but even so there
have been many cases of suspected hybridisation so that some very
doubtful cases exist. The pied should have a definite area of black,
mantle to rump, during his breeding season.

Habitat
As for the pied wagtail.

Aviary
As for the pied wagtail.

Food
As for the pied wagtail.

Breeding
As for the pied wagtail.

Yellow Wagtail (*Motacilla flava*)†***

General Description
There are many variants of this bird, the head plumage differing
very widely in some cases, while in others handling seems the
only way for true identification. It is a little slimmer than the
other wagtails. When describing the yellow race, we have in mind
the green-headed bird; there are also ashy-headed, blue-headed,
grey-headed and black-headed races in Europe and their management differs not at all. It has brilliant yellow underparts, with
yellowish-green above, and a yellow eye-stripe. The females of
the various races are difficult to identify and the juveniles almost
impossible. A very dainty bird, it measures sixteen and a half
centimetres in length. Due to a certain amount of hybridisation
which has almost certainly occurred, it can at times be hard to
state categorically the race of some birds observed in the field: I
once had the young of a male bird brought to me; the sire was
almost canary-like, and of the six young birds some were named
as one race and the balance as another, and as this was by two

very experienced ornithologists it illustrates how these races can be confused.

Habitat
It is found in pasture land and open grassland often near water but not essentially so. The nest is built in a depression of the ground where it is hidden by overhanging grass or other vegetation.

Aviary
As for the grey wagtail but provide long grasses over half the aviary base and omit the man-made nest sites.

Food
As for the grey wagtail.

Breeding
As for the grey wagtail.

WOODPECKERS, WRYNECK, NUTHATCH, TREECREEPER, WALLCREEPER

These birds, although grouped together as climbers, vary greatly in management; as would be imagined, the needs of the diminutive treecreeper differ greatly from those of the great spotted woodpecker.

All the woodpecker family, even to the close relative, the wryneck, are coarse feeders; they are long lived when housed wisely and provided with a diet which suits their needs. The woodpeckers themselves, and here I have described only the great spotted and lesser spotted, having only hand reared the Green and Black races in experimental feeding and released them when completed, can all be given the staple mixture to which one can add coarsely grated steamed ox heart and liver, and grated Cheddar cheese. Give them a certain amount of soft fruit and minced vegetable matter, both root crop and greenfood. They do not seem too fond of fish in their diet, whether steamed or raw, but will take it if it is kept to the barest minimum. They enjoy hammering locusts to pieces, even the fully grown ones which, depending upon the race, may grow to twelve centimetres long; indeed they will take everything offered in the way of livefood from the common insects of Europe.

The wryneck is better hand reared as then it will also take everything offered. For adult specimens refer to Part One, 'meating off'. When hand raising these birds give a reliable insectivorous mixture moistened with milk. Every other feed give livefood: if cut-up mealworms are included with the softfood, then between these meals they can have wax-moth larvae and a certain amount of wood ant larvae but the latter must be kept to a minimum, not because of any deficiency or over-richness of the food but due to a habit of the wryneck to become too keen on it and show a tendency towards dependency upon it. Such items as earwigs and caterpillars, may all be given but of most importance is the inclusion of the cheese and minced steamed ox heart and liver. These birds will also take a small percentage of steamed fish and roe if well stirred into the basic mixture.

Treecreepers and wallcreepers can be 'meated off' but once again I much prefer to obtain such birds as nestlings and hand raise them. I would always rather bring up nestlings where a natural rapport is formed, than take adult birds and force them to accept me. These birds can be raised on the same diet as wrynecks, and the rule of keeping ant larvae to a minimum still applies in their case. Always resist that temptation to offer a mealworm to show how tame the birds are; give them only chopped up in the food and be more sure of healthy stock: if cut finely they will flavour the food yet not prove addictive in themselves. Treecreepers will benefit also from a small amount of soft fruit and vegetable matter such as brassica and dandelion being minced and included in their diet.

The nuthatch is odd to this group in that in the winter, as well as taking small quantities of its normal insectivorous food it will become very dependent on its sunflower supply.

Great Spotted Woodpecker (*Dendrocopos major*)†
General Description
This variegated plumage is very beautiful and also distinctive: black is the predominating colour but the addition of white and red makes this a striking bird to view. The breast and underparts are a pale but warm mushroom shade; the throat and cheeks are white but separated beneath the cheek by the black mantle; the crown, back and wings are black, a large white patch is clearly seen on the latter which also show a series of dots giving the impression of wing bars. The male has a red nape and both sexes show the crimson of the under tail coverts. In all other respects they are alike, the male being a little stouter in general appearance and the young having both crown and nape red; the central tail feathers are black and, as with the wings, the outer feathers are dotted with white. The length of this bird is twenty-three centimetres.

Habitat
Broad-leaved forests and coniferous areas both will shelter this bird and although a special preference for coniferous trees is

shown he is still frequently heard 'drumming' in parks and orchards where well-matured trees exist. The nest is in the hole of a tree at any height between two metres and twenty metres from the ground; the base will be covered in wood chippings.

Aviary

In consideration of this bird's long bounding flight, it is a pity to house them in too small an enclosure. They will certainly nest in an aviary of two metres high, but give a greater height where able. The length should really not be less than six or eight metres to fully appreciate their flight and provide them with adequate exercise. I would suggest, after some ghastly experiences of my own, that the enclosure be either made from railway sleepers or metal angle; if the former, it will only have a limited life before some part will require renewal. If of metal, then one can add lengths of fallen birch or other heavier timbers for them to 'play' with, replacing them as required. These charming birds can make debris of a fine enclosure in a very short while. I would erect this bird's shelter in the actual aviary, once again suggesting such solid materials as wooden railway sleepers or telegraph poles.

Food

This is no problem: make the mixture a crumbly consistency or a small lumpy texture, using a little honey to give the right 'feel' to it when mixing. All the additives previously mentioned can be given and the normal daily quota of mealworms chopped up and thoroughly mixed with this. Soft fruit, berries and greenfood such as Brussels sprouts, dandelion, sowthistle heads are suitable; green peas also can be added in a minced condition; a few grated walnuts and brazils can be given when available and a small number of sunflower seeds daily. Some birds will ignore these and others enjoy them. This is one bird that I find does take a fair amount of peanut butter when mixed with its food but, it can be fattening and unless the birds are housed in a large enclosure should not be over-done.

Breeding

My birds always took great delight in taking the nest box to pieces; the bottom was first to go and there they used to roost, inside the box, their tails protruding from the hole; the only consolation was that it didn't need cleaning. These birds were very entertaining, becoming quite good friends. I learned what I could from their presence but as I could not specialise in them to the extent of providing what I conscientiously considered vital for their successful breeding, they were released. I can well imagine these birds accepting a portion of a tree bole that had previously held the nest of one of their kind.

Much patience would be needed on the part of the bird keeper, and if fortunate enough to have young result, then some busy moments supplying the livefood diet for the nestlings. My own birds have always been hand-raised specimens, consequently learning to accept that diet which was provided, to my knowledge suitable for their needs and to them a tasty mixture readily accepted. I have little doubt that they could be reared successfully and probably hand-raised birds would be willing to give certain of the man-made mixture to their offspring.

Lesser-Spotted Woodpecker (*Dendrocopos minor*)†

General Description
Merely the length of hedge accentor, fourteen and a half centimetres, this may lack the red under the tail coverts but it makes up for it in its dainty appearance. The upper parts are black, heavily barred with white; the underparts are brownish-white lightly streaked; only the male has the red crown; the face and sides of neck are white in both sexes; both sexes of the juvenile show the crimson cap. It is not so destructive as the greater bird.

Habitat
A rather shy elusive little bird, it may be seen very high in the branches of conifer and broad-leaved trees, in lightly wooded areas and even orchards; the 'drumming' can be heard in spring but to a far lesser degree than that of the great spotted race.

Aviary
Although quite small, it is an extremely active bird and should therefore be given an enclosure at least three or four metres square, by a height of three metres; the structure, whilst not needing to be quite so fortress-like as that of the previous bird, should still be constructed of metal where possible. If using timber it is always a useful precaution to cover all wooden posts and horizontal timbers with a small mesh wire netting. Once again, where possible, I have always had hand-raised specimens of this bird; it becomes very confiding when reared in this manner and this gives one so much greater opportunity for study or even

general pleasure in watching their behaviour. Whilst not migratory, I have always thought a shelter for their use in the colder months a useful addition to their aviary; it can be built inside the enclosure and allows them to avoid the worst weather if they so wish.

Food
Treat as for the great spotted woodpecker, but offering smaller locusts where these are bred for their use.

Breeding
The inclusion in the aviary of suitable lengths of fallen birch will normally provide them with a nest site to their liking, but man-made boxes will be accepted; the use of the birch is purely a personal preference as I have enjoyed watching them very often excavate a rotten log of birch.

In all manner of feeding the adult birds or for preparation prior to the breeding season, and for nestling feeding, treat as for the great spotted bird but offer correspondingly smaller livefood should nestlings be hatched.

Wryneck (*Jynx torquilla*)†
General Description
I cannot resist allowing a personal preference for this bird to show itself here. It is a bird which has always fascinated me since the time as a child when my father pointed out a nest in a nearby orchard, situated in the hole of an old apple tree: it contained eggs at the time. I was lifted shoulder high to have a quick peep and nearly fell backwards when the brooding hen hissed snake-like at me and darted her head forward fearlessly. Since those days I have hand-reared a number of nestlings and 'meated off' many adult specimens. Where a pair have not nested within a certain time or when a single bird was being held, I have liberated them, readily confessing a sentimental fondness for this bird. Brown all over, a slim elongated bird of sixteen centimetres, it tends to look longer due to the slender build. The plumage varies from a rich dark brown to pale greyish-brown, the background being formed of the latter with the darker shades forming the beautifully marked patterns over the whole body, wings and tail. The breast is decorated with hundreds of small crescent-like markings and the crown, mantle, back, wings and tail have their share of spotting and barring, making this one of nature's won-

ders of camouflage: to see this bird against the bark of a tree is a rare picture; it has a tendency to 'freeze', staying motionless and watching one if alarmed.

Habitat
Open woodland, certainly a tendency more towards broad-leaved tree areas, old over-grown neglected orchard often provides just the right type of natural hole for nesting.

Aviary
To fully appreciate the beauty and gracefulness of this species, an outdoor enclosure of at least three metres in length by two metres both in width and height should be given to a pair. This outdoor aviary must have an adjoining draught-proof shed-type shelter attached; gentle warmth should be provided during the cold months in addition to extra light for feeding later in the day. Both shelter and outdoor aviary will require more vertical old tree boles, with bark intact, than horizontal perching arrangements although the latter should be included. I would suggest two bark-covered posts in the shelter, in opposite corners so offering an individual roost for each bird. The outer enclosure could have a vertical bark-covered pole or tree bole in each corner and one centrally, the latter being shorter, with at least half a metre between the top of the post and the wire roof. This all wire-breeding area should have the four corner sections lightly roofed with rigid plastic so covering the corner posts or tree trunks; the most easily acquired tree boles are the old rotting silver birch trees, they can easily be cut to the lengths needed when in this decayed condition. A shallow pond should be included when constructing this aviary and the base covered with a deep layer of peat or leaf mould. Little growing vegetation is needed but hops growing on one side of the wire enclosure will provide much insect life as well as forming an effective wind-break.

Food
Just so long as one gives a fairly high percentage of animal protein in the diet, the livefood can be almost disregarded for hand-reared specimens. One could not acquire an adult specimen and immediately treat it thus; certainly they can be gradually changed to accept such foods but this takes time and patience. The standard insectivorous mixture, with a minimum of fruit and vegetable matter, generous servings of grated cheese, steamed and

minced ox heart and liver, small quantities of fish and fish roe treated in a like manner will be suitable. Any livefood should be cut very small and mixed well into the food. When wood-ant larvae is obtainable take as much as can be gathered and freeze this for all the year round feeding: not much at a time will be required a pinch per bird mixed into the food will suffice. Greenfly can be shaken over their food dish and will be readily taken.

Breeding
One of my biggest thrills in bird keeping was to watch a pair of these birds go through their mating display: sitting on a perch facing each other they raised their heads high, crests raised, bills open; they shook their heads in nodding fashion up and down for minutes on end, only stopping when they realised that I was watching them. That year I had great hopes of breeding them but an attack of botulism that was experienced by many put paid to this. I have experimented a great deal over the years with various diets for this bird, and have a greater confidence now than ever before; perhaps one year I may be fortunate again. One problem is to know a true pair: in the many that I have studied, each loud calling specimen was the male; each of these was just a little heavier built too. Were these birds given a section of tree which held a natural site, they might well, as mine did, enter and accept this; I had placed decayed wood chippings in the hole in readiness for their inspection.

The rearing of nestlings if ever fortunate enough to have some hatch would be a challenge, but I see no reason why success should not result. Our failing in general, as bird keepers, and would-be breeders is to keep too many species; the breeding time stretches to the limit our insectary production. Specialisation in a limited number of species is a more likely recipe for success.

Nuthatch (*Sitta europaea*)†****
General Description
This was one of my first ever insectivorous species as a child, and they still give me as much pleasure to watch today. Bluish-grey above, crown, mantle, back and tail, the chest should be a rich warm timber-brown; the flanks of the male are a bright reddish-chestnut hue and the ventral area is heavily spotted with the same colour. The female has far less of the chestnut on the flanks and

not so deep chestnut flecks over the vent. The black stripe through the eye and the whitish throat, indeed the general colouring, make them an attractive subject for a garden aviary. The birds' length is twelve centimetres.

Habitat
High in the branches of trees, broad-leaved being the favourite haunts, they can be seen anywhere. It feeds lower in the winter, and will then often visit gardens and take the foods hung up for the tit family. It nests in a natural hole in a tree and will normally mud-up the entrance to allow just sufficient space for their own entry.

Aviary
Allow them an enclosure at least three metres long by one and a half metres wide by two metres in height. Secure two or three log-type nest boxes around the aviary. A shallow pond is always welcome since they enjoy bathing as much as any bird. The remainder of the aviary floor space can be evergreen shrubs and flowering decorative bushes; a few ferns, and for attracting insect life the old favourite climber, hops, may be planted at the rear. These birds will winter outdoors quite well but should have a small roofed section at each end of their enclosure to roost beneath, and keep free of severe frosts.

Food
One of the simplest of insectivorous birds to cater for, provide it with the usual mixture, with all the normal recommended additives. During the winter months this can all be supplied in very small quantities as the nuthatch becomes almost a seedeater at this time; sunflower seed will then form its main diet, together with the cut-up mealworms and adhering particles of softfood, cheese, etc., of which it is extremely fond.

Breeding
A most entertaining bird during the breeding season, the male becomes quite an ardent wooer, calling, and fetching livefood for his mate from dawn to dusk; as the female becomes aware of what is expected of her, she will increase her visits to one of the sites, often having to follow her mate inside to obtain the proffered insect. The nest, if one can call it such, consists of dead leaves, small thin particles of bark and rotting wood chippings all forming a shallow bowl in which she will lay her eggs.

Here again we have a species which, if hand raised, will pass on
to nestlings a certain amount of softfood: the provision of extra
mealworms, cut into small pieces and well mixed, will add their
flavouring to the food and encourage its use. Much livefood in the
form of spiders, earwigs and aphids will be collected from a
climber such as the hop if its growth is encouraged. Other insects
can include maggots, after having been cleaned properly and
treated with the additives. Offer almost anything at this time: it
seems it is hardly ever refused. Give small locusts at first, but if
the size is gradually increased fully grown specimens can eventually be offered and they will hammer them to pieces for their
constantly hungry and calling young. The wax-moth larvae and
other smaller, more soft items are ideal for the bare nestlings just
hatched.

Treecreeper (*Certhia familiaris*)†****
General Description
A brown bird of twelve and a half centimetres length, attractively
marked, rather like a wryneck in pattern, the plumage is palish-
brown on the upper parts, and darkly dotted and streaked in very
evenly marked patterns; the throat, breast and belly are white; the
bill is slender and slightly curved; tail is brown.

Habitat
Of woodland areas, frequenting both broad-leaved and coniferous
trees, it often roosts in bark cavities of red cedar where this exists.
They nest in a cavity behind raised bark, a natural tree crevice or
even behind bark and ivy wherever there is space to hold their
nest of grass, rootlets, moss, wool and feathers.

Aviary
The standard minimum recommended size enclosure will be
adequate to house a pair of these birds; it is advisable to build to
this a frost-proof shelter, which, although it may not be heated,
can provide extra feeding time by having electricity laid on for
the lighting. There is widespread destruction of elm trees due to
the Dutch elm disease and this makes the collection of suitable
large 'sheets' of bark a simple matter: these can be firmly attached
to a dry rear wall of the aviary to form one or more natural
nesting sites. The inclusion in the aviary of a few old rotting
birch tree boles will give these birds a near wild setting and
provide quite a lot of insect life. The growth of a climbing plant

such as the hop will also afford a normal way for them to bathe in the foliage, although these birds will also use a shallow bath.

Food
A very fine mixture is to be supplied with the cheese grated small, the steamed ox heart and similar all minced very fine, four or five mealworms per bird daily chopped finely and well mixed in. The moth larvae can be given alive but also stirred into the food. If obtainable give a pinch of defrosted ants 'eggs' from a frozen source; the dried variety offer little more than roughage and even when soaked first in milk containing Abidec they introduce only what one can quite easily get the bird to take in other simple ways. Fruit can be kept to a minimum but greenfood should be minced finely and added daily; try to offer this in variety, not always giving the same vegetable matter.

Breeding
Breeding these birds for the first time ever gave me great satisfaction. I had experimented with various foods over a number of years, having been granted licences for research work and I had on occasions reared from the day after hatching. It is a time-consuming task and one must ensure warmth at night, this being the vital ingredient to success. To raise birds on a food mixture, to keep them living upon this as a basic food intake, before attempting to breed from them, does help to a certain extent because they are already accepting it as a basic food requirement. I am positive that my pair used some of this mixture daily when rearing their own nestlings. We did, of course, supply quite large amounts of moth larvae in particular and the mealworm content of the softfood was greatly increased too.

Wallcreeper (*Tichodroma murina*)†
General Description
An exceedingly attractive specimen, the crown and mantle are bluish-grey; wings are dark brownish-grey but with very large crimson red patches extending from wing butt almost to the tip, the edges being dark and white spotted; the tail too is very dark with just the outer feathers tipped white; the throat during the breeding season is black like the breast and belly; during the winter months the throat is a very pale greyish-white. The sexes are very alike but on close inspection one finds the female just a little less bright in the crimson and the beak of the male is a

fraction longer. With such slight sex differences one must have two or three birds for comparison. The flight is rather butterfly-like, resembling the hoopoe's. The bill of the nestling is much shorter, not growing to its full length until it reaches independence. The overall length of adult birds is sixteen centimetres.

Habitat
A species of mountainous Southern Europe, it rarely perches on a tree but uses steep rock faces, and gorges where crevices abound, replacing the rock nuthatch at a certain altitude. It nests in rock holes and cavities.

Aviary
Because of its manner of flight and in order to appreciate the beauty of the bird climbing I would suggest an enclosure at least four metres square, with a height of two and a half metres being the minimum. If the aviary walls are constructed to these suggested dimensions giving an area of ten square metres per wall, a natural ornamental rock-faced wall could be built on one, two or three sides, or, using the usual wire mesh, a central large rock pillar-type block could be built in the middle of the aviary and allowing all round flight by the birds. Whichever type of aviary is constructed it must be for the general well being of the inmates and it should always be remembered that this bird rarely uses the normal perch, preferring, as does the nuthatch, a rough-surfaced face to climb. When building a rock face in this manner, it will be found a far simpler matter if an ordinary brick wall is first erected and the ornamental rock built to this when fully dry: cavities for roosting and nesting can then easily be incorporated in such a structure. These birds do appreciate bathing facilities, and I mention this because with a little planning a very attractive setting could be provided for the inmates with shallow pools at different heights, with pumped water cascading from one to the other; advance planning of this nature can make a tremendous difference in providing a near natural habitat and appreciably raises the standard of aviculture. Extra hours of light, for additional feeding time, in a frost-free shelter should not be denied this bird, although artificial heat is not vital.

Food
As this bird almost reaches the snow-line high in the mountains, the food taken by this species in the wild might be imagined as

rather on the coarse side. However, at that height there are many types of insects, even butterflies, and they spend most of their time in nuthatch-like movements darting to crevice after crevice in search of some hidden insect in between the rocks. On the standard insectivorous mixture as previously advised for the tree-creeper they will live for a number of years; if an ivy can be grown in their aviary and trained up a rock face it will encourage many insects: even so, one must tempt these birds to visit the food dish frequently, otherwise they tend to spend all their time searching. The addition of mealworms, moth larvae and small locusts, all cut into small pieces and mixed into the food will normally ensure a healthy daily food intake.

Breeding

The nests that I have seen in the wild were all in rock holes and crevices and constructed of grasses, moss, rootlets, some animal wool and hair and then lined with feathers. I have never had such a bird nest in my possession, the majority of the birds that I have handled being purely for a study of dietetics. The near relative, the treecreeper, nested when I was carrying out feeding experiments and I confess that I really had to do very little to assist them.

STARLINGS, WAXWING, BEE-EATER, ORIOLE, HOOPOE, ROLLER, KINGFISHER, SHRIKES

Though grouping these birds by size some require specialised treatment whilst others can be very coarse feeders.

The starlings will certainly exist on an austere diet, but being a firm believer that 'we are what we eat' and having seen the excellent colours resulting from good feeding I could never condemn this bird to anything less.

Waxwings again have a very hard time in the wild during some winters, not just in Britain but in many countries when a natural harvest of berries fails. These birds will keep in wonderful condition if given, as well as the basic insectivorous mixture, soaked household currants and a piece of eating apple. In the basic mixture should be grated plenty of vegetable matter, brassica and dandelion.

Bee-eaters and hoopoes need plenty of animal protein: build up their basic softfood with extras such as steamed and minced ox heart and liver, fish or fish roe, treated in a like manner. They will also benefit from eating a small amount of vegetable matter daily, plus the usual locusts, mealworms and moth larvae which should be cut and mixed well into the food.

The oriole and roller, whilst sharing this preference for live insects, should also have a few soaked currants, and grated fruit, with the normal daily additions of grated cheese, ox heart and other protein food. These larger birds will also take live locusts but although it is pleasant to observe birds feeding naturally, it is far better for the bird in the long run, for longevity and general fitness, to have all such livefood cut up and mixed with their food.

Starling (*Sturnus vulgaris*)†****‡
General Description
In case any whetting of the interest is needed for this bird, let me

state immediately that the tame starling is very different from wild birds. Especially if hand raised, the plumage itself is a mass of colours high-lighted when hit by the sun: the daily bathing; better food; clean roosting site all add up to making this a more colourful specimen than its wild kin. At twenty-one centimetres this bird is largish and therefore shows a greater expanse of colour to advantage: it is blackish at first glance maybe, but the iridescent hues of green and purple with the spangled spots make this bird quite handsome. If hand raised and housed near a good songbird when they become self-supporting, they will learn to mimic extremely well: we had one male that imitated a goat so well that people used to ask who had a goat nearby. It makes a good parent and I have used one as a foster parent for other birds, one being the rose-coloured starling (*Sturnus roseus*) which a friend brought to me as eggs to place under these birds. It is also a fascinating bird to study.

Habitat
It frequents gardens, woods, cultivated areas, villages and towns throughout Europe.

Aviary
The minimum-sized enclosure is suitable for a pair but these birds have a habit of breeding, so unless wishing to change later, it is advisable to start off with as large an enclosure as one can manage. Bathing facilities are essential and the amusing bathing habits can honestly provide one of the best reasons for keeping these birds. Make sure the aviary floor is a well-drained one. These birds will turn over the soil better than any cultivator. Give a few large nesting boxes: some individuals will roost in them, others will choose the open. Roof over a small portion at each end of the enclosure for comfort.

Food
I am well aware that one can keep these birds on scraps, but when providing the usual diet of insectivorous mixture plus all the usual additives recommended, the gloss on the plumage and hues which reflect the light are all improved. Quite apart from this, if hand raised they remain remarkably tame and confiding, very mercenary really, and will go to most any lengths to obtain meal-worms from their keeper.

Breeding
With the provision of nest boxes, and a bundle of materials hanging up so that one can watch their antics they will soon go to nest. The sexes look very alike at first glance but the male is the brighter of the two. Also when they are in breeding condition study the base of their bills: the male is blue where it joins the head and the female is pink.

When rearing is in progress, they will need the usual multitude of insects; locusts of all sizes are wonderful for starlings; also provide cut-up mealworms in a fair number in their food. Wax-moth larvae just seem to disappear as soon as they are seen. They will rear on worms, and I have seen many acquire various complaints through a diet of these so they should be watched carefully and made to revert to softfood if trouble occurs: this is one bird which will give its young vast amounts of softfood and rear successfully on same.

Rose-Coloured Starling (*Sturnus roseus*)****
(Common Starling reared)

General Description
This is of the same size as the common starling, twenty-one and a half centimetres in length. Although black of head and throat, with wings, rump and tail of the same colour, the mantle, chest and belly are pink. Sexes are similar but the female is paler. Juveniles are very much like the young of the common starling. These birds are crested, but this is not always noticeable as it is not held in the raised position at all times. The female has a slightly shorter crest than her mate.

Habitat
It belongs to Russia and Eastern Europe, dwelling on the grassy steppes, and low surrounding hills and breeds in colonies. It nests in rock crevices.

Aviary
As for the common starling.

Food
As for the common starling.

Breeding
As for the common starling.

Waxwing (*Bombycilla garrulus*)****

General Description

The smooth greyish-brown plumage of this bird must be touched to fully appreciate the softness which exists in a number of northern varieties: it is almost comparable to the feel of goose-down. It has a rich chestnut head crest; pale underparts of grey, slightly tinged with pink; the throat is black; the lower back and rump are grey; the red, yellow and white markings on the wing show up to perfection when close by. The red is of a coral hue and for all the world as though composed of wax; the tail is tipped with yellow; legs and bill are black and there is an eye-stripe of the same colour. The length is twenty-three centimetres, and, seen as a silhouette against the sky when perching, it can resemble a starling until one sees the crest. The sexes are very alike, but upon close observation one will see a longer and wider crest in the male, and this may be perhaps a shade darker. The black throat bib in the male is wide and deep, ending very abruptly, whereas that of the female is more narrow and tends to fade out on the upper breast. The yellow 'tick' marks in the wing also differ: both the downward stroke of the tick and the upward 'cast-off' are far thicker in the male than the female.

Habitat

In the birch forests and tundra areas of Scandinavia and Russia, it may nest colony style in one place one year and a hundred miles away the next.

Aviary

Give a pair an enclosure measuring four metres long by two metres wide and high. Place perches at each end and their food in the centre but shielded from strong sun or rain; each end of the aviary should be roofed for rather more than half a metre and have a small amount of side shelter to prevent driving rain reaching a roosting bird. No other winter quarters are necessary, and providing they are fed correctly they should live for many years. As I write I have a specimen about fifteen years old and still as fit as ever. Site the aviary in a cool spot: it should not be too sunny.

Food

Give daily a handful of soaked household currants, previously steeped in water for twenty-four hours: during summer keep these in a refrigerator to prevent any fermentation due to heat.

Sweet apple should always be available with a small quantity of insectivorous mixture into which has been mixed a little grated carrot, cheese, brassica and about two cut-up mealworms per bird. Never at any time feed worms or live mealworms to this bird. Maggots will often pass straight through this species without being digested. It raises its young in the wild on mosquitoes and cranefly. Under controlled conditions, the first time they were ever bred we managed to obtain large amounts of wood ants' larvae: one hen in particular was so tame that she took these from a moistened finger, raised herself and regurgitated them to the newly hatched young. From this point we had little difficulty: within an hour or so they were using wax-moth larvae and the ants 'eggs' and continued with these foods along with softfood until the young were about seven or eight days old.

Breeding
Since they nest on the colony system in the wild, there is nothing to prevent one attempting this method of breeding them under controlled conditions. In fact at one stage I had seven hens all with nests at the one time and there were about five males in the enclosure, but this was a well-proportioned aviary.

The nesting sites may range anywhere between a metre and two metres from the ground. My birds have nested at all heights within that range and wild specimens frequently have to nest this low because of the stunted trees in the tundra areas. Shelves, clusters of branches and shallow boxes will be used when a female is in breeding condition. At this time the problem is to make them choose a safe site, rather than one in the open or in full view of owls or cats; they have little fear at any time and with breeding condition they assume the tameness expected of northern species. Provide grasses and moss: mine often used dry chickweed and other plant stems; give animal hair and vegetable down: that from sowthistle is frequently used; a few feathers and wool will also be used for the lining.

These birds are late fliers and often at dusk they will hunt moths or small insects and probably mosquitoes as we have always been in the habit of having a pond in their enclosure; they will at this time fly from one end to the other continuously calling their low 'si - i - i - t - si - i - i - t', a low trilling sound.

Their mating behaviour is most interesting and their gift-offering procedure can be fascinating to observe: they will select an item, anything from food to a small piece of twig or leaf, then pass this back and forth between themselves: this can go on for many minutes at a time and all the while they hold a grotesque shape, puffing their feathers from the body like a large ball, raising the head and pointing the tail vertically downwards giving themselves a very exaggerated size and shape. I would say without hesitation that up to the present time I have not found better rearing items than wood ants' or wax-moth larvae for these birds; day-old locusts will be taken but they disappear very quickly in a large aviary, especially if one has a colony of these birds on the look-out for insects. The larvae recommended can usually be obtained or cultured in such vast numbers that one can freely offer them at frequent intervals.

Bee-Eater (*Merops apiaster*)†

General Description

Once this bird has been hand reared one does not forget it easily, not merely because of the vivid hues of its plumage but also because of the mannerisms peculiar to this bird: the enormous gape; the habit of almost swallowing one's fingers if left in the close proximity of the bill; the greed with which they bolt their food at the nestling stage. Despite these failings in etiquette, it grows into an attractive bird of harlequin plumage: the greater part is blue-green; the head and mantle are chestnut, the latter fading on the back to the yellow rump; the throat is yellow and the forehead yellowish-green; it has a dark, almost black, eye-stripe and below the yellow throat a black breast band which separates the throat coloration from the blue of the breast; the shoulder is dark greenish; there is a chestnut patch on the wing and the flights are blue with black trailing edge; the tail is greenish-blue with the central feathers projecting to two separate 'swallow' tail points showing clearly against the shorter remaining tail feathers, which spread on each side. The length is twenty-eight centimetres and the sexes are very similar. I feel that the hen is a shade more dull of plumage and perhaps a fraction shorter in the bill; she is certainly the quieter, or rather, least noisy, when being hand raised.

Habitat

A bird of Southern Europe, mainly Italy and Spain, they colony breed using holes in the banks of streams, sand pits or similar straight faced, sandy soiled terrain.

Aviary

Having considered its habitat, one should give much thought to the shelter to be used during the winter months: this should adjoin the outdoor breeding aviary and will need to be well glazed, preferably from above to allow maximum light to enter; it should have both heating and lighting facilities. Although great warmth is not necessary, a gentle warming of the air is a good thing; artificial lighting will have to provide extra feeding time for these colder months. I would suggest that these birds be allowed the use of the outdoor aviary all the year round, but be able to return to the warmth of the shelter when wishing to do so; a well-illuminated shed will draw them inside even if only to eat from their food dish and this should always be sited indoors. The outdoor aviary should be three or four metres long, by at least two metres wide and high. Where the aviary joins the shelter the roof should be covered for the space of one metre with a clear plastic building material; beneath in the dry, site a large bale of peat which should have a few holes made in it at the sides near the top. If it can be managed, I would suggest this bale be stood on a wooden platform in an effort to keep it vermin free. The holes should be the diameter of a fist. If these are not to the birds' liking they will amend them to suit their needs.

Food

The friendly apiarist will now be needed: ask for any wasted brood comb, or try to obtain a few wasp nests. This is covered in Part One under the heading of insect culturing. Some wasp nests are treated with chemicals and so could be useless but others may in any case be safe as all the grubs, which we now wish to obtain, are sealed in their own little chamber. With a pair of tweezers one can soon draw out these grubs for immediate use or for freezing for later use. These items are extra to our basic softbill food which should receive liberal quantities of the many nutritious additives, plus a little more honey. The mealworms can also be given, a dozen a day per bird, cut into small pieces and mixed well with the other foods. The use of locusts and wax-moths and their larvae should be watched carefully: ensure that the birds are taking softfood and if they seem to drift from it, cut down on the live insects and increase those cut up and mixed with the food.

One cannot of course operate such persuasive methods when the birds have young: then they must have a maximum supply of all possible.

Breeding

The beginnings of the tunnels in the bale of peat would be sufficient for nest sites if a pair of these birds reach breeding condition: they will then excavate this further to the shape and angle they require. No nesting material is needed. The entrances should be started in the end of the bale so that the nest chamber can be situated at a maximum distance from the entrance itself.

Hand-raised specimens are more likely to rear than wild adults taken from liberty: they should also keep to their rearing food to a certain extent and subsequently be less reluctant to offer it at an early stage to any nestlings one is fortunate enough to breed. So many foods can now be stored by freezing that one can build up supplies to quite large stocks in preparation for such events as breeding: it is then a simple matter to de-frost them as required, add to the softfood and offer them together with any live insect specimens.

Golden Oriole (*Oriolus oriolus*)†

General Description

Migrant. A bird of twenty-four centimetres long, the male is a bright yellow with wings and tail of black but showing yellow on the tail's outer feathers; from the bill to the eye it has a small black eye-patch. The female is considerably more dull in appearance, being of a greener hue and only yellowish on the belly. The juveniles are darker still and more dull of plumage. In captivity, without colour feeding it tends to lose some of the sheen despite every effort to maintain the bloom on the plumage.

Habitat

Watching this bird in its native haunts is a thrilling experience in Southern Europe's broad-leaved woodlands, forests and parks, where there are scattered trees. The nest in the wild is a work of art, suspended between the branches of a tree.

Aviary

I have had only one pair of these birds and that was when obtaining them abroad and keeping them until their owner could collect them. I would suggest that a five-metre long enclosure would not be too generous; the height should be above average, perhaps three metres and the width the same, but one must realise that this, if ever obtained, is something very special in aviculture. A real effort would have to be made to breed from them to even justify having them in the first place.

Food

In addition to the basic food supply of man-made softfood, one should include locusts in this bird's diet. It may well be that fresh vegetable matter assists the coloration and we should certainly increase the greenfood included, together with plenty of soft fruit. The usual mealworms should be added daily and despite this bird's size, such items as wax-moths and even smaller insects, are readily taken.

Breeding

I would think that the inclusion of two small apple trees in the aviary would assist one to specialise in the study of this bird and do all possible in persuading it to breed. The nest is slung between two branches; the rim of the nest is woven twigs and vegetable stalks; the nest itself is of grass, plant stems and pithy bark, all interwoven, binding the nest to the rim; the lining of the one I investigated was of fine grass, vegetable down and seeding grasses; quite possibly the materials could vary with the locality.

Any young of this species could be given fairly large insects from hatchings, or newly hatched locusts, cut up mealworms and wax-moth larvae; even small fish could be tried. I have often been surprised to see various, even far smaller, birds, take minnow fry from an aviary stream and have seen some young birds reared on them almost entirely. I have also seen many take tadpoles and small frogs.

Hoopoe (*Upupa epops*)†***

General Description

Unmistakable for any other bird, the hoopoe has, with adulthood, a long curved bill, and a crest which, although often relaxed in the flattened position, can be raised in moments when curious, alarmed or displaying. This when erected as a fan shows the black tips, and a white bar between this and the general colour of pinkish-beige of the lower crest; the head, neck and body, the wings and tail are barred black and white; in flight this bird really does look like a very large fluttering butterfly. The female is very like the male but slightly smaller in stature: the bill, too, is just a shade shorter and the crest not quite so prominent, but these differing features must be seen when in comparison: the sexing of one bird can be difficult. The main call, in other than the breeding season, is 'hoop – hoop' with an extending of the throat; with the completion of the call, the air seems to be expelled with a sound of 'kh-u-u-u-r'. With the attaining of breeding condition in the male he seems to add an extra 'hoop', making it a series of three in his call: the exhaling sound also becomes louder. Two of our hens laid at opposite ends of a long horizontal nest box and the one male present could be heard half a mile away so loud was his call at that time.

Habitat
Orchards, vineyards, wooded areas are its haunts. It is a hole nester, usually using a tree, or hole in a building wall.

Aviary
The enclosure we gave our birds, which were all hand-raised specimens, was about eight metres long. Prior to this we had at one time eight young which we allowed out of their hand-rearing box to fly around indoors. They are a fascinating bird whilst young; their bills are far shorter but these gradually grow so that when ready for liberation into an outdoor enclosure this is almost full length. Bearing in mind their manner of flight, one should endeavour to give them as large an aviary as can be managed. Some frost-free winter quarters are advisable but we allowed our birds the use of outdoor flights all the year round. A little warmth may be necessary but extra feeding time is certainly necessary for complete fitness. The beauty of their flight often drew me to their enclosure after dusk to see them.

Food
Although many aviculturists say that these birds do not drink, and I believe they may get all their required moisture from their food supply, and I have never seen them drink, I did at all times see that they had bathing facilities in their aviary: despite this they continued to dust bathe as always.

The hoopoe throws back its food in a manner similar to a toucan or hornbill: holding the required item between the tips of the bill, it will toss its head back, at the same time releasing the morsel of food so that it arrives at the back of the throat as the head reaches its furthest point back. Remembering this, it will be seen that any softfood taken must be anything but fine: it should be rather lumpy. We gave the usual softfood with all additives such as ox heart, liver and fish with very little fruit, but kept up to the usual quantity of vegetable matter; we also gave a very little finely minced beef and fish, both in the raw state; a little honey was also added and the whole, together with about six cut-up mealworms per bird, became a rather lumpy mixture. Pieces the size of a pea were very easily thrown back by the young birds and this carried on throughout their adult lives.

Breeding
Our birds did not use any nesting materials on any occasion. The nest boxes all contained a few inches of peat, slightly moistened beforehand and the birds merely formed their own depression and laid in this.

For rearing purposes, offer locusts of all sizes; whilst nestlings are very small give newly hatched ones together with any other small insects available. With the pond in these birds' aviary they had a large number of tadpoles and small frogs: we saw them take these on many occasions, much to my wife's dismay, but apparently to the delight of the hoopoes.

Roller (*Coracias garrulus*)†
General Description
Migrant. The roller is very conspicuous in flight or perching, the brilliant plumage immediately identifying it from all others. The head, nape, breast and underparts are blue; the tail is blue with black tips, the central feathers of which are a much darker blue; the wings are dark blue and black tipped and edged; a large bright but paler blue wing patch is very prominent; the back is chestnut. The overall length is thirty-one centimetres. The sexes are very alike, but when compared side by side the female is slightly less bright of plumage and also slimmer. The young are more dull and remind one more of the Indian roller which is far browner in appearance.

Habitat
It likes open country with scattered trees, and usually nests in a tree hole or in a building wall, but is found also in rock crevices. It breeds in Eastern and Southern Europe.

Aviary

The aerial acrobatics of this bird in the wild cannot be performed fully in the normal aviary. Due to the size alone, however, it should be given as large an enclosure as possible; I would suggest that a breeding pair would need an aviary at least eight metres long by four metres both high and wide. These birds will winter outdoors but a draught-proof shelter should be given them, where they can avoid the worst of the frosts and feed in comfort.

Food

All of the birds I have kept have been hand raised: we used locusts, mealworms, and our own insectivorous mixture moistened with milk; steamed fish was mixed into the food at first, and later added raw but minced. Later, when adult, their food varied little but was given drier, of a more crumbly nature, and with added maggots.

Breeding

Although never having attempted to breed from this species, I have seen a number of nest sites: most had a certain amount of old plant stalks, feathers and the usual debris one finds in the case of such hole nesters. There is no true nest. A large box with a suitably sized entrance hole, would, I imagine, be acceptable to these birds: the floor of this should be about eight centimetres deep with a mixture of peat and dampened sawdust or wood shavings.

For rearing one could offer all the usual rearing foods and, due to the appetite of the larger type of birds, I would suggest maggots be made use of after having been treated with a few drops of cod-liver oil, and various powders made up from calcium lactate, Vionate, Casilan and Complan.

Kingfisher (*Alcedo atthis*)†

General Description

Apart from the bee-eater, this is the most colourful British bird: in the sun the upperparts look a brilliant mass of cobalt blue and green metallic hues; beneath it is rich chestnut; the throat is white and a patch of white is very conspicuous each side of the neck; a chestnut stripe runs through the eye and just in front of the eye is a small white splash which even though quite minute, is easily seen when near the bird. The length is sixteen centimetres.

Habitat
It may be found along clean fresh-water streams and lakes where fish abound.

Aviary
I have kept only one family of young kingfishers: these I hand raised while still at school, and I vowed then never to do so again. A suitable enclosure for a pair would have to be six or seven metres long and at least two metres in height and width. We can consider keeping these birds on a natural or on a man-prepared diet: if one were able to collect discarded fry from a trout-breeding establishment or obtain small fish in any other way, in large and regular quantities, the former would be well worth considering; it is useless and cruel, however, to embark on any exercise like this if there is any likelihood of a supply failure occurring half-way through a programme. The reason I mention this under the above heading is that were one keeping these birds under very natural conditions, they should have a pond in the aviary, shallow but long, covering about half the area. If keeping them on a basic man-made preparation, then bathing facilities only are needed. An open-fronted shelter will be necessary where fed on a softfood with a variety of additives but a closed-shed shelter if to be fed indoors during the winter on small fish: this would again have to have some form of shallow indoor pool and very roomy quarters.

Food
When hand rearing a bird it is very easy to give food which would otherwise rarely if ever be eaten; it is a simple matter to persuade a young bird to eat a man-made diet, to grow up on this and so accept it in later life as a natural course.

The five kingfishers which I had were dug from a bank during the excavation and erection of a riverside building not so very far from where the Magna Carta was signed. I took them home and we were fortunate that at that time some damming of a minor stream was going on, with the diversion of the water into another: this meant that the lower reaches were mere mud and shallow pools in which we could gather hundreds of small fish; the pools were so thick with them that a dip into the moving mass with a net meant the capture, literally, of hundreds and buckets were soon filled in this manner.

The first time I gave a feed of freshly killed fish, one bird

passed its excreta, expelled as is normal, but at that time un-
known to me, for a distance of about half a metre; I queried it with
my father as I thought the bird was ill or that I had done something wrong in my feeding method. The smell was not too pleasant and my mother's carpet not exactly the way she most appreciated it. I suggested returning them to the site but my father
replied with, 'You took them, now you look after them.' We
found that by rolling up a sheet of paper and attaching this to the
side of their now three-sided box, they turned each time with
their backs to this make-do tunnel and all was well if one held
one's breath and concentrated deeply upon the end being fed; my
mother's trance-like expression remained aloof for many days but
fortunately my father's sense of humour and appreciation of birds
won the day. The birds thrived despite a young lad pushing
mealworms, fish and soft pellets of a food mixture down their
throats. Every member of the family had a rather pained look
about them when I brought out the birds for a feed: most would
suddenly remember an urgent job elsewhere, or think it time to
take a walk in the garden among the lavender and roses.

With the increase in size came appetites to match. I was young
but can well recall the food mixture prepared by my father for all
our softbills in those days; these birds ate the very same but had
more mealworms, grasshoppers, minnows, sticklebacks and
minced larger fish than any others. The pellets were being thrown
up as fast as I could manage to keep the place clean. I do not
know how many fresh new clean boxes those birds had. The
disapproving looks of all pursued me everywhere; the 'go and
wash yourself' instructions came far more often. I cared little at
the time because these birds, despite their more dull juvenile
colours, were in wonderful condition; I recall well that when my
father gave me a 'well done' they must have really warranted such
congratulations; their bills grew fast, and until we liberated them
were still completely black without the orange on the base of the
lower mandible.

Eventually, despite their quite high food intake of the basic
softbill mixture, we began to give them live fish in an old hip-
bath; they would perch all around the rim, all being housed now
outdoors in a small two-metre long aviary; the heads would each
point at a fish and suddenly, as though the bird had been fishing
all its life, one would make a dive and hammer the fish on the
metal bath rim. The next bird, in such circumstances, would first

beg, then snatch. When all were feeding well they were liberated, but up to that time they had still been eating large amounts of softfood containing minced fish, and cut-up mealworms.

Breeding
Although never having attempted to breed from this species, because of being unable to provide suitable bird accommodation (the ideal would include natural running water), I imagine that with hand-raised specimens, it need not be impossible if one perseveres and specialises in this effort. Few if any species are impossible to breed if first studied thoroughly, then persevered with—this has always been my contention and why I have achieved so many first breedings over the years. Where even pumped water forms a stream and sufficient fish fry can be obtained—perhaps the discarded fry from a commercial operating trout farm—the 'fabricated bank' of one or more bales of peat, well holed, might well provide a suitable nesting site. My own specimens, whilst I kept them, took softfood containing extra fish meal, fish roe, minced fish, cut-up mealworms and a number of other insect items as acquired; I see no reason why, with a regular and plentiful supply of minnows, etc. in the stream such an aim should not be achieved. However, it is certainly not an ambition to be taken lightly.

Great Grey Shrike (*Lanius excubitor*)†
General Description
The largest of the shrikes, at twenty-four centimetres long, the forehead, crown and mantle are a dark pearl-grey; the throat is white; the chest is pale grey fading to white at the vent; a black eye stripe runs from the lores to the ear coverts and this is very prominent, as are the black wings and tail, the wings having a white stripe. The female is more dull and the young even more so: both have slightly barred breasts, though that of the young is more heavily marked.

Habitat
It is found in wooded country, orchards and open forest, normally nesting in thorny bushes or in trees.

Aviary
As it has a strong long flight, rarely settling on the ground, the aviary should be six or seven metres long and two metres in

height and width. At the rear an open-fronted shelter will provide all the necessary seclusion and winter warmth. If one can have a dense hawthorn hedge immediately outside this shelter, but to one side so that it does not limit their flight, it will form a more or less natural nesting site; a little clear plastic roofing over this could prove an advantage. The ground cover should be short, and fairly bare; provide a small pond for bathing. The only specimens of this variety have been hand-raised birds and so were tame. Having handled wild ones abroad, I somehow cannot see a wild bird settling sufficiently to breed in an aviary.

Food
Due to mine having been reared by hand, I have always been able to feed them a basic softbill mixture, with a maximum of animal protein added; in addition we have given full-sized locusts and small mice. They are simple to cater for.

Breeding
Although I have kept about a dozen specimens over the years, I have never attempted to breed from this bird. Certainly much livefood would be required but much of this could be in the form of young mice especially reared for the purpose. They always emptied their softfood dish and they readily accept this once reared upon it.

Provide dry grasses, twigs, rootlets, plant stalks, animal hair, tufts of wool, teased out finely to avoid accidents, and finally feathers. I lost a hen once through becoming entangled with sheep's wool and apart from the regret at a loss through care-lessness, it is extremely frustrating to raise a bird to reach this peak condition, only to see it die.

Red-Backed Shrike (*Lanius collurio*)*
General Description
Migrant. A handsome bird, the male has a blue-grey head and rump, rich chestnut back, a long graduated tail of black with white feathers at the side; a wide black stripe runs through the eye from lores to ear coverts; the throat is white, this becoming a pinkish-cream on the breast and underparts. The female lacks the facial stripe and is mainly brown. Juveniles and the female share small crescent markings on the underparts. The adult length is seventeen centimetres.

Habitat
It frequents scrub and heathland with scattered trees, frequently nesting in hawthorn or shrub.

Aviary
In a small aviary one would lose much of this bird's natural beauty particularly of the flight, the hovering when spotting a morsel of food on the ground. It rarely stays on the ground for long. Provide an enclosure similar to that for the great grey shrike, but remember this bird should have either a frost-free shelter or be moved into an indoor flight during the winter when extra feeding time will be greatly appreciated.

Food
As for the great grey shrike.

Breeding
As for the great grey shrike.

Woodchat Shrike (*Lanius senator*)†**

General Description
The male is a most striking specimen when in full breeding plumage, with rich chestnut crown and nape, the black forehead and cheeks, the underparts, rump and wing bars white like the nostril patch and outer feathers and under-flue and tip of tail. The female, although bearing the same colours, is far more dull and less conspicuous. The juvenile is very similar to the young red-backed shrike but shows very pale patches on the wing where the white will be at a later date. The length of an adult is seventeen centimetres.

Habitat
Woodland areas, orchards, olive groves, open ground with scattered trees provide haunts. It builds a rather clumsy typical shrike nest in the outer branches of a tree.

Aviary
As for the great grey shrike, but with a closed shed-type shelter for winter use where it can have extra feeding time and a little gentle warmth if necessary. This variety seems to feel the cold a little more than the red-backed shrike.

Food
As for the red-backed shrike.

Breeding
As for the great grey shrike.

DIPPER, SWALLOW, MARTINS, SWIFT, MOORHEN, LAPWING, PARTRIDGES, PLOVER, SPARROW

Rather than have many separate groups, these birds have been placed together for convenience, since all are a little out of the ordinary for the usual aviary inmate and rarely studied in aviculture and although the diets are varied with none apart from the dipper has any difficulty been experienced.

The dippers were hand-reared birds which grew well, and the plumage looked perfect as they reached their self-supporting age: in fact they were as good as any wildling. A little later, however, I despaired of them; whether at liberty they have a state of untidiness just prior to the moult I do not know but I have never seen one looking quite so like a feather duster as mine did.

Swallows, martins and swifts all prove excellent subjects to hand raise: so many fall out of nests that I feel sure many others have shared my experiences with these birds but perhaps not many have wintered them, releasing them as fully adult specimens the following spring.

Plovers and moorhens are interesting to rear and having humans as foster parents seems to appeal to them far more than to most species. The swallows and martins chattered excitedly in groups upon the arrival of a human with food, but the plovers and moorhens were devoted, almost dog-like, in following one, their little legs working nineteen to the dozen and falling over in the panic to follow and keep up.

Dipper (*Cinclus cinclus*)†
General Description
Eighteen centimetres long, this bird is easily identifiable when seen in midstream on a rock where it spends much of its time bobbing and curtseying then diving into the fast-running water to

appear some distance from where it went under. Shaped rather wren-like but far larger, it is very dark brown above, with the throat and chest pure white; the belly is rufous, rich in colour but fading to dark brown in the ventral area.

Habitat
It is found near fast-flowing hill and mountain streams where pebbles, never mud, cover the bottom.

Aviary
I have kept a few of these birds, but have never been able at the time to provide a natural setting of shallow running water over a stone-strewn stream bottom. I would suggest, however, that some considerable thought is given to the planning of an aviary with much research being done on their natural habitat and general needs. A two- to three-metre stretch of water by one or two metres wide, pumped in a re-circling motion, with the introduction of a host of wild water insects, could well make these birds feel more at home. Mine were all hand-raised specimens and took our standard food mixture with the usual additives. After providing them with a daily bath, they would after a period of months look a little wet and miserable: they were not unhappy but something was evidently not quite right physically. On the other hand, when offering a bath for short periods, or only twice a week, they looked dry, but still miserable after the same length of time. The appetite was good and I varied the food extensively. I believe that the correct aviary conditions could make a vast difference. Give plenty of ornamental rock surroundings. The rear and sides of the aviary, if constructed of brick, could be rock faced and have nesting sites, holes about twenty-five centimetres in diameter built into them; this, covered in ivy, would be ideal and far from unattractive. I would suggest an open-fronted shed-type shelter be attached for their use, when they so wish, and perhaps extra light in winter, but they require no heat.

Food
I gave our standard mixture, with ox heart and liver steamed and minced, fish both raw and steamed and fish roe in its natural state. Cod-liver oil was added, along with plenty of calcium to replace the crustaceans taken in the wild, plenty of vegetable matter, even increased amounts of sea-weed in lieu of algae and also for the extra minerals so provided; many freshwater shrimps

were given in shallow dishes but at that time I did not offer small minnow fry. I was not altogether happy with the results: the birds ate well and visitors used to congratulate us upon their appearance but when one has lived for years with birds, eating, sleeping and dreaming them, a niggling feeling that all is not quite as it should be grows until a decision is made to release the subjects and start again another time when one has had more time to study the wild specimen. Perhaps one day another opportunity will arise.

Breeding
The netting of a wide variety of water life is a simple matter and the dedicated bird keeper will never hesitate if a bird such as the dipper is being kept. The stream as previously advised must be well stocked and perhaps one or two smaller inlets could be added so that these stillwater sections could encourage more prolific breeding of insects. If the hand raising, as I experienced, was so simple, why should adulthood bring problems when normally the reverse occurs; maturity, after rearing on a good basic food, is usually a trouble-free time.

The nesting materials in the wild are grasses, moss and dead leaves; the nest is a large domed structure with the entrance hole pointing to the water just below it. Perhaps I was too self-critical at that time; we sometimes expect too much; had I kept the birds, instead of releasing them, they may have moulted into perfect adult specimens.

Swallow (*Hirundo rustica*)†*
General Description
Migrant. The long wings and forked trailing tails are probably well known to most people observing wild birds. It has glossy blue-black upperparts, a rich chestnut throat and forehead; the tail with the long outer streamers is marked with white; the underparts are white, softly tinted with pink. The juvenile has noticeably shorter tail fork. The adult length is nineteen centimetres.

Habitat
Seldom a city bird, they frequent more open country, where they are to be seen soaring elegantly whilst taking insects on the wing, or swooping low over water where much of their food is taken

from the surface. I had a pair nest over my bed in a Nissen hut when in the army: they swooped in through a broken ventilator to a shelf where I kept a few books, and there they nested. Stables, mills, granaries, anywhere that entry is available through an open window or door are the favourite sites: there they will use the upper surface of a beam or rafter, or even a brick ledge.

Aviary
Unless being kept for some sphere of research, or being hand reared if fallen from the nest, or for some special project, any aviary always seems to limit them too greatly. All mine over the years have been hand-raised specimens: some we have wintered in roomy birdroom flights, liberating them in spring, but when housed outdoors the great consideration was given to their needs, and the maximum I could allow them was about nine or ten metres, by something like three metres wide. Ours used taut string perches and shelves, and the enclosure had a small pond where they frequently swooped to gather flying mosquitoes. Not once did I see them grounded outdoors: I did see it once indoors when entering the birdroom very early; one was waddling, and I can explain it no other way, across the floor.

Food
When these birds are hand raised, diet is no problem: it is provided by a good basic softfood, a little finely minced dandelion or similar vegetation, steamed and minced ox heart and liver, a few chopped-up mealworms and moth larvae all well mixed together into a crumbly moist food. The food receptacle should be placed only just below the perches, not beneath them: they can be some way away, but only a little below their perch level. Their water dish, too, if indoors, should be at least a metre from the floor, and be a large shallow container: they will frequently do a 'belly flop' into this, hardly pausing in their flight but getting sufficiently wet to satisfy their wish for a bath. With regard to these containers for food and water, I found that the most convenient forms were wide and shallow but having a definite upward pointing rim: mine were the white-enamelled metal-type used for cooking in the oven. Mealworms cut up small, and wood ants' 'eggs' seem favourite items when fed to this bird over a long period. When hand raised, the swallow will readily adapt to a man-made food and I have always endeavoured to keep them on as much softfood as possible, with all insects cut small and mixed

well in it, for fear that they might revert quickly if given the opportunity to hawk for livefood. I must admit that this has never happened with those that I have kept: ours invariably took the mixture even after having been flying in the outdoor enclosure and brought in for the winter.

Breeding
The only birds we have wintered were hand-raised specimens: wild adults have always recovered from their accidents prior to the migratory departure time and been released; there have been occasions when young birds handed in to us as casualties have been so badly soiled and ill through well meaning people trying to keep them for a short period, that their plumage, even upon becoming self-supporting, was not considered adequately airworthy for migration. These birds were the ones wintered in the birdroom; in early spring they were released into an enclosure which housed waxwings, a very docile bird and all went well until the swallows (there were three on that occasion) began taking nesting materials to a shelf beneath the roofed section. As fast and as hard as they worked, so the clumsy waxwings knocked down the nest foundations from the shelf: it had always been one of their favourite roosting or resting sites. The swallows were taking insects on the wing so we liberated them and as it was then only the end of March it is well possible that they bred that year.

House Martin (*Delichon urbica*)†
General Description
Migrant. At one time it was extremely common but is nowadays far less so. It cannot be mistaken for a swallow since it lacks the tail streamers of that bird; the tail in this instance is a very short fork. The upper parts are a dark blue-black except for the white rump; the underparts are pure white. Juvenile plumage is browner. The adult length is twelve and a half centimetres. I always feel that swallows and martins have rather pretty faces: large eyes and dainty bills give them a most attractive look.

Habitat
They will be found near human habitation, using the under-eaves of a house to build their nest. In more open terrain they will use outcrops of cliff or rock face. They are a little more gregarious than the swallow, frequently nesting in large colonies on houses close together. They are most familiar to all as a bird that wheels

and dives in its acrobatic flight after insects or when about to
enter its nest.

Aviary

Apart from keeping 'fall outs' which have been handed in for safe
keeping and the odd adult or so from accidents, I have never had
these birds from choice, for, like the swallow, they seem to suffer
from confinement. Once again they have, when being cared for,
had as large an enclosure for their needs as could be spared. On
one occasion I could only offer an indoor flight of two metres
square but even in this very limited area the birds circled and
dived, 'belly flopped' in their water and even landed to bathe
daily. The few that I have wintered have been simple to care for
since these were hand reared, but even adults can be persuaded to
take a surprising amount of softfood when they realise plenty of
insects are mixed in with it.

Breeding

I have had no experience of them breeding other than being
aware that two birds had paired and were carrying mud: at this
point they were released. Their behaviour at this time was interesting: my whole family, more or less, happened to be in the garden at
the time and my wife and daughter each released one or two
birds. For what must have been ten minutes afterwards, the
house martins flew low backwards and forwards over our heads in
gradually increasing flight distances. They commenced with
about three or four metres in a to and fro movement, gradually
increasing this till they were almost out of sight, only to reappear
for a few seconds over our heads before vanishing in the other
direction. With a suitable aviary and an acceptable diet, I have
always said that any breeding is possible and it may well be with
house martins but the enclosure would certainly have to be a
comfortably spacious one.

Sand Martin (*Riparia riparia*)†

General Description

Migrant. The smallest of this family and probably the one least
seen, its tail is only slightly forked and is rounded at the outer
limit; the underparts are white, except for a broad brown chest
band; the upper parts are a sooty-brown. The length of this bird
is twelve and a half centimetres.

Habitat
It is found near water in open country where it excavates a hole in a vertical sand bank or disused gravel pit or quarry.

Aviary
Having only hand raised these birds when they were brought to me, and only housed them in an aviary for a short period, just long enough to be sure that they were taking wild insects, I am not very familiar with them. They would need a very large enclosure.

Food
For some reason they do not seem to take as much softfood as either the swallow or house martin: they will eat it readily enough when being reared as young but once fully self-supporting they tend to scorn the mixture and select from it all the insect life. They would probably eat a large enough amount if gradually introduced but I have always liked to see birds eat a softfood with a hearty appetite. Feed as for the swallow.

Breeding
Breeding this bird would be quite a challenge. If one decided to study these birds closely in confinement, even the presence of a large expanse of water would encourage far less insect life than they would require; even a suitable nesting bank would be hard to construct and whether, being a colonial nester, they would require more than one pair to 'trigger off' any breeding impulse is difficult to decide.

Swift (*Apus apus*)†
General Description
Measuring sixteen and a half centimetres in length, this bird has a forked tail but it is far shorter than that of the swallow, with no streamers, and the fork is held very close together. The long wings are scythe shaped. Predominantly dark brown, at the throat it shows greenish-white. The aerial performance is so fascinating as a group wheel and dive with the excited squealing so well known to the villager, that a description seems wholly inadequate to convey its beauty.

Habitat
It is extremely widespread, nesting in cavities of cliffs and buildings in much the same manner as a swallow. A shallow cup is

built on some supporting ledge and made from straw, feathers and a wide variety of materials all collected during the bird's aerial acrobatics and whilst the material itself was airborne. These materials are stuck together with saliva.

Aviary

On the very few occasions I have hand raised these birds and kept them until they were completely self-supporting, they were barely in an outdoor aviary for more than two or three weeks, and I have noticed that they seem to pick up the habit of catching a moving insect even quicker than swallows or martins; the head swivels and by the time one has pin-pointed what the bird is looking at, it is eaten. They are so quick, even whilst being hand reared, that the movement of a fly in the vicinity will cause all the heads to swivel, following every movement of the insect. Anyone having seen this bird will appreciate that a large enclosure would be vital: my indoor flight for a brood of these was only about two metres long by one metre wide and they managed to manoeuvre extremely well in this small space but it was obvious that anything small outdoors would be totally inadequate for their needs.

Food

As for the swallow, but double the mealworm content of the softfood.

Breeding

My knowledge of their breeding habits, limited to observations of wildlings, does not really permit me to advise on the subject. The collection of materials for the swift, the fastest flying of the group of small aerial species, poses immediate difficulties and one would encounter many more. An open-fronted shelter adjoining an exceptionally long outdoor aviary, and a keeper willing and wishing to specialise—a person dedicated to the needs of the birds, with time to spare—may make a possibility of breeding the swift. It was not so very many years ago that the keeping and breeding of many native birds, where success has been achieved, would have been doubted and considered well beyond one's wildest dreams.

Moorhen (*Gallinula chloropus*)****

General Description

This is so common everywhere that I feel sure most can identify this bird upon sight: the upper parts are almost black, seen to be a dark brown when handled; slate-grey underparts with a distinct white line along the flanks join the white undertail coverts; the bill is red at the base and this colour extends to the forehead. The female is more dull in appearance. The length is thirty-three centimetres. It is very territorially inclined where other moorhens are concerned.

Habitat
It is found in town or country wherever there is a stretch of fresh water or swamp, where it feeds upon the grassland adjoining water.

Aviary
Providing the aviary is at least four metres long by about two metres in both height and width, and most important, a pool of water is provided, a pair can be kept and studied quite simply. A pair will breed in a small enclosure of this size but if kept for other than educational purposes where one wishes to watch them at close quarters, they should have a far larger enclosure consisting of grass and pond only. An open-fronted shed will be used by them during the colder months.

Food
Our young birds were incubator hatched, then housed under an infra-red heater, where they received finely chopped dandelion leaves, comfrey, brassicas, watercress, chopped mealworms, maggots and crushed turkey starter crumbs. As they grew we gave them the standard softfood mixture, trying always to give a little more vegetation than normal. They grew particularly fond of mealworms and would follow me in dog-fashion wherever I went in the garden. They ran so fast when small that their little legs would trip them up. If I walked at a normal pace the length of the garden path, they would almost all have fallen over somewhere *en route*, in their efforts to follow as closely as they could.

Breeding
Until I kept these birds I had never realised to the full just how pugnacious they can be towards their own kind with the arrival of spring. Almost as soon as the Christmas season was over so they began in earnest. The two birds which we retained cannot be called a true breeding pair; they used an old mud patch in the garden which we kept topped up more or less daily with the hose. I suppose it would have been in the region of two metres in

diameter, certainly well under half a metre deep and was situated just rear of a lawn behind some bushes; since they were more or less reared by hand, these birds were remarkably tame. Even the specimens we released in a local park had not wanted to stay behind when we walked away. We had selected the two most confiding of them and they roosted that first winter in an old dog kennel given to me by a neighbour. We kept this beneath the bushes adjoining their 'pond'.

As a child I appreciated their first nesting attempts as it coincided with my birthday and at that age it conjured up all kinds of thoughts. I was led to expect no successful rearing by my father who said it was quite possible they would not succeed in fertilising any eggs until two years old. Seven eggs finally appeared on a typical moorhen nest which had been built on our foundation of old bean sticks, broken, and pushed well into the mud bottom of the pool: we gave them old flag and iris leaves but I think they used as much other plant vegetation as these. Seven young eventually hatched but within two days three had disappeared without a trace, whether one of the crow family (we were living in very rural surroundings at the time) was responsible, I never knew. When we moved from that area to a far more suburban locality we had to release the adult pair and the young, the last I recall seeing of them was the pair sedately walking towards their new pond abode with the four young running behind in much the same way as I remembered the older birds following me the previous year.

Lapwing (*Vanellus vanellus*)

General Description

This bird, with the long curved crest and plaintive call in the fields, should be familiar to all. Seen in their groups, quite large flocks at times, in my own childhood, I cannot imagine them being strangers. At a distance it looks merely black and white but upon close inspection it will be seen that the mantle, wings and breast are dark green with a rich metallic purple sheen; the underparts are white as too are the cheeks. During the breeding season they have a black throat which moults to white afterwards. They have a splash of chestnut in the wings and also on the upper and tail coverts. The length is thirty centimetres.

Habitat
They frequent fallow and cultivated ground, marshy fields, open moorland and are often seen on mud-flats.

Aviary
A six-metre length by two metres both in height and width, would hold a pair of lapwings. The base should be well pebbled over two-thirds of the area and a shallow pond and a few sedges and clumps of reed should be provided. To the rear of this allow grass to grow. At the far rear of the aviary should stand an open-fronted shed and it is here that one provides their food.

Food
To simplify feeding we gave these birds our standard softfood plus all the usual additives. A wide dish held their daily ration and they always finished it apart from a few fine crumbs. When using a basic mixture it is a fairly simple matter to add or exclude certain items as one goes the rounds of the aviaries with the numerous small containers. To feed lapwings on such a rich diet may seem on the lavish side, but they were in excellent condition and bred in the collection to which I gave them.

Breeding
If the aviary is laid out as suggested above, little difficulty should be encountered. The insect content of the food will have to be increased considerably once young are hatched, but the chicks will soon learn that the dish contains what they are looking for and grow quickly, becoming completely independent in about five weeks.

Partridge (*Perdix perdix*)
General Description
It has brown upper parts, with the head, tail and flanks more chestnut hued; the breast is grey with an upside-down chestnut horseshoe on the lower breast; the legs are blue-grey. It is thirty centimetres in length.

Habitat
It is found on moorland, heaths and arable areas but also in semi-desert.

Aviary
As for the lapwing.

Food

Partridges eat an enormous amount of vegetable matter, but also take seeds; we offered very little except screenings, but our staple softfood mixture was taken readily at all times, probably because the chicks had been brought up on it. Needless to say we gave extra vegetables such as brassicas, dandelion, spinach and grated carrot as well as plenty of animal protein. Maggots seemed always a favourite, and though we rarely gave mealworms, we found that they like young locusts.

Breeding

If the aviary is arranged as for the lapwings, the tall grass at the rear will serve their purpose for nesting: with the arrival of young increase the livefood supply and give plenty of greenfood.

Red-Legged Partridge (*Alectoris rufa*)

General Description

The white throat and black spotting on the upper breast just below the black breast band identify this bird at a glance. This bird is larger than the common variety at thirty-four centimetres long. The underparts are chestnut and the bluish-grey flanks show heavier barring in black and chestnut. The bill and legs are red.

Habitat

It has a taste for rather wilder country than the common partridge.

Aviary

As for the lapwing.

Food

As for the common partridge.

Breeding

As for the common partridge.

Little Ringed Plover (*Charadrius dubius*)

General Description

Migrant. This bird has a narrow white line above the black forehead-stripe; it has a black bill with yellow on the lower mandible; the upper parts are light-brown; the underparts are white. When not in breeding condition and showing the black crown and ear coverts the male is much browner. The sexes are alike but the female's black head markings are browner during the breeding season. Their length is fifteen centimetres.

Habitat
They frequent freshwater shingle slopes, river and gravel pit banks.

Aviary
As for the lapwing.

Food
As for the lapwing.

Breeding
The shingle area of the aviary will be readily accepted once the inmates are sufficiently tame. Any young hatching will need a considerable increase in the livefood, as well as the chopped mealworms in the softfood; offer maggots and very small locusts, with wood ant 'eggs' and similar food.

House Sparrow (*Passer domesticus*)†****‡
General Description
When viewed closely, watching a tame specimen, this bird is found to be not unattractively marked. It has a chestnut mantle and grey crown and rump; the male's black throat, the cheeks and underparts are greyish-white. The female lacks the grey crown and black throat but both are darkly streaked on the back in a pleasant pattern. The length is fourteen and a half centimetres.

Habitat
Wherever humans work or dwell so too will this sparrow; it can be a cluster of shacks miles from anywhere but they will soon join the community.

Aviary
A caught house sparrow is very wild and shy and in fact many aviary-bred specimens are just as unruly and nervous. The best method is to hand raise a nest of them if wishing to obtain a pair. An aviary for one pair can be the standard minimum enclosure. A wooden nest box as supplied for the tits should be placed in position well in advance of the breeding season. Ensure the hole is sufficiently large for entry. The layout of the aviary need be nothing

special and can be decorated purely for visual pleasure, roses are always useful in so far as they attract greenfly which this bird welcomes when breeding, and hop plants at the rear will also serve this purpose.

Food

I suppose that I have had quite a number of house sparrows over the years. On two occasions I have had quite large collections of the fawn mutation, and at one time a silver. Our method of feeding was to offer the waste seed from the finch enclosures and, as a basic diet the same insectivorous mixture that we gave our softbills. If this diet is maintained throughout the year and one commences with hand-raised specimens, the aviary inmates can provide quite a lot of interest and pleasure.

Breeding

When the aviary is laid out as above and nesting materials comprise grasses, moss and feathers nesting should occur. They will use bits of tissue paper, string and much rubbish when at liberty, but some of these items cause the entanglement of young in the nest.

When young are being fed, they will require plenty of livefood: young locusts, greenfly and moth larvae have been used successfully.

Tree Sparrow (*Passer montanus*)

General Description

Measuring fourteen centimetres in length, it differs from the house sparrow by the chestnut crown, yellowish rump and far smaller throat marking: in this case there is a mere black bib; there is also a small black cheek patch which is absent from the other bird.

Habitat

Orchards and parkland where scattered trees exist provide favoured haunts. It nests in tree holes, thatched roofs and similar sites.

Aviary

Being a rather shy and retiring bird by nature, it is better to hand-raise a pair than take wildlings. Bearing this in mind one can provide the minimum-sized enclosure so that their behaviour can be observed. It is advised that hops are grown against a rear wire section.

Food

This is another instance where the waste seed mixture from the finch aviaries can be put to good use. Together with this we have provided a dish of softfood as supplied to the insectivorous species. Screenings when available are eagerly turned over by the tree sparrow, but many insects are taken as well and any chopped mealworms in the softfood are soon removed; locusts at the twenty-four hour stage seem a favourite; this may well be because they resemble a grasshopper so much.

Breeding

Treat as for the house sparrow.

CORVIDS, HAWKS AND OWLS

The crow family make quite intelligent pets; they are well capable of having a sense of humour and can be as mischievous as a kitten. One or two flying loose that have been hand raised, just so long as the garden is large enough and no neighbours feel belligerently inclined towards them, can give a great deal of pleasure. Never tease them or allow children to do so as they are not noted for their patience and if hurt can become aggressive in their ways; it is only through such maltreatment that I have ever known one to be spiteful. They can certainly be kept in a large aviary, and be bred from, the diet causing no problems whatsoever.

Hawks are a really specialised subject. I have kept kestrel, sparrow hawk, buzzard and merlin but only the first for any length of time: the others were hand reared and passed over to other people. I am not in favour of liberating predatory species when hand raised: it certainly can be done but the training enabling the bird to hunt and live by its catch is a considerably long and involved procedure and requires someone to have a close affinity with these birds: too many such birds starve when freed by well meaning but not fully understanding people. All of these species can be housed in aviaries, long enclosures six or seven metres long by two metres wide and high, which should have a shelter attached with an entrance hole large enough for the bird to effortlessly pass through when in flight; they will invariably breed in the shelter if a box is secured in position for them.

Owls are birds which one seldom keeps just a pair of: having hand raised a fair number over the years, I must admit that I am not really very fond of these birds: the only variety which I have kept for any length of time and had young from were scops owls: these were hand reared like all the others, but when my wife hand fed eight of them from their fluffy stage when they looked like dandelion heads she fell head over heels in love with them.

Whereas hawks have a shed-like shelter with an entrance hole, crows and owls need only an open-fronted type of shelter: it should lead off to a long flight. Apart from the exercise essential to a healthy bird, the beauty of their flight, of any bird in flight, is one of the great pleasures of keeping and studying them.

Small children ought not to enter the enclosure housing hawks or owls unless they have played an active part in hand rearing the birds concerned and there has been no time break in that contact or relationship. Especially during the breeding season, all these birds can become very territorially minded and some hand-reared specimens will then attack purely from instinct. Others, where a rapport exists, will allow themselves to be lifted from eggs and gently replaced.

Carrion Crow (*Corvus corone corone*)**
General Description
This differs from the rook in that it has no bare face patch between eyes and bill. The crow shows a glossy green sheen, not so black and has thigh feathers which fit tightly as compared to those of the rook which resemble rather baggy plus-fours. This large all black bird measures about forty-seven centimetres but I have seen them larger. Although rather ungainly in movement on the ground and of heavy flight both taking off and when in the air, it makes up for its clumsiness by becoming very attached to anyone hand raising it; the sidling up and nuzzling are all very mercenary of course.

My wife once found a young crow, a 'fall out', whilst out walking with the dogs and the very first thing she could lay her hands on upon returning home, for the poor creature was nearly starving, was some cream crackers: these she quickly dipped in milk and the bird gulped the pieces down as though there was no tomorrow. Every day of that bird's stay with us it had to have some of this food: my wife would place four or five dishes in its cage, one containing softfood and minced ox heart or liver, one holding bread sop, another with mealworms and maggots and so on; the bird would sidle along the dishes looking in each and if there were no cream crackers it would turn and get a little piece of skin of my wife's hand and twist it and then just stand and look at her, waiting for the hidden dish containing its firm favourite. Fond as I am of this biscuit with cheese, it is not very nutritious for bird feeding and I cannot advocate its use!

Habitat
Farmland, parks, moorland and fields adjoining cultivated land
are all frequented where they find much of the carrion, vegetable
matter, insects and small animals that form their diet. They often
take small game birds on the ground.

Aviary
An aviary of at least six metres length, with the height and width
both being about two metres and an open-fronted shed at one end
to provide a shelter will provide all this bird will require. Where
the bird roosts or sits outdoors, I would suggest a perch at each
end of the enclosure; the immediate underneath should either be
cemented to allow daily hosing or have large pebbles to a depth of
30 cm, which can also be hosed and raked over now and again.
The shed also should have a concrete base: if one or two courses of
bricks are laid before the shelter is erected on top, the hosing will
in no way cause deterioration of the timberwork. The perches
should consist of natural branches; try to give them of varying
thicknesses, with the bark still on and renew them once a month.
A pond in their aviary will always be much appreciated; this need
be just a hollow in the soil with a cement covering, with the water
renewed daily.

Food
I have often used our own softfood as a base and added a wide
variety of other foods but a more economical manner of feeding
is to use turkey crumbs, moistened with milk, to which can then
be mixed raw grated root crop, swede, turnip, carrot, parsnip,
greenfood such as grated Brussels sprouts, dandelion, spinach and
comfrey. Almost any left-overs from the table can be put through
the mincer, and these may include meat and gristle, bacon rind,
liver, fish, sausage, any fruit, cheese and rind. Stale milk can
always be used on their food, and a little wholemeal bread or cake
and broken biscuits given in moderation; the occasional portion of
canned dog meat will also be taken. Needless to say maggots and
mealworms are accepted at any time. Small fish will be taken
from a shallow dish; an angler friend often used to give us a few,
up to about fifteen centimetres, which were soon broken to pieces
and eaten.

Breeding
In the shelter at the rear secure a box about sixty centimetres

square and fifteen centimetres deep; cover the base with thin beech or birch twigs and supply many more twigs in the outdoor aviary where the rain can keep them supple. The nesting box should be about half a metre below the shelter roof allowing plenty of room for entry when flying straight to the nest from outside. Once the twigs are being carried inside offer plenty of moss, plant stems and dried chickweed, then animal hair, wool and feathers; always keep any wool cut into small lengths to avoid accidents and entanglement. If a pond has been included in the aviary and allowed to keep the surrounding earth damp, they will collect their own mud for the construction when binding the twigs and other coarse materials together in the initial stages.

For the successful rearing of young one must increase the animal protein: day-old chicks from the sorting sheds of a hatchery, mice, minced offal, fish and a rabbit cut into small sections can be offered; almost anything is taken at this time. To the basic food add some Abidec, calcium lactate, Casilan and Complan.

Jackdaw (*Corvus monedula*)†****
General Description
This is the smallest of our crows, and another bird which makes a wonderful pet. As a child I do not think that I was ever without one or two around the place: I suppose many of them reverted to nature with the arrival of the breeding season but there were always others to take their place. It is black, with the nape grey and this silvery-grey in comparison to the jet glossy black gives the bird a most attractive appearance; the eye too is very intelligent looking. They are well known for the manner in which bright objects catch their eye and the way in which they have often taken and hidden such items. It is about thirty-five centimetres in length.

Habitat
Towns and villages provide its main haunts and it is often found in the vicinity of very large buildings such as cathedrals. It nests in tree holes, cavities in rock faces when on the coast in particular, and even buildings where entry may be gained to a well-secluded ledge; it quite often breeds in a colony.

Aviary
As for the crow.

Food
As for the crow.

Breeding
As for the crow but omit chicks from the diet and substitute mealworms, fully grown locusts and maggots.

Jay (*Garrulus glandarius*)†****
General Description
Measuring about thirty-four centimetres in length, this member of the crow family, although considered a villain, is one of our most colourful species. It is no friend of the game-keeper, or of small birds whom it robs of eggs and young. The body is rosé wine coloured; black and white feathers on the crown are frequently raised forming a crest; the wings are bright blue barred or checked with black, with a white patch between that and the wing tip; the tail is black. Although having earned itself a bad name for its robbing of small birds' nests, the jay also eats a tremendous amount of nefarious insect pests.

Habitat
The jay haunts are in woodland and forest, frequenting also orchards and parks where it nests in the fork of a tree very near the bole.

Aviary
As for the crow.

Food
As for the crow.

Breeding
As for the crow.

Magpie (*Pica pica*)†
General Description
This today is one of our worst pests for taking the young of smaller birds. An exercise carried out on three properties involving over eighty nests provided us with conclusive evidence of this bird's deeds: not one young bird ever fledged and magpies, in large numbers were witnessed time and again over the whole area and were seen actually removing the young in many cases. Meas-

uring forty-six centimetres long, the tail being about twenty-five centimetres, it is a striking bird in appearance, having a purple-blue gloss of metallic sheen to the black of the body and greenish gloss to the black graduated tail; the underparts are white and the wing has a large white shoulder patch.

Habitat
A town, village and country bird, it even enters gardens now and one was seen robbing a wren's nest within a few feet of a window in a suburban garden a few doors away from my own home. The numbers bred, and the necessary food required for their young gives rise to considerable thought as to how best to control this pest.

Aviary
As for the crow.

Food
As for the crow.

Breeding
As for the crow.

Azure-winged Magpie (*Cyanopica cyanus*)†

General Description
The birds which I have kept were all hand-raised specimens, the majority having been reared in twos or threes. However, in one instance, a single bird was reared and became 'imprinted' in no mean fashion, remaining to this day extremely attached to me, but disliking females; it has been tried on many occasions with a mate but to no avail. The azure-blue wings and tail, the latter being graduated as the common birds', the shining black head and nape, the body and mantle brownish-grey, and the throat white, make it most distinctive. The length is thirty-four centimetres.

Habitat
The open woodlands and olive groves of Spain form its habitat.

Aviary
As for the crow.

Food
As for the crow, but omit chicks and mice and give more locusts in the fully adult stage with more beetles, mealworms and maggots.

Breeding
As for the crow, with food as above.

Rook (*Corvus frugilegus*)†

General Description
The plumage is all black with a purplish metallic sheen; the face is grey and devoid of feathers; the thigh feathers are loose. It has a much more stately way of walking than the crow. It is very nearly half a metre in length.

Habitat
Farmlands and fields cultivated or fallow where a few tall trees stand will be preferred. It feeds in open country on grain, seeds and insects.

Aviary
As for the crow.

Food
As for the crow.

Breeding
As for the crow.

Kestrel (*Falco tinnunculus*)†**

General Description
The male measures about thirty-five centimetres and the female between thirty-six and thirty-eight; she is invariably a little larger. The male has a chestnut mantle and wings, spotted with black; a blue-grey head and tail, the latter having a black bar and then being tipped with white; the underparts are buffish with black spots. The female lacks the blue-grey of the head and tail and has a general tendency to be a shade paler. The juveniles resemble the female. The wings of the kestrel are long and pointed; the tail, too, is longish, but the most familiar characteristic is its constant hovering while watching the ground below.

Habitat
It can be found in both wooded and open landscapes.

Aviary
As for the crow, but the shelter should be of a shed type with open entrance hole.

Food
As for the sparrow hawk.

Breeding
As for the sparrow hawk.

Sparrow Hawk (*Accipiter nisus*)†

General Description
In flight this bird is seen to have short rather blunt wing tips. The plumage varies enormously in this bird: there are darkish grey upper parts in the male and russet under parts barred in white; the female has far browner upper parts and is more white beneath, she lacks too the russet except for a little on the flanks. Males usually measure in the region of thirty to thirty-three centimetres whilst the female is at least thirty-eight centimetres.

Habitat
Wooded country provides its main haunts.

Aviary
As for the crow, but with shed-type shelter and large entrance hole.

Food
When keeping hawks, one must eventually contact a hatchery and try to acquire the dead day-old chicks which are always present. If this is impossible white mice will have to be bred specifically for feeding purposes. When using day-old chicks it is best to remove the yolk sac as this is too high in cholesterol for longevity in the subject. As a 'makeshift' meal, one can offer a little very lean minced beef. I tried to introduce fish but my birds would not take it; perhaps others may do so if it is minced with or inserted into the carcase of a small animal or bird. Remember that one rat is not equal to its weight in mice: with the former the bird gets only one set of offal whereas with the equivalent weight in mice he gets a number of these organs together with the greater undigested food content.

Breeding
Increase the mice and day-old chicks, make an incision in them and put a drop or two of Abidec in each with some calcium lactate as well.

Barn Owl (*Tyto alba*)†
General Description
The upper parts are a golden-brown; the under parts are white; the back and wings are softly flecked with grey and the face is white and circled by an almost orange-coloured ring. The male will normally measure about thirty-three centimetres, and the female is a couple of centimetres longer. Apart from the slightly heavier build of the female the sexes are alike in appearance.

Habitat
A farm barn, church tower or derelict building can house a pair of these birds. They frequent scattered trees and are ever alert for vermin which form the bulk of their food.

Aviary
As for the crow.

Food
Mice and day-old chicks will form the staple diet. Offer also the mealworm beetles after they have finished their egg laying lifetime; mealworms will also be taken and fully grown locusts will be eaten once the taste has been acquired.

Breeding
The nest site should be a half open-fronted box with wood chippings to a depth of eight centimetres. Increase the above foods with the arrival of young.

Little Owl (*Athene noctua*)†
General Description
The upper parts are greyish-brown streaked with white; the under parts are similar but lighter. It is a rather stout little bird, measuring from twenty to twenty-three centimetres. The female is invariably the larger. The large yellow eyes give it a rather fierce expression.

Habitat
The little owl frequents parkland and open country.

Aviary
As for the crow, but with a shed-type shelter and large entrance
hole.

Food
Mice, day-old chicks cut in two, mealworms and beetles will
suffice.

Breeding
As for the barn owl, or place a nest box on the shed floor; it
should be a complete box with an entry hole on one side. Food
should be as above, but increased.

Scops Owl (*Otus scops*)†***

General Description
Measuring a mere nineteen centimetres long, it is a very attractive
little bird with its ear-tufts and kitten-like eyes. The beautifully
marked and camouflaged plumage makes them almost invisible
when standing in front of natural tree bark. There appear to be
two phases, brown and grey. It is a far more slender owl than the
little owl. The male looks a regular little guardsman, in the way
he stands so erect and slim. He is more slender than his mate, but
one must have both birds for comparison purposes to sex them
with any degree of certainty; the female has a more rounded look
about her: even the head of the male seems smaller, but this only
because of his manner of pulling in all his plumage so tightly.
The plumage is patterned very attractively with silver, grey and
brown; the wings and tail are barred and thighs feathered. The
call of 'pheu' at fairly short intervals is heard more as the breeding season approaches.

Habitat
It is found in France, Spain and Italy in broad-leaved trees,
parks, farms, towns and villages.

Aviary
As for the crow, but with a shed-type shelter and large entrance
hole. The nest site will be a box with an eight-centimetre hole for
entry; the base inside should be covered with moist saw-dust or
shavings; a natural site of hollow log can be offered but ensure
this is adequately large enough inside for their use, at least eighteen centimetres in diameter and containing a layer of saw-dust or
wood shavings.

Food

Day-old chicks, mice, mealworms and the beetles of this insect and locusts can be given in all sizes.

Breeding

All of our birds have been hand raised and so were exceedingly tame; the mating took place at dusk after considerable calling by both sexes. The hen seemed to come off her eggs only with the going down of the sun. In the wild, this owl eats mainly insects; very rarely indeed would it have small mice and never anything as large as a day-old chick.

This is a very different bird to the pygmy owl of Scandinavia and Russia, which is very fierce for its size, so much so that one can find the remains of waxwings (*Bombycilla garrulus*) in their nest boxes.

INDEX OF ENGLISH NAMES

INDEX OF SCIENTIFIC NAMES

287